QUICK ESCAPES®
CLEVELAND

Help Us Keep This Guide Up to Date

Every effort has been made by the author and editors to make this guide as accurate and useful as possible. However, many things can change after a guide is published—establishments close, phone numbers change, facilities come under new management, etc.

We would love to hear from you concerning your experiences with this guide and how you feel it could be improved and kept up to date. While we may not be able to respond to all comments and suggestions, we'll take them to heart and we'll also make certain to share them with the author. Please send your comments and suggestions to the following address:

> The Globe Pequot Press
> Reader Response/Editorial Department
> P.O. Box 480
> Guilford, CT 06437

Or you may e-mail us at:
> editorial@globe-pequot.com

Thanks for your input, and happy travels!

QUICK ESCAPES® SERIES

QUICK ESCAPES® CLEVELAND

25 WEEKEND GETAWAYS
FROM OHIO'S NORTH COAST

BY

MARCIA SCHONBERG

The Globe Pequot Press

GUILFORD, CONNECTICUT

Quick Escapes is a registered trademark of The Globe Pequot Press.

Cover photo by Jerry Sieve/Index Stock
Cover design by Laura Augustine
Text design by Nancy Freeborn
Maps by M.A. Dubé
Interior photos by © Marcia Schonberg/ViewFinders

Library of Congress Cataloging-in-Publication Data

Schonberg, Marcia.
    Quick escapes Cleveland : 25 weekend getaways from Ohio's North Coast / by Marcia Schonberg. — 1st ed.
        p. cm. — (Quick escapes series)
    Includes index.
    ISBN 0-7627-0709-7
    1. Cleveland Region (Ohio)—Guidebooks. 2. Ohio—Guidebooks. I. Title. II. Series.

F499.C63 S335 2000
917.71'320444—dc21

                                                                                        00–030867

Manufactured in the United States of America
First Edition/First Printing

In memory of my mother, Helene Albert, who, like many readers, enjoyed close-to-home treasures.

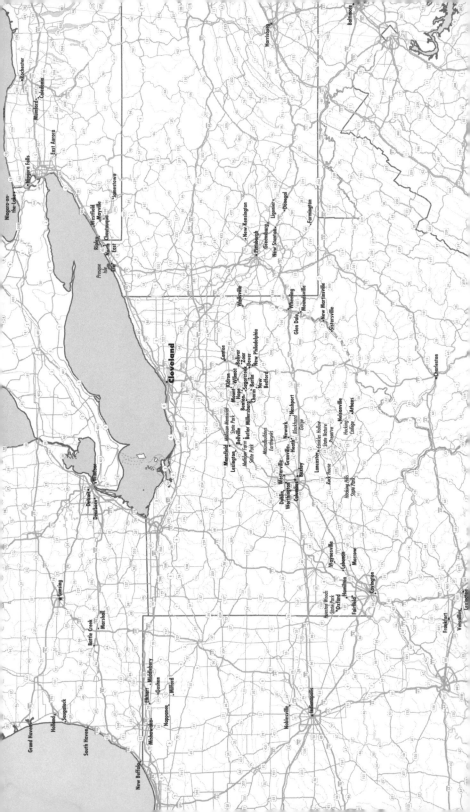

CONTENTS

ACKNOWLEDGMENTS

My heartfelt appreciation goes to the many tourism professionals I met along my Quick Escapes research journey. A special thanks to my husband and best friend, Bill, for your endless bounty of support and pride and to you, the readers, for allowing me to share my joy of travel.

INTRODUCTION

I f you live in Cleveland or nearby, it's but a leisurely drive to exciting getaway destinations in Ohio and beyond. In addition to quick trips within Ohio, *Quick Escapes Cleveland* offers intriguing excursions into our five bordering states, plus fun-filled weekends in New York and Ontario. All are within a six-hour drive from Cleveland—and many much closer than you think.

Most of the getaways in this guidebook are no more than three or four hours' drive, leaving time for exploring new cities and towns along the way. Three quick escapes—to Chicago, Nashville, and Baltimore—require a flight from Cleveland Hopkins International Airport. I included them because they are often quicker than motoring (about an hour airtime), inexpensive (usually under $100) and easy (non-stop), but mainly because they give you the flavor of vacationing, of really getting away, and they are vibrant, sexy, and romantic.

As you use this guide to plan your getaways, you'll find variety to match your moods and favorite pastimes. If you're feeling like taking in some music, there's no better place than Rochester, New York, where a free concert is on tap nearly every day of the year. Hikers can't resist Ohio's Hocking Hills region, just a few hours away in the southeastern quadrant of the state. The same spot is perfect for romantics looking for a secluded weekend in the woods. If you'd rather "lose yourself" in the city, say in the shops lining Chicago's Magnificent Mile or in a cozy French bistro there are itineraries here for you, too. Most also make great family getaways, with only a few modifications required (must-see attractions for families are duly noted).

Then there are pleasant surprises such as discovering the perfect cup of tea (and all of the accouterments that go along with it) in the midst of Kentucky's Blue Grass or a supreme spa just one hour south of Pittsburgh. Seafarers will want to add nautical interests, perhaps maritime museums, lighthouses, lakeside retreats or a canal boat ride, while antique lovers can choose among destinations that brake at antique shops along the way.

I offer these ideas merely to whet your appetite for the twenty-five weekend getaways you find fully described in this guide. If you follow my suggestions, you'll fill each day with personally recommended activities. They are tried and true, providing a natural sequence to exploring must-see sights for first time travelers and out of the way stops for return visitors and natives.

Many readers will want to tailor their trips to fit their personal goals. With this guide, adjusting times and events is easy. I have tried to include more suggestions than you might be able to use. You might choose to sleep in and get a later start than I recommend. Or spend the morning at one museum and the afternoon leisurely walking the promenade around the inner harbor in Baltimore, for example.

Let each itinerary pique your interest. While spontaneity may sound like fun, I strongly suggest arranging your trip before setting out. Once you've decided on a destination and the dates you'd like to travel, make reservations. It's also a good idea to book dining and entertainment at the same time, not to mention airline tickets where applicable. Naturally, the more lead time you allow, the more likely it will be that you'll get your first choices, but don't hesitate to check for last-minute openings. I often find that cancellations do crop up and spur of the moment excursions work out as nicely as those planned long in advance. But do call ahead so you won't be disappointed. I have included a wide range of accommodations, eateries and sights, as you will soon discover. Prices for each vary, too. You'll find luxury and value options, along with some downright bargains.

Personally, I enjoy the unique surroundings of B&Bs and small inns. Their character often reflects the entire ambience of the area. The most perfect example might be the Roycroft Inn in East Aurora. It exemplifies the architecture and style of the Arts and Crafts Movement that sets this area apart from others in the book. On the other hand, I occasionally include national chains and large hotels when it makes travel easier. For instance, in Nashville, I suggest you stay downtown in a major hotel not only because of the comfortable amenities and reasonable week-end rates, but also because of the convenient location. To me, being able to get around without worrying about driving, complicated driving directions, and parking fees is important. I opt for a taxi over paying for valet service.

Of course, ten city blocks may mean a walk to some readers, but a taxi ride to others. Use common sense when it comes to your safety. It may be perfectly safe to walk to a restaurant before dark, for example, but more prudent to catch a ride back to your lodging.

The restaurant recommendations within this guide also focus on unique offerings. I generally avoid the chains that are prevalent everywhere across the United States. Occasionally I include a restaurant with several locations, ones that are regional, and others like McCormick & Schmick's Seafood Restaurant, because the food is delicious.

In addition, you'll find a listing of some of the more prominent and quirky annual events for each destination. I hope you will read between the lines a bit here. Race fans should realize they need to plan well in advance to include the Indianapolis 500 in their Memoria! Day weekend, while others will know to avoid Indianapolis then. Generally, I limit sports talk to those who know it best: you, the fans. I am sure you know who you are and where the stadiums are located—ticket information and availability will be up to you. Still, I have provided telephone numbers and nearby hotels and restaurants in many cases.

Does a listing in the "There's More" section sound irresistible? On this menu substitutions are permitted, even encouraged, to make your getaway the perfect personal blend for your individual tastes. The only essential ingredients that you must bring are your enthusiasm for traveling and your love of new experiences. So pack lightly, tuck in your camera, and don't forget to carry *Quick Escapes: Cleveland*. Bon appetite and bon voyage!

The information and rates listed in this guidebook were confirmed at press time. We recommend, however, that you call establishments before traveling to obtain current information.

NORTHEASTERN
ESCAPES

Greater Buffalo
and into Ontario
MORE THAN NIAGARA FALLS

2 NIGHTS

Antiques • Art • Architecture

Think of Buffalo and you automatically think of Niagara Falls. Innkeepers and concierges agree that most tourists, at least first timers, want to see the falls, from either the American or the Canadian side, when they visit. Because they are so close and such a natural wonder, a side trip into Canada is included here, but you'll have the chance to venture beyond Niagara Falls, up to Niagara-on-the-Lake, Ontario, for an afternoon of browsing quaint shops, wine tasting, and an evening's entertainment.

Your accommodations are in the midst of a former artists' colony. The Roycroft Shop, as the community was known, was founded by writer Elbert Hubbard and played an important role in the the Arts and Crafts movement of the early 1900s.

With so much to do in and around Buffalo, especially if you enjoy the three A's—art, architecture, and antiques—you might not have time for much else, except for some good meals. You'll also discover some pretty scenery, so take comfortable walking shoes and a shopping list, because you'll find unique shops with great gift ideas.

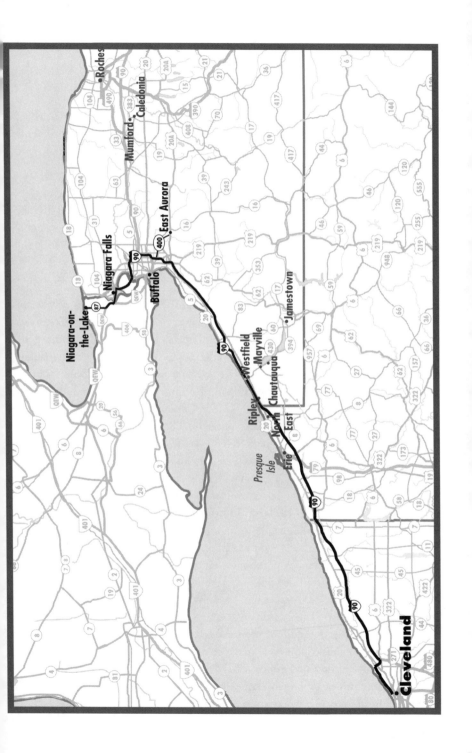

DAY 1

Morning

Take off early to have the afternoon for exploring your first stop, **East Aurora,** New York. The freeway drive (I–90 north toward Buffalo) is an easy one, taking around three hours for the 200-mile journey. From I–90 north, take exit 54, State Route 400 east. Exit at U.S. 20A, turning right onto Main Street.

LUNCH: Take a seat at the counter of **Sweet Memories Ice Cream Parlor** (701 Main Street; 716–655–1630) for lunch and an ice-cream soda. It's a good stop for chocoholics: They sell fudge. Moderate.

Afternoon

The red and white awning in front and the fact that the original store has sprawled into neighboring properties make **Vidler's 5 & 10** (676–679 Main Street; 877–843–5377) the most prominent historic facade along Main Street. Inside you'll find old-fashioned items, the kind that originally stocked this general store in the 1930s, as well as many current-day necessities. There are laughs and memories aplenty as you browse the nostalgic aisles on three floors. It's open daily Monday through Thursday plus Saturday, from 9:00 A.M. to 5:30 P.M., Friday from 9:00 A.M. to 9:00 P.M., and Sunday from noon to 4:00 P.M.

East Aurora has two notable home museums. The **Elbert Hubbard Roycroft Museum** (363 Oakwood Avenue; 716–652–4735) provides a close look at Elbert Hubbard and the Arts and Crafts style he developed. He was well known for his philosophical mottoes. They are printed and framed in their distinctive style and hang throughout the home, which is furnished with authentic period furniture. Nearby, you'll find the **Millard Fillmore House** at 24 Shearer Avenue (716–652–8875). The Fillmores' honeymoon cottage was moved to its current site and became a studio for local artist Margaret Price (of the Fisher-Price Toy Company). Some of her remodeling still remains, but the local historical society is trying diligently to refurnish it with original and period pieces. Both museums are open from 2:00 to 4:00 P.M. on Wednesday, Saturday, and Sunday only, June through October, so plan accordingly.

Then head out for a walking tour of the **Roycroft Campus** on South Grove Street. The complex of fourteen architecturally significant buildings is listed on the National Register of Historic Places. From 1895 to 1939, as many as 500 artists and artisans created finely crafted items here. The buildings now house retail shops and galleries with works created in the earlier style. The original Roycroft pieces are highly prized by collectors. You'll see pottery, glass, furniture, antiques, china, and art. You may get a chance to meet or watch artisans at work. They belong to the Roycroft Renaissance Master Artisans, obliged to carry on the early traditions of the artists' colony.

DINNER: You can expect a romantic and delicious dinner at the **Roycroft Inn** (40 South Grove Street; 716–652–5552). Entrees include fresh pasta dishes (less than $15) and lamb chops (about $25). The inn and restaurant are very service oriented, with a friendly, accommodating staff. If you haven't left room for dessert, order it later and a waitperson will likely offer it to you in the comfortable guest area, the original foyer. Soothing classical background music and Fournier murals, conserved during the inn's recent $8 million restoration, serve to further inspire guests.

LODGING: The Roycroft Inn has twenty-two three-, four-, and five-room guest suites. Each reflects the patterns, color, and furnishings of the period and is identified by a name carved on the wooden door. Rates range from $130 to $230. The standard rooms are spacious but the Disraeli, the bridal suite, sports a luxurious double whirlpool and other amenities. One midweek special, the Preservation Package, includes dinner for two for $180.

DAY 2

Morning

BREAKFAST: A continental breakfast is provided in the inn's cheery dining room, but guests can also enjoy it outdoors at one of the tables on the veranda.

Before leaving for a day in Buffalo, a half-hour away, stop at the **Toy Town Museum** (636 Girard Avenue; 716–687–5151). It's in the Fisher-Price Headquarters' complex, but is not part of the company. Self-guided tours are free, or let a docent provide the details for a $2.00 trip through your childhood. Fisher-Price toys are displayed (including a collection of all the Little People), and exhibits show off one-of-a-kind antiques and toys from the 1930s to today. There's also a hands-on area for children. Hours are 10:00 A.M. to 4:00 P.M. Monday through Saturday. Needless to say, there's a nice gift shop and wonderful posters here. Check out the **Fisher-Price Toystore** next door if you want a huge selection of the current line. One section, "Bits & Pieces," is the place to find the lost parts for both old and new toys. Phone (716) 687–3300.

The drive to **Buffalo** is about 20 miles. Off Main Street, head north on Maple Road to the entrance of State Route 400. Follow Route 400 north to I–90 east.

At exit 53 you will pay a 50-cent toll as you enter I–190 north. At exit 11 you will enter State Route 198 east. Take the Elmwood Avenue exit and follow signs to the Albright-Knox Art Gallery for a day of art and antiquing. You won't return to East Aurora until evening.

LUNCH: Begin with lunch at the **Garden Restaurant** in the **Albright-Knox Art Gallery** (1285 Elmwood Avenue; 716–882–8700). The light, modern eatery is operated by a local restaurant, Just Pasta, and, as you would expect, offers a variety of pastas, including a great baked macaroni with four cheeses. Prices are moderate. The restaurant is open Tuesday through Saturday, from 11:30 A.M. to 3:00 P.M., and serves Sunday Brunch from 11:00 A.M. to 3:00 P.M.

Afternoon

The gallery's mission is presenting modern contemporary art; expect to see works by most of your favorite nineteenth- and twentieth-century artists, including some unusual pieces. Although the gallery has many strengths, the abstract expressionists are particularly well represented. As you stroll the galleries, take your shoes off and walk into one piece of art, called *The Mirrored Room,* on your way to the pop art exhibit.

The gallery shop stocks a wonderful selection of books and gifts. The museum is open Tuesday through Saturday from 11:00 A.M. to 5:00 P.M. and Sunday from noon to 5:00 P.M. Admission is $4.00 for adults, $3.00 for seniors and students.

The museum is next to **Hoyt Lake,** a good spot to enjoy some peaceful scenery before heading to **Allentown,** the city's historic preservation district.

Follow Elmwood south and, as you approach the busy shopping district, park on or near North Street. From here you can conveniently hit many of the shops clustered together. An interesting and unusual shop, **Great Waves Antiques** (27 Allen Street; 716–881–1164) combines its eclectic vintage collection with **Tiger Lily & Wing,** an Asian bakery and cafe. It's a wonderful find for an inexpensive lunch, but is especially fun for a midday snack. You'll find sweet baked buns stuffed with Asian fillings like almond choy and red beans. They're perfect with tea.

Continue on the browsing spree, but leave time for a stop at the **Theodore Roosevelt Inaugural National Historic Site,** at 641 Delaware Avenue (716–884–0095). The home, which belonged to Roosevelt's friend Ansley Wilcox, became the inaugural site when he took the Presidential Oath following William McKinley's assassination in Buffalo. The furnishings of some rooms give visitors a look into the past, while other rooms interpret the time at the turn of the last century. Open Monday through Friday 9:00 A.M. to 5:00 P.M., Saturday and Sunday

*Stop at Buffalo's Albright-Knox Art Gallery, renowned for its collection of nineteenth-
and twentieth-century art.*

noon to 5:00 P.M.; closed on Saturdays January through March. Admission is $3.00
for adults, $2.00 for seniors, and $1.00 for children 5 to 12.

DINNER: Head over to **Buffalo**'s theater district, a few more blocks south, and
park in one of the public lots for an evening of dinner and theater. **Brownstone
Bistro** (297 Franklin Street; 716–842–6800) is a bustling dinner choice conveniently located near the downtown theaters. The name describes the easily recognizable exterior, a vintage structure that went through several personality changes
before becoming an upscale eatery. Several pastas (with a choice in portion size),
steaks, poultry, seafood, and first courses accompanied by innovative toppings and
sauces offer delectable choices. Prices are moderate to expensive after wine and
soup or salad are added.

Performing arts are thriving in the theater district. There are many theaters in
close proximity, so the area is lively, crowded, and well lit. The new **Irish Classical Theatre** (625 Main Street; 716–853–4282) is a good choice due to its sched-

ule of international works, but also because of its design. The circular center stage provides an up close and personal relationship between the audience and performers. No nosebleed section here. Tickets range from $10 to $25. Evening performances begin at 7:30.

LODGING: The drive back to the Roycroft Inn will take about a half hour. From downtown, take Tupper Street, which is one way, to State Route 33 east and then to I–90, retracing your route from this morning.

DAY 3

Morning

BREAKFAST: The Roycroft Inn.

Check out of the inn before leaving to see the falls. It's an easy drive via Route 400 north to I–90 east, I–290 west, and I–190 north to the Robert Moses Parkway. It sounds longer than it is and will take less than an hour to reach the **Niagara Falls Reservation State Park,** where you can find picturesque views from the American side.

If you want to venture into Canada, just follow the signs to the Rainbow Bridge and prepare to pass through customs. Before entering Canada, you should be aware of the procedure. You may be asked to prove your citizenship upon crossing the border so carry a voter registration card, birth certificate, or passport. Your driver's license is not adequate. You will be asked for your destination, purpose for visiting, and expected length of stay. Upon re-entering the United States within forty-eight hours, you may bring in $200 worth of goods, ten cigars, fifty cigarettes, and four ounces of alcohol, duty free. Keep receipts. The U.S. agent will ask you to describe any purchases upon your return. For more information, contact the U.S. Customs at (716) 551–4368.

From customs, continue along the Niagara Parkway, stopping at the **Horseshoe Falls** and continuing north as time permits. Even if you drive only a short distance from the falls, park and walk along the **Niagara Parks Recreational Trail,** a multipurpose path running about 35 miles between Fort Erie and Niagara-on-the-Lake, for a glimpse of the beautiful scenery. The trail runs alongside the highway with access all along the route.

The drive to **Niagara-on-the-Lake, Ontario** is about 10 miles from the Rainbow Bridge. This quaint community full of shops, cafes, B&Bs, and historical sites is a picturesque side trip. Between April and October, the Shaw Festival's repertory theater series presents three simultaneous productions during matinees and evening performances. Shows by George Bernard Shaw and his contemporaries range from $34 to $70 a ticket; (905) 468–2153.

LUNCH: The Oban Inn, 160 Front Street, Niagara-on-the-Lake, Ontario; (905) 468–2165. Views of Lake Ontario, English-style gardens, and delicious cuisine make this one a favorite. Inn and meal prices are reasonable considering the U.S. exchange rate. Afternoon tea is also available. For lower prices, but the same menu as in the main dining room, opt to eat on the patio or near the piano bar.

Afternoon

There are twenty-seven wineries on the Niagara Peninsula with eleven in Niagara-on-the-Lake. Many have wine-tasting rooms that are open year-round and quite a few offer vineyard tours seasonally. Try an ice wine, if you've never tasted this sweet and limited (therefore expensive) production. Ask for a map nearly anywhere to make finding them easier than just following the road markers. Often several are clustered together, making it easy to get directions from one to the next. Right off the Niagara Parkway, for example, you'll see Reif Estate Winery, (905) 468–7738; Inniskillin Wines, (905) 468–3554; and Marynissen Estates, (905) 468–7270.

The return trip to Cleveland takes about four hours. Take the Niagara Parkway to the Lewiston Queenston Bridge into the United States. After customs, take I–190 south to exit 16, which leads to I–290 east. Follow it to I–90 west and straight into Cleveland.

DINNER: For a meal in historic surroundings, stop in **Painesville,** Ohio, about 30 miles east of Cleveland. Exit I–90 at State Route 44 and head north to State Route 84, turning right off the ramp and then left immediately onto Chestnut Street. The road dead-ends at the **Rider's Inn** (792 Mentor Avenue, Painesville; 440–247–1200). Once a stagecoach stop and an Underground Railroad station as well, it's now a full-service inn with an English-style pub complete with darts. Prime rib is the house specialty. Sunday brunch ($14.95) is available from 10:00 A.M. to 3:00 P.M. and dinner is served from 5:00 to 8:00 P.M.

THERE'S MORE

Burchfield-Penney Art Center, Rockwell Hall, Buffalo State College, 1300 Elmwood Avenue, Buffalo; (716) 878–6011. Located across from the Albright-Knox Art Gallery, this is another stop for seeing some of the Roycroft objects you've learned about over the weekend. You'll also find watercolors by the gallery's namesake and other regional artists. Hours are Tuesday through Saturday 10:00 A.M. to 5:00 P.M., Sunday 1:00 to 5:00 P.M. It's free, but donations are accepted.

The Buffalo & Erie County Historical Society, 25 Nottingham Court, Buffalo; (716) 873–9644. This is the other museum in the Elmwood Museum District, a must-see for history buffs interested in learning the region's past. Admission is $3.50 for adults, $2.00 for seniors, and $1.50 for children; families are $7.50. Hours are Tuesday through Saturday 10:00 A.M. to 5:00 P.M., Sunday noon to 5:00 P.M.

Architecture. Drive along Buffalo's Delaware Avenue, once called "Millionaires' Row," for a look at the mansions of the Gilded Age. Frank Lloyd Wright spent some time here, designing five houses, but as you tour Buffalo you'll also see Eliel and Eero Saarinen's work if you visit the Kleinhans Music Hall (71 Symphony Circle; 716–883–3560), home of the Buffalo Philharmonic Orchestra and other masters. Guided tours of Frank Lloyd Wright's Graycliff are offered from April through November, 11:00 A.M. to 4:00 P.M. on Saturday and from 1:00 to 4:00 P.M. on Sunday. From June through September sunset tours are added at 7:00 P.M. on Friday. Tours last one hour and include the picturesque grounds. Downtown walking tours (one-and-a-half-hours long, $5.00 per person) are available May 1 through October 31 and bus tours, every day except major holidays, last two hours, and cost $18 per person. Contact the Friends of the School of Architecture and Planning at Buffalo University (716–829–3543) for required reservations.

SPECIAL EVENTS

May–October. Downtown Country Market, Main Street between Court and Church Streets. Farmers' market. (716) 856–3150.

June. Allentown Art Festival, Delaware Avenue and Allen Street. More than 400 artists from all over the United States sell their work. (716) 881–4269.

July. Waterfront Summer Concerts Series. Tuesdays and Saturdays bring live music of every style to Lake Erie shores for family entertainment. (716) 884–8865.

July. Taste of Buffalo, Main Street, downtown. Live music on four tages, food from the city's leading restaurants, and wine from nearby wineries. (716) 831–9376.

August. Toy Fest, Main Street, East Aurora. East Aurora becomes Toy Town, U.S.A., with a parade, life-size toys, entertainment, and activities. (716) 687–5151.

November. Festival of Lights, Niagara Falls, New York. Ice skating and laser light shows; free transportation aboard the People Mover amid thousands of twinkling lights. (716) 285–8484.

OTHER RECOMMENDED RESTAURANTS AND LODGINGS

Buffalo

Beau Fleuve B&B Inn, 242 Linwood Avenue; (800) 278–0245. Within walking distance of shops and eateries on Elmwood Avenue. Five rooms, two have shared bath. Rates are $75–$95 and include a gourmet breakfast. Innkeepers are architectural buffs and direct guests on walking and driving tours of the area. The new commercial kitchen is a showplace, reflecting the home's Arts and Crafts influence.

Le Metro Cite, 520 Elmwood Avenue; (716) 885–1160. One of the restaurants in the Elmwood District, this one also has a hearth bakery and pizza bar. Gourmet and upscale pizzas, pastas, and entrees, mostly comfort foods like chicken and biscuits, steak and pommes frites. Moderate.

Niagara-on-the-Lake, Ontario

The Olde Angel Inn, 124 Regent Street; (905) 468–3411. Original inn burned during the War of 1812; it was rebuilt and still reflects the early 1800s, with exposed beams and plank floors. Pub-style furnishings and menu. Moderate.

FOR MORE INFORMATION

East Aurora Chamber of Commerce; (800) 441–2881.

Buffalo Visitors' Center, 617 Main Street (Market Arcade Building), Buffalo, NY 14203.

Niagara-on-the-Lake Chamber of Commerce, 153 King Street, Niagara-on-the-Lake, ON; (905) 468–4263.

Erie and
the Chautauqua Region
WATER, WATER EVERYWHERE

2 NIGHTS

The Battle of Lake Erie • Summertime learning
Quaint towns • Lighthouses

After driving an hour and a half northeast, you'll be ready to begin a weekend that winds through two states and offers an especially inviting repose for nature lovers. If you enjoy quaint villages, antiques, wineries, and beautiful scenery, you won't be disappointed.

Most weekend destinations in this guide provide one-stop lodging for a two-night getaway, but the region surrounding Presque Isle State Park in Erie, Pennsylvania, and the charming towns in New York's Chautauqua County are full of diverse possibilities. A sampling of both are provided. If you prefer to unpack only once, consider a day trip to the other region, or divide the itinerary into two separate sojourns. No matter what your choice, you'll want to return again and again.

DAY 1

It's about 100 miles from Cleveland to **Erie.** Leave by early afternoon, if possible, to allow several hours of sightseeing before dark, depending on the season. To get to Erie, take I–90 east to I–79 north, which will become Bayfront Highway. Then turn left onto Holland Street to begin exploring Erie's maritime history.

Your first stop, the **Erie Maritime Museum,** sets the mood. This state-of-the-art facility in the midst of Bayview Commons (150 East Front Street;

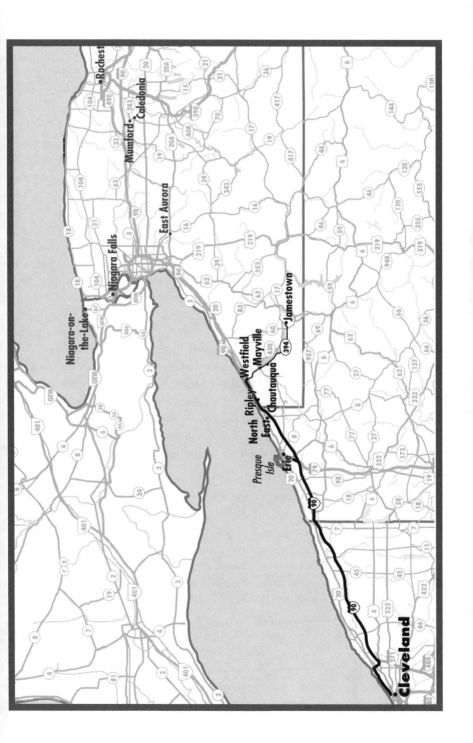

814–452–2744) harbors the home port of the U.S. Brig *Niagara*. Unfortunately, this reconstruction of the vessel that won the Battle of Lake Erie in 1813 will be on the seas all of 2000, which has locals up in arms. If you want to see the *Niagara,* you'll have to visit port towns along the Erie Canal as she heads for Philadelphia, Annapolis, and then on to others, including Halifax, Montreal, and Boston. Even if the slip outdoors is empty, the museum, with an array of exhibits devoted to her battle, sailing ships, and Commander Oliver Perry, explains the story.

Begin with the award-winning video, a side-by-side British and American interpretation of the battle events. Then take as long as you want on a self-guided visit or take the guided tour. An interactive light-up map describes the battles of the War of 1812 and integrates their events. You'll also learn about the saying "Don't give up the ship," the difference between a sloop and a brig and other rigging terms, and how to tie those great sailing knots. This state museum shares its new and old space with the Erie County Public Library. The Maritime Museum is open Monday through Saturday, from 9:00 A.M. to 5:00 P.M., and Sunday from noon to 5:00 P.M. Admission is $6.00 for adults, $5.00 for seniors, $3.00 for youth, and $15.00 for a family. Prices include tour of Brig *Niagara* when in port. Prices are $4.00, $3.50, $2.00, and $10.00 respectively when *Niagara* is out of port.

When you finish at the museum, drive west along Bayfront Parkway, turning left on State Street. Drive two blocks to the **Bicentennial Tower** (Dobbins Landing; 814–455–6055). This 187-foot observation tower was built for the city's bicentennial celebration in 1995 and provides great views of the Presque Isle Bay. Open seven days a week April through October, and weekends only January through March. Admission is $2.00 for adults and $1.00 for children ages six through twelve; free on Tuesday.

DINNER: Return to the Bayfront Parkway and continue traveling west to West Twelfth Street. Turn right and watch for **Oscar's Pub and Restaurant** (2147 West Twelfth Street, at the end of a strip mall; 814–454–4325). Once you pass the huge moose hanging above the doorway, you'll find yourself in a pub atmosphere complete with an extensive beer selection, reflecting the owner's tastes as a beer connoisseur. To go along with the imported beers, the menu offers international specialties (try the fresh sliced Wiener schnitzel served with delicious red cabbage and apples). The portions are large and moderately priced.

Drive west on Twelfth Street to Peninsula Drive. Turn left and continue to a right-hand turn on West Twenty-sixth Street (U.S. 20). This road gets local traffic, but still has the look of the highways that were popular before the creation of interstate freeways. It has a history as a stagecoach route, too, but bears no resemblance to that era. Just 2 miles from Presque Isle State Park, the thoroughfare offers visitors overnight stays at the small family-owned motels of its heyday.

LODGING: One such motel is the **Glass House Inn** (3202 West Twenty-sixth Street; 800–956–7222). The owners are the third generation to operate the colonial-style motel. The family business began in 1955; Grandma often had to turn off the phones by three o'clock because there were no vacancies. With clean, inexpensive rooms and the friendliness of a bed-and-breakfast, it still fills up quickly, especially during the summer. A complimentary continental breakfast cheerfully served in the family dining room adds to its popularity. Rates range from $49 to $94.

DAY 2

Morning

BREAKFAST: Dress appropriately for a morning outdoors. After a self-serve continental breakfast at the motel, check out and depart for Presque Isle.

Turn left out of the motel and left onto Peninsula Drive, heading north to **Presque Isle State Park** for walking or biking along the paved path, relaxing at the sandy beach, boating, or enjoying other outdoor activities. Just off the main road to the right is the Stull Interpretive and Visitors' Center. Stop to pick up a park map and glean information about the six ecological zones from the displays. The park is a great place for bird-watching. Located along the Atlantic flyway, more than 350 species have been recorded here. You'll want to browse the gift shop, but might save that for your departure.

Make sure to see the lighthouse and *The Feather,* landscape art situated just off the paved 12-mile multipurpose path running along side the road. The park sports a handicapped-accessible fishing area and 15 miles of hiking trails along with free interpretive pontoon rides. Lighthouse excursions aboard the *Lady Kate* (800–988–5780) operate from the park, but are privately consigned. Two-hour tours are $13.00 for adults and $9.00 for children and run every day in season, rain or shine. There are also pontoon and canoe rentals at the marina. It takes some seventy-five lifeguards to patrol the sandy beaches. Concession and changing facilities are located among the various beaches; picnic areas, with grills and some pavilions, are tucked throughout the park.

As you explore, you'll learn more of the Battle of Lake Erie. Stop at Perry's Monument at Crystal Point at the tip of Misery Bay, where many of Perry's soldiers were quarantined with smallpox and died. They were buried nearby in Grave

Yard Pond. During winter you can enjoy ice fishing, skating, and other outdoor activities as well as finding serene beauty in the ice dunes along the lake's edge.

LUNCH: Leave by noon, traveling south on Peninsula Drive and west on Eighth Street to the **Colony Pub and Grille** (26770 West Eighth Street; 814–838–2162). This inexpensive family-run eatery features fresh Lake Erie perch; salads are served family-style.

Afternoon

Continue east on Eighth Street for 4½ miles, turning left on East Avenue and right on East Lake Road (State Route 5). You'll pass several wineries in North East, about 15 miles from Erie. One of the first you'll come to is **Mazza Vineyards** (11815 East Lake Road, North East; 800–796–9463). If you have never tasted ice wine, stop for a sample of this rare and expensive variety, produced in very small quantities right after the first freeze.

Soon you'll be in **New York.** In Barcelona, about 10 miles east of the state line, turn right on State Route 394, driving through Westfield and continuing south into Mayville. As you follow Lake Road, you'll want to stop at the **Chautauqua Institution** (800–836–ARTS). Families have been recreating and learning here during the summer's lecture and concert series for more than a century. During the season, you'll have to park and hop on a golf cart or walk into the gated community, but other times cars are permitted. Among the classes are sailing, special studies classes, music concerts, and seminars. Classes range in length.

Continue on your loop drive around Lake Chautauqua, stopping in Lucille Ball's hometown, **Jamestown,** to visit the **Lucy-Desi Museum** (116 East Third Street; 716–484–7070) in her honor. The small museum highlights the couple's careers and offers a down-home flavor to celebrity fame. Admission is $5.00 for adults, $3.50 for students and seniors. There is a family rate of $15 for four or more.

From Jamestown take State Route 430 around the other side of the lake, stopping at artists' galleries and antiques shops along the way.

DINNER: When the road intersects Route 394, head north to **Westfield** and drive to the **William Seward Inn** (6645 South Portage Road, Westfield; 800–338–4252). Dinner is a gourmet experience here. The innkeeper/chef prepares a four-course prix fixe dinner ($38) at a 7:00 P.M. seating; during the summer, two seatings are offered. Guests choose from a menu of several choices, all elegantly presented.

Expect scenic marina views along Lake Erie's coastal drives, such as this one overlooking Barcelona Harbor.

LODGING: The William Seward Inn. This historic inn was purchased by William Seward in 1837 while he served as agent for the Holland Land Co. The house has since been moved in three sections to its present location. The current innkeepers have elegantly redecorated each of the twelve guest rooms (eight in the main house and four in the carriage house) and serve up a made-to-order breakfast each morning. Rates range from $70 to $185.

DAY 3

Morning

BREAKFAST: Breakfast at the inn is nearly as elegant as dinner. Fresh baked muffins and fresh fruit appear before your order is taken. Check out after enjoying a leisurely meal, but plan for a few more stops before heading home.

As you drive into Westfield on State Route 394, turn left on Main Street and stop at **Lincoln–Bedell Park,** where a larger-than-life bronze statue of Abraham Lincoln awaits. It was here in Westfield that eleven-year-old Grace Bedell met the new president when his train bound for Washington braked. She had previously written to him suggesting he would be a more appealing candidate if he grew a beard, adding that women would convince their husbands to vote for him. After taking her advice, President Lincoln stopped to meet her.

Follow State Route 394 to State Route 5. Just east of Barcelona Harbor, you'll arrive at a unique and interesting maple-grape farm, **Vinewood Acres,** and its **Sugar Shack** (7904 Route 5, Westfield, New York; 716–326–3351 or 888–563–4324). On weekends the pancake house here features the twenty flavors of syrups produced from the farm's orchards and vines. If you arrive before 2:00 P.M., pancakes are waiting and the "wall of fame" boasts the pancake-eating prowess of the heartiest appetites. Otherwise, samples of the fruit syrups are given atop ice cream. You'll get a free tour of the state-of-the-art maple sugaring operation and an interpreted nature walk to the lake's edge thrown in for good measure. The gift shop's jams, jellies, and syrups (some in imported "grape" glass) are too sweet to resist. Hours are 10:00 A.M. to 5:00 P.M. Thursday through Tuesday, Wednesday by chance or appointment.

Pause at the Barcelona Lighthouse and Harbor for your last views of Lake Erie from New York shores before heading back to Cleveland via I–90 West. Your trip back is roughly 150 miles or about a 2½-hour drive.

THERE'S MORE

Erie Art Museum, 411 State Street, Erie; (814) 459–5477. Located in the historic bank building that later became the Customs House in 1839; most exhibits are changing ones. Admission is $1.50 for adults, $.75 for students and seniors, and $.50 cents for children under twelve.

ExpERIEnce Children's Museum, 420 French Street, Erie; (814) 453–3743. Hands-on exhibits and activities for children ages two to twelve. Two floors of educational yet fun things, especially well suited for younger children. Admission is $3.50. Open Wednesday to Saturday 10:00 A.M. to 4:00 P.M., Sunday, 1:00 to 4:00 P.M.

Roger Tory Peterson Institute, 311 Curtis Street, Jamestown; (716) 655–2473. Hiking and birding trails, nature store, and exhibit of this noted naturalist's collection. Open Tuesday to Saturday 10:00 A.M. to 4:00 P.M., Sunday 1:00 to 5:00 P.M.

Johnson Estate Winery, Route 20, Westfield; (716) 326-2191 or (800) 374-6569. The state's oldest estate winery, open year-round for tastings. Tours are conducted in July and August.

McClurg Museum and Chautauqua County Historical Society, Village Park, Routes 20 and 394, Westfield; (716) 326–2977. Restored 1818 mansion filled with a variety of artifacts and period furnishings.

SPECIAL EVENTS

February. Currier & Ives Sleigh Rally, Chautauqua Institution. Horsedrawn sleigh rides. (814) 789–5804 or (800) 242–4569.

June–August. Chautauqua Institution season; write P.O. Box 28, Chautauqua, New York 14722 or call (800) 836–ARTS for schedule. The Chautauqua Institution offers programs from late June through August. During this season a gate fee is charged.

July. Discover Presque Isle, Presque Isle State Park. Fund raiser for the Friends of Presque Isle, the auxiliary responsible for most of the projects in park. Bonfires, music, arts and crafts, boat rides, and nighttime events. (814) 871–4251.

July. Westfield YWCA Arts and Crafts Festival, Moore Park, Westfield. The largest in area, with more than 250 vendors. Free shuttle service to the park from off-site parking. (716) 326–2011.

OTHER RECOMMENDED RESTAURANTS AND LODGINGS

Chautauqua County

Athenaeum Hotel, Chautauqua Institution, Chautauqua, New York; (800) 821–1881. Daily rates at this 1880s Victorian queen range from $258 to $330 based on double occupancy. The wide veranda offers magnificent views of the lake and the community.

The White Inn, 52 East Main Street, Fredonia, New York; (888) FREDONIA. Beautifully appointed and restored mansion. Full-service inn provides gourmet meals; breakfast is included in lodging rates, which range from $59 to $169.

Lakeside B&B, 8223 East Lake Road, Route 5, Westfield, New York; (800) 454–8237. Windows from this B&B show off the Barcelona Lighthouse and Harbor across the street and beautiful views of Lake Erie just beyond. Innkeepers pamper guests with tea, snacks, and breakfast featuring local syrups. Rates: $75–$110 for the lake view.

The Grainery, 1494 County Road 66, Cherry Creek, New York; (716) 287–3500. Surprisingly imaginative selections for being in the heart of Amish country. Fresh produce and products from the surrounding farms, served in a century-old renovated barn. Located across from the Cockigne Ski Resort, each table offers great views. Before you leave, pick up a free map detailing local Amish merchants.

Italian Fisherman, 61 Lakeside Drive, Bemus Point, New York; (716) 386–7000. Great views, even a floating clam bar. Outdoor dining on the waterfront. Seafood and pasta are among the specialties. Moderate.

Erie

Bel-Aire Hotel, 2800 West Eighth Street, Erie, Pennsylvania; (800) 888–8781. Even this more luxurious hotel near the Lake Erie shore started out as an old-fashioned motel, typical of the area, but renovations and upgrades have added exercise facilities, restaurants, and a uniquely styled atrium pool. Rates: $85–$93.

Shakespier's Bar & Grill, 726 West Bayfront, Erie, Pennsylvania; (814) 452–6607. Wide variety of choices, but try the fondue for an appetizer or snack while enjoying the beautiful bay view or sunset. Alfresco dining, weather permitting. Sunday brunch. Moderate.

Webb's The Captain's Table, West Lake Road, Mayville, New York; (716) 753–3960. Moderately priced sandwiches, soups, and salads are typical lunch fare, with entrees offered at dinner.

FOR MORE INFORMATION

Chautauqua County Visitors' Bureau, P.O. Box 1441, Chautauqua Institution Main Gate Welcome Center, Route 394, Chautauqua, New York 14722; (716) 357–4569 or (800) 242–4569; www. tourchautauqua.com.

Erie Area Convention and Visitors Bureau, 109 Boston Store Place, Erie, Pennsylvania 16501; (814) 454–7191 or (800) 524–3743.

Erie Area Fund for the Arts provides schedules of events at the various musical and performing arts venues in the Erie area; (814) 452–3427.

Rochester and More
BIG APPLE AMBIENCE
CLOSER TO HOME

2 NIGHTS

History • Music • The Magic Black Box

Spend a weekend in Rochester, New York, and you'll undoubtedly leave wishing you had more time to explore this visitor-friendly city. A few days will only provide the flavor of this area, smaller than Buffalo and just an hour farther east on I–90. It's a pivotal point between activities on Lake Ontario to the north and the Finger Lakes to the south, and still enjoys the scenery and activity along the Erie Canal and the Genesee River.

Rochester has a rich history, which you will soon discover. With its location on the water, it was a booming community during the canal era. It became known as the "Flour City" when the milling industry thrived, and then changed to the "Flower City" as master designers added parks and horticulturists brought new industry. Each spring the lilac festival in Highland Park celebrates the city's profuse display, with ten days of family-inspired events; the formal gardens of the community's various estates color the landscape throughout the seasons.

Speaking of estates, the George Eastman House, considered a mecca for photographers, is worth the trip alone. But do allow time to peruse other museums and lend an ear to the musical performances and performing arts as well. Classical music lovers can find a concert or recital by the gifted students at the Eastman School of Music any day they visit.

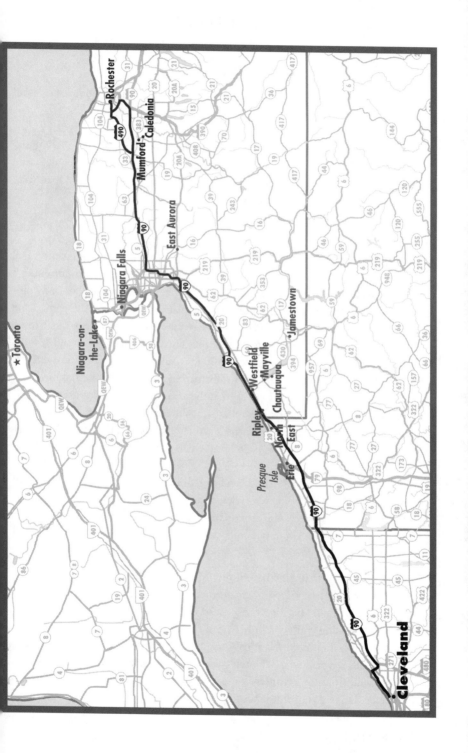

DAY 1

The 250-mile trip is a straight shot on I–90 east from Cleveland, but it takes about four hours.

LUNCH: Stop for lunch at the **Coal Tower Restaurant** (9 Schoen Place, Pittsford; 716–381–7866) right on the Erie Canal. You'll find an extensive burger and sandwich menu and homemade desserts in a restored canal coal bin. Open daily with lunch prices from $3.00 to $8.00.

Afternoon

Head out to explore the **Erie Canal.** The tour boats running along the canal operate mid-May through mid-October. If you're traveling then, plan for either a one-and-a-half or three-hour excursion aboard the *Sam Patch,* a replica of a nineteenth-century packet boat like ones that regularly maneuvered the canal. One point of departure is Schoen Place in the village of **Pittsford,** a canal town founded before Rochester. Sightseeing cruises, including passage through a lock, depart at 2:00 and 4:00 P.M. and cost $10.00 for adults, $8.00 for seniors, and $5.00 for children. Call (716) 262–5661 for information and other cruise options.

If you don't have time for a cruise, visit the area anyway. A multipurpose Rails-to-Trails path follows the towpath, and quaint shops and eateries abound in towns along the canal. Rent a bike, perhaps a tandem, at **Towpath Bike Rental** (7 Schoen Place, Pittsford; 716–381–2808). Rentals are $7.00 to $10.00 an hour or $50.00 per week.

From Schoen Place in Pittsford head to **Rochester** by turning right onto East Avenue. Continue for about two miles, turning right onto Fairport Road. Take I–490 west to I–590 north and exit at Blossom Road. Turn right onto Blossom. The Daisy Flour Mill is about two miles further on the right as you drive through the park.

DINNER: Stop off at the **Daisy Flour Mill** (1880 Blossom Road; 716–381–1880). The moderately priced menu features American favorites like prime rib, chicken, and seafood. The Blue Daisy Salad combines bacon bits and homemade blue cheese dressing and costs only $1.50. The restaurant occupies the site of an 1809 gristmill and is on the National Register of Historic Places. These and more historic details are printed on the reproduction flour sacks used as menu holders.

Turn right from the restaurant onto Blossom Road. It will turn into University Avenue. Drive 3 to 4 miles, turning left onto Goodman and then right onto

East Avenue at the next block. The Strathallen Hotel is one block down on the right at Strathallen Park.

LODGING: The Strathallen Hotel, 550 East Avenue; (800) 678–7284. You'll appreciate the roomy size of your suite accommodations and the great location, minutes from the museums and bustling neighborhoods full of shops and restaurants. The hotel started out as a luxury apartment building for former residents of elite East Avenue, but missed its mark with rental rates even the affluent balked at. Now the full-service all-suites hotel has apartment-size rooms equipped with microwave, refrigerator, complimentary snacks, and plenty of room at reasonable prices. Rates: $135–$145 before AAA or AARP discounts.

DAY 2

Morning

BREAKFAST: There are several breakfast options after your first cup of coffee in your suite, but one you'll surely enjoy (even if you have to wait in line) is **Jine's Restaurant** (658 Park Avenue; 716–461–1280). A wide variety of breakfast fare, including lots of omelettes and frittatas, is available anytime. It opens at 7:00 A.M. and prices are moderate. There are other restaurants for every budget and palate along Park Avenue, a great example of Rochester's preservation efforts. The area is noted for its many unique shops and boutiques interspersed with eateries.

Head 1 block north to East Avenue, turn left, and drive to the **George Eastman House International Museum of Photography and Film** (900 East Avenue; 716–271–3361). Five first-floor rooms are furnished as they were when Eastman built the mansion and entertained his friends, including Thomas Edison. The "floating" staircase (a great photo op) leads visitors to other rooms that have been converted to exhibition spaces. The home, containing some 85 percent original artifacts, is a "picture-perfect restoration," as one exhibit explains, because of the profuse number of photographs available for reference.

In the Discovery Room, sophisticated photographic techniques become child's play. You'll see works by many leading photographers, as well as famous photographs made by lesser-known photographers, and you'll learn how the name Kodak came about. Film history and archives are also part of the picture here. Admission is $6.50 for adults, $5.00 for seniors, and $2.50 for students, and includes a one-hour docent-led tour at 10:30 A.M. or 2 P.M.

Outdoors, manicured gardens are open to guests. You can take a walk here, even if you don't visit indoors.

The Skyliner Diner is just one of the family friendly stops at the Strong Museum.

LUNCH: The **Strong Museum** (One Manhattan Square; 714–263–2700) is the place for lunch and hours of educational entertainment for adults, children, or both. Located in the museum's atrium, the **Skyliner Diner,** a stainless steel '50s original, is the place for reasonable diner fare before enjoying the exhibits. Breakfast is served anytime. Prices aren't the same as they were in the '50s, but reasonable nonetheless. Just beyond the diner, Louie's Sweet Shoppe, inspired by the Rochester landmark, serves up ice-cream concoctions.

The museum itself is a state-of-the-art historical time machine. Even the elevator offers changing commentaries, allowing you to imaginatively take trips to the future and back to earlier periods. Children will enjoy the Sesame Street interactive segments, where toddlers will want to play endlessly. For adults, *When Barbie Dated GI Joe: Toying with the Cold War* takes guests back to the '50s and earlier. Then there's the world's largest doll collection. About 7,000 of the 27,000 dolls in the collection are displayed at any one time.

Extensive displays of decorative arts and furniture, even kitchens from various decades, make up the 500,000 objects of Americana on display on the upper level. There's also an on-site lending library. Hours are Monday to Saturday 10:00 A.M. to 5:00 P.M. (until 10:00 P.M. on Friday) and Sunday noon to 5:00 P.M. Admission is $6.00 for adults, $5.00 for students with ID and seniors, and $4.00 for children three to seventeen. Parking is free.

After visiting the museum, stop at the pedestrian bridge overlooking the High Falls on the Genesee River just east of the Frontier Field, the community's baseball and soccer field across the street from the world headquarters of Eastman Kodak Company. To reach the bridge, turn left onto Manhattan Square Drive from the museum parking lot. Turn right at Chestnut Street and drive approximately five blocks to Andrews Street. Turn left and drive on Andrews until it ends, turning right onto State Street. You'll find a parking garage about two blocks further. Walk out the Platt Street entrance to the bridge. You can also walk over to an observation area for a closer vantage point or return after dark, mid-May through mid-October, for a free nightly laser light show. Call (716) 325–2030 for a full schedule.

DINNER: From the bridge, take State Street south, turning left onto Andrews Street. At Chestnut Street, turn right and drive about 4 blocks to East Avenue, turning left and then left again onto Winthrop Street to **Restaurant 2 Vine** (24 Winthrop Street; 716–454–6020) for an upscale dinner in a lively bistro atmosphere. Daily specials depend on what's fresh and available, but entrees averaging $15 to $20 are innovative and interesting and there's a good wine list.

After dinner, opt for a flick at the **Little Theatre** (240 East Avenue; 716–232–3906). This newly renovated "art house theater" bills highly acclaimed art and foreign films. Tickets are $6.50 ($4.50 for seniors and matinees).

LODGING: Strathallan Hotel.

DAY 3

Morning

BREAKFAST: Enjoy a leisurely breakfast at the hotel's Five50 Pub & Grille, then drive downtown to the **Susan B. Anthony House** (17 Madison Street; 716–235–6124). This pioneer for women's suffrage was arrested here in 1872 for voting. The museum and education center next door are open Thursday to Sunday 1:00 to 4:00 P.M. Admission is free.

Before leaving Rochester, take a drive through Rochester's parks to **Mt. Hope Cemetery,** touted as the largest Victorian cemetery in the country. A self-guided walking tour, or a guided tour on weekends, leads visitors to Frederick Douglass's family grave. Susan B. Anthony and other less notables, like George Washington's driver, are interred within this 200-acre parklike setting. To get there from downtown, take State Street south (it will turn into Exchange Boulevard) to the Ford Street Bridge. Turn left and drive over the bridge and turn right onto Mt. Hope Avenue. The North Cemetery entrance and office are located on the right about one-half mile ahead. The Friends of Mt. Hope Cemetery offer free tours May through October, Sunday only at 2:00 and 3:00 P.M. Gates are open daily from 8:00 A.M. to 6:00 P.M.

LUNCH: Wegman's, a unique New York–based grocery chain, Pittsford Plaza, 3195 Monroe Avenue; (716) 586–6680. Have lunch in the "cafe" and pick up a few snacks for the ride back. Prices are moderate.

Afternoon

Take I–590 west to I–390. Head south to I–90 for the four-hour trip back to Ohio.

THERE'S MORE

Genesee Country Village and Museum, 1410 Flint Hill Road, Mumford, New York; (716) 538–6822. This living history museum, the country's third largest collection of historic buildings, is a must-see. Located a half-hour west of Rochester, just south of I–90, it's an easily accessible stop if you're visiting between May and October. "Villagers" in many of the fifty-seven buildings moved from nearby towns show visitors what life was like from the 1790s to the 1870s. There's something cooking every day, perhaps a full meal in the frontier home or cheese making in the farmhouse. There are log homes, Greek Revival and Italianate mansions, the birthplace home of George Eastman, and the first dwelling built by Nathaniel Rochester, the city's founder. Call ahead for special events, like the Hearthside cooking and dining experience, for which participants don period costumes for an authentic step back in history.

Performing Arts. Whatever you're in the mood for, you'll find it in Rochester. Contemporary and classic films are screened six times a week at the Dryden and Curtis Theatres, located in the George Eastman House International Museum of Photography and Film. The Rochester Philharmonic Orchestra

(RPO) performs classical, pops and family concerts year-round. Tickets run $24 to $39, depending on the concert. Box office: Ticket Express, 100 East Avenue; (716) 222–5000. At the Eastman School of Music (60 Gibbs Street; 716–274–1110), more than 700 free concerts are on tap annually. Check the arts and entertainment section of *City,* a free weekly guide, for an eclectic range of jazz, blues, zydeco, folk, and world beat, as well as comedy and dance clubs around town.

Memorial Art Gallery, 500 University Avenue; (716) 473–7720. Peruse a panorama of 5,000 years of world art, from antiquity to contemporary compositions and works by regional artists, with a long stop at the museum's American galleries. Admission is $5.00 for adults, $4.00 for college students and seniors, and $4.00 for children six to eighteen. Open Tuesday noon to 9:00 P.M., Wednesday through Friday 10:00 A.M. to 4:00 P.M., Saturday 10:00 A.M. to 5:00 P.M., and Sunday noon to 5:00 P.M.

The Frederick Douglass Cultural Museum, 300 East Main Street; (716) 546–3960. Located in the same building where Douglass published his famous newspaper, *The North Star,* this new museum celebrates Douglass's achievements and inspires others by his example. It depicts not only Douglass's abolitionist contributions, but African-American culture past and present, with exhibits by artists of color. Open Tuesday to Thursday noon to 5:00 P.M., Saturday until 3:00 P.M. Admission is $4.00 for adults, $2.00 for children.

Historic Homes. Those interested in the Underground Railroad can retrace some of history by adding visits to the Harriet Tubman Home (180 South Street; 315–252–2081) and the Seward House (33 South Street; 315–252–1283) in Auburn, New York.

Shopping. Monroe Avenue, beginning downtown at the Strong Museum, One Manhattan Square, and continuing several miles east, is a shopper's delight. Stroll or drive part of the street lined with a mix of restaurants and boutiques. A brochure is available from the Greater Rochester Visitors Association (800–677–7282) or the Monroe Avenue Merchants Association, 219 Monroe Avenue, Rochester, New York 14607.

SPECIAL EVENTS

May. Lilac Festival. Ten-day celebration of spring flowers, one of the largest of its kind in North America. Parades, musical performances, entertainment, and flowers throughout the city's parks and the Lamberton Conservatory make this a colorful and lively event. Free. (716) 256–4960.

June. Maplewood Rose Festival, Maplewood Rose Garden, Lake and Driving Park. Rose culture workshops, tours, and a celebration of the more than 5,000 historical rose bushes found here. (716) 428–6677.

July–August. Park Avenue Summer Art Fest. The street becomes a happening as artists from all over the country set up shop. Music, food, and entertainment. Free. (716) 244–0951.

July–August. Civil War Reenactment, Genesee Country Village and Museum, Mumford. Confederate and Union armies meet on the great meadow. (716) 538–6822.

September. Clothesline Festival, Memorial Art Gallery grounds. Weekend event is largest arts and crafts festival in the area with 600 artists exhibiting. (716) 262–3142.

October. Rochester River Romance along the banks of the Genesee River and banks of Lake Ontario. Spend the weekend hiking, boating and touring the Genesee Gorge. A special event is an invitational collegiate regatta. (716) 428–6677.

December. Yuletide in the Country: Tours through Holidays Past, Genesee Country Village and Museum. Reservations are required for these candlelight walks through the village. Holiday buffet is also available. Tickets are $13.00 for adults, $9.00 for youth. Buffet meals are $18.50 each. (716) 538–6822.

OTHER RECOMMENDED RESTAURANTS AND LODGINGS

Rochester

Cutler's Restaurant, 500 University Avenue, in the Memorial Art Gallery; (716) 473–7720. Light cafe-style choices make this a perfect accompaniment during an afternoon of gallery browsing. Moderate.

Charlie's Frog Pond, 652 Park Avenue; (716) 271–1970. Located along historic Park Avenue, this upbeat eatery offers daily specials and a weekly all-you-can-eat pasta and salad combo for $7.95. Also noted for its Sunday brunch, served from 8:00 A.M. to 3:00 P.M. Moderate.

Highland Park Diner, 960 South Clinton Avenue; (716) 461–5040. If you're on a mission to visit '50s diners, you won't want to miss this classic taste of Americana. It's an original, moved to this site from Williamsport, New York, and offers another good spot for Sunday brunch.

428 Mt.Vernon, 428 Mt.Vernon Avenue; (800) 836–3159. This bed-and-breakfast is located in a private setting on two-and-a-half acres above Rochester's Highland Park. This Arts and Crafts Style home has seven guest rooms with private baths, some with queen-size beds. The $115 rate includes a full breakfast, selected from a menu of choices and cooked to order.

Crowne Plaza Rochester, 70 State Street; (716) 546–3450 or (800) 243–7760. All the amenities of the Crowne Plaza group, including an outdoor pool. Overlooks the Genesse River downtown. The "Best Break" weekend rate is $89, including a full breakfast for two.

Hyatt Regency Rochester, 125 East Main Street; (716) 456–1234 or (800) 233–1234. This 27-story high-rise towers over downtown and offers ongoing weekend promotions, including breakfast for two for $99; often there are even lower weekend specials.

FOR MORE INFORMATION

Greater Rochester Visitors Association, Inc., 45 East Avenue, Rochester, New York 14604-1102; (800) 677–7282 or (716) 546–3070; www.visitrochester.com.

SOUTHEASTERN
ESCAPES

Pittsburgh

WHERE THE OLD MEETS THE NEW

2 NIGHTS

Dinosaurs • Architecture • Pop art

Pittsburgh is an easily accessible two-and-a-half-hour turnpike drive, yet visitors will soon discover cultural and sightseeing opportunities that might remind them of more distant spots, possibly even different eras. The skyline's tall buildings and bridges display a gamut of old and new facades. Most brim with activities and reasons to take in an active weekend in Pittsburgh, as well known now for its environmental and urban renewal as it once was for its production of iron, steel, and glass, and its bituminous coal mining.

From Mt. Washington, formerly called "coal hill," visitors can take in a breathtaking view of the city filled with diverse neighborhoods, cultural opportunities, and educational arenas that all mix stories of its past with pride for present times. Only the smoky part of the heritage is gone. Whether you stroll the wide streets in "The Strip District" or visit one of the Carnegie Museums in Oakland just east of the city, dine in a microbrewery where names on the draft spigots provide a history lesson or sleep in the former home of Bavarian Benedictine priests and brothers, you'll discover parts of the past and too many activities to leisurely fit into a weekend escape. You'll have to return for the spectator sports and many of the cultural experiences you'll likely miss. Bring children back another time too. There's plenty to explore with them, but for now, join in the bustle and get ready to take in the sights.

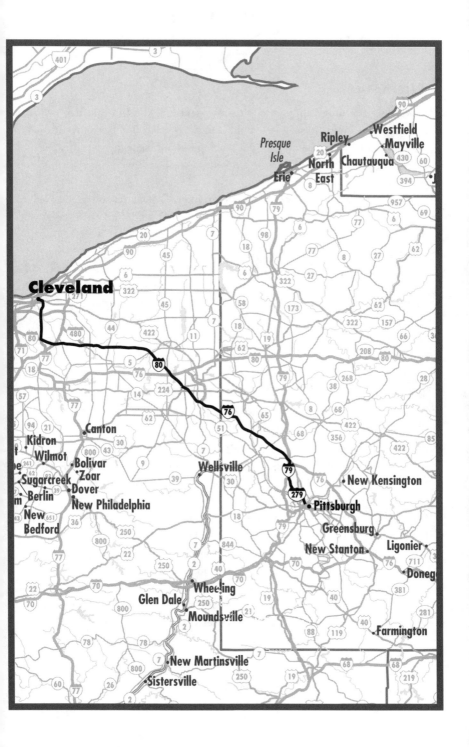

DAY 1

Afternoon

Leave right after lunch for your adults-only weekend. The 143-mile trip will take just over two hours. Head east on the Ohio Turnpike (I–80), connecting with I–76 south of Warren before crossing the Pennsylvania state line. As you approach **Pittsburgh,** take I–79 south to I–279 south, which will take you right into the heart of the city.

Exit I–279 at Grant Street. Turn left, driving northeast toward Sixth Avenue. Turn left onto Seventh Avenue, following it to the Seventh Street Bridge, staying in the left lane. Turn left at the end of the bridge onto Isabella Street. The Warhol parking lot entrance will be on the right about 500 feet ahead.

Start exploring at the **Andy Warhol Museum** (117 Sandusky Street; 412–237–8300). The museum is one of the most comprehensive single-artist museums in the world, with 900 Warhol paintings, 1,500 drawings, 500 prints, and the list continues. Open Tuesday through Saturday 10:00 A.M. to 5:00 P.M. and Sunday from 1:00 to 5:00 P.M., with a cocktail party each Friday from 5:00 to 7:00 P.M. Admission is $6.00 for adults and $4.00 for children three to eighteen.

Turn left onto Sandusky Street and then right onto East General Robinson Street to State Route 28 north. Turn right onto the Thirty-first Street Bridge, which becomes Thirty-first Street. Turn left onto Liberty Avenue and watch for the Church Brew Works about a half-mile further on the left.

DINNER: It's a fifteen-minute drive to **The Church Brew Works** (3525 Liberty Avenue; 412–688–8200). At first you might be aghast at seeing the shiny copper and stainless steel brewing tanks situated on the altar and diners caught in the glow of magnificent stained glass windows encircling the sanctuary. However, you'll soon recover after learning a little of the restaurant's history. It was formerly St. John the Baptist Church until it was purchased by the current owners who turned it into a brew pub, thereby saving its bell tower, courtyard, and magnificent interior from the wrecking ball. So take a seat in a pew (now shortened to become more manageable dining seating) and order your favorite brew: maybe a Celestial Gold, a Pious Monk Dunkel, a Bell Tower Brown Ale, or the Pipe Organ Pale Ale. Enjoy a little California cuisine, Southwestern spice, a neighborhood specialty, or wood-fired pizza, all moderately priced.

After dinner, allow some time to stroll the quaint streets nearby. Then head to your lodging. From the brewery turn left, driving southwest on Liberty Avenue toward downtown. Turn right onto Thirty-first Street, which becomes Thirty-first

Street Bridge, and turn left onto State Route 28, taking the North Canal Street ramp. Turn right onto Cedar Avenue and right onto Pressley Street. The Priory is the last building on the left with parking across the street.

LODGING: The Priory—A City Inn, 614 Pressley Street; (412) 231–3338. The inn is really two historic landmarks, an 1852 St. Mary's German Catholic Church and an adjacent 1888 residence of Bavarian Benedictine priests and brothers. At the Priory evening wine with light snacks and continental breakfast are included in rates ranging from $67 to $147.

DAY 2

Morning

BREAKFAST: Continental breakfast is included with your lodging at The Priory. During nice weather, opt for outdoor seating in the courtyard with views of the historic steeple and turrets.

Then it's off to the Strip District to join the mecca of early Saturday morning shoppers along Smallman Street, where the city's main railroad switching yard once sprawled the wide street. In those days the produce was sold right from the railcars.

It's still the center for the city's wholesale markets—Italian bakeries and espresso bars, an old world fish market, and more—but your destination is the **Senator John Heinz Pittsburgh Regional History Center,** housed in a spectacular nineteenth-century warehouse at 1212 Smallman Street (412–454–6000). It's large enough to hold a 1949 restored trolley, a Conestoga wagon, and the massive city fire bell cast after the Great Fire of 1845—and that's just on the first floor. Upstairs, *Building a Life in Western Pennsylvania, 1750–Today* features three life-size reconstructions of homes, depicting various stages in the state's development. There's a log home, an immigrant worker's courtyard home, and a suburban ranch home. Admission is $6.00 for adults, $4.50 for students and seniors, and $3.00 for children three to eighteen.

The **Society for Contemporary Crafts,** on Smallman Street at Twenty-first Street (412–261–7003), showcases works of more than 200 nationally known craft artists in its small intimate gallery, sells many pieces in its shop, and also has a small cafe.

LUNCH: A local, somewhat gritty place for lunch is the legendary **Primanti Brothers** in the Strip District, where local workers originally met in the wee hours after work. Now tourists and office workers line up at three locations (also in Southside and downtown) for the famous deli sandwiches. Tomatoes and deli meats are stuffed between thick slices of Italian bread along with the coleslaw and french fries. A little advice: don't knock it until you've tried it and don't try to order it any other way.

Afternoon

With more than fifty museums from which to choose, the most difficult task is deciding on just one or two. First timers shouldn't miss the **Carnegie Museum of Natural History** (4400 Forbes Avenue, Oakland; 412–622–3131). Just look for the dinosaur out front.

Inside you'll visit one of the largest dinosaur fossil collections in the world in the famous Dinosaur Hall. Look to the ceiling to see a model skeleton of the largest flying animal ever in existence. Open Tuesday through Saturday 10:00 A.M. to 5:00 P.M. and Sunday 1:00 to 5:00 P.M. Also open Monday in July and August. Admission is $6.00 for adults, $5.00 for seniors, and $4.00 for children and students.

Another must-see is the University of Pittsburgh's **Nationality Classrooms** encircling the Gothic Commons Room on the first floor of the Cathedral of Learning (4200 Fifth Avenue, Room 157; 412–624–6000). These twenty-four rooms, authentic examples of Classical, Byzantine, Romanesque, Renaissance, Tudor, and Empire styles, were gifts to the University from the various ethnic groups that settled in Allegheny County. During December, holiday decorations reflect the rooms' ethnic origins. Guided and self-guided audio tours are available by reservation.

It's but a five- to ten-minute drive east to Shadyside's Walnut Street, where little boutiques and some of the top national stores like Williams & Sonoma, Talbots, and Gap call home. A host of eateries and coffeehouses caters to shoppers and students who like to congregate here.

Rejuvenate yourself back at The Priory and enjoy complimentary wine in the library or out in the courtyard before motoring across the Ninth Street Bridge for dinner, only a half mile away. If you really need a stress reliever, call ahead and book a predinner spa treatment, perhaps an hour-long Swedish massage for $60 or an aromatherapy massage for $70, at the Spa Uptown (412–281–5400). It's located in the Pittsburgh Marriott City Center.

DINNER: The **Steelhead Grill** at Pittsburgh Marriott City Center (112 Washington Place; 412–394–3474) features signature seafood dishes prepared any way you like, great desserts and service, and an extensive wine list. The warm breads served can be purchased for taking home. It's definitely not the usual hotel fare and worth the trip to Pittsburgh by itself. Moderate to expensive, entrees are in the $20 range.

After dinner more choices abound. Pick up the *Pittsburgh City Paper* or *In Pittsburgh* to check goings-on in the downtown Cultural District. Cornerstones of the area are the Byham Theater (101 Sixth Street; 412–622–8866) where local productions and touring companies take center stage; Heinz Hall for the Performing Arts (600 Penn Avenue; 412–392–4900), home of the Pittsburgh Symphony Orchestra; and the Benedum Center for the Performing Arts (719 Liberty Avenue; 412–456–6666), for opera, dance, and first-run Broadway touring productions. The newest spots are the Harris Theater (809 Liberty Avenue; 412–682–4111), where visitors will find independent and foreign film showings, and the O'Reilly Theater (621 Penn Avenue; 412–316–1600) for Pittsburgh Public Theater performances.

LODGING: The Priory—A City Inn.

DAY 3

Morning

BREAKFAST: Have a first cup of coffee at the inn, but save room for a luxurious array of breakfast delicacies at the Sunday brunch at the **Grand Concourse Restaurant** at Station Square, across the Smithfield Bridge (412–261–1717). Located in the waiting room of the former Pittsburgh & Lake Erie railroad station, tall vaulted ceilings and natural lighting streaming through stained glass windows provide an elegant atmosphere for gourmet fare anytime, but the New Orleans–style Sunday brunch is a favorite among locals and visitors alike. Brunch costs $17.95 for adults, $7.95 for children four to twelve; free for children under age four.

After brunch stroll the shops at **Station Square** (800–859–8959). The shops are open on Sunday from noon to 5:00 P.M. Then take a round-trip up to the top of Mt. Washington and back on one of the two remaining funiculars or inclines. The **Monongahela Incline** (8 Grandview Avenue; 412–442–2000) is the closest, right next to Station Square, but the **Duquesne Heights Incline** (1220 Grandview Avenue; 412–381–1665) is more interesting, retaining its original 1877 cars and housing a small museum indoors. For $2.00 round-trip, you'll catch a panoramic view of Pittsburgh and all the spots you visited. It runs until 12:45 A.M. daily, in case you'd rather see the view under starry skies.

From Station Square drive east on West Carson Street, following signs to I–279 north. I–79 links to I–76 west at exit 3 in Warrendale for your return trip.

The Golden Triangle, several bridges, and downtown Pittsburgh can be seen from the cable car on the famous Duquesne Incline.

THERE'S MORE

The Carnegie Museums of Pittsburgh, 4400 Forbes Avenue; (412) 622–3131. Andrew Carnegie's perpetual gift to the city. Located in Oakland, east of downtown between the University of Pittsburgh and the Carnegie Mellon University, the museums consist of the Carnegie Library, the Carnegie Music Hall, the Carnegie Museum of Art, the Carnegie Museum of Natural History, and the Andy Warhol Museum. All museum hours are Tuesday through Saturday 10:00 A.M. to 5:00 P.M., Sunday 1:00 to 5:00 P.M. Admission is $6.00 for adults, $4.00 for children three to eighteen.

The Mattress Factory, 500 Samposnia Way; (412) 231–3169. Its name comes from the former use of its space. Now it exhibits contemporary site-specific installations. Open Tuesday through Saturday 10:00 A.M. to 5:00 P.M., Sunday 1:00 to 5:00 P.M. Admission is $4.00 for adults, $3.00 for students; free on Thursday.

The Frick Art & Historical Center, 7227 Reynolds Street; (412) 371–0600. A short distance from downtown, but worth the drive and time spent discovering the grand Victorian era. The complex comprises several buildings—including the restored home of industrialist Henry Clay Frick and the art museum housing the collection of his daughter, Helen Clay Frick—and acres of manicured lawns and gardens. High tea is served in the garden. Hours are Tuesday through Saturday 10:00 A.M. to 5:30 P.M. and Sunday noon to 6:00 P.M., with tours given Wednesday, Saturday, and Sunday at 2:00 P.M. Admission is free.

Pittsburgh Children's Museum, 10 Children's Way; (412) 322–5058. A recent $600,000 expansion added more interactive exhibits like *Great Heights* for exploring vertical space: Children make and launch flying machines and pull themselves up using their own human-powered elevators. Parents and kids can create art in the multimedia studio and then relax in the cafe. Open September through June on Tuesday, Thursday, and Saturday, 10:00 A.M. to 5:00 P.M., and Sunday, noon to 5:00 P.M. Summer hours vary. Admission is $4.50 for adults and $3.50 for seniors and children.

Phipps Conservatory and Botanical Gardens, One Schenley Park; (412) 622–6914. Just the place to visit during winter for a quick pick-me-up amid bright blooms. Admission is $5.00 for adults, $3.50 for seniors and students, and $2.00 for children ages two to twelve. Call for hours.

Shopping. Don't forget Pittsburgh's downtown when looking for great shopping. You'll find Kauffmann's at 400 Fifth Avenue, Saks Fifth Avenue at 513 Smithfield Street, and Lazarus at 301 Fifth Avenue. Look beyond these major stores for specialty and designer shops at PPG Place (Third and Stanwix) and The Shops at One Oxford Centre (Grant and Fourth Streets). Two levels of boutiques await at Fifth Avenue Place (Fifth and Liberty Avenues). If that's not enough, try the outlying malls and, believe it or not, the AirMall at the Pittsburgh International Airport.

Professional Sports. Visitors come to share the excitement of Pittsburgh's sports teams: the Pirates (412–323–5000), the Penguins (412–642–1800) and the Steelers (412–323–1200). By 2001, the Steelers and the Pirates are scheduled for new stadiums on the city's North Side. The new football stadium will built near the site of the existing Three Rivers Stadium.

SPECIAL EVENTS

February. Pittsburgh Automobile Show, David Lawrence Convention Center, downtown. (412) 565–6000.

March. Annual St. Patrick's Day Parade, downtown. (412) 621–0600.

March. Spring Flower Show, Phipps Conservatory and Botanical Gardens, Oakland. (412) 622–6914.

May. Pittsburgh Folk Festival, I. C. Light Amphitheater, Station Square. More than twenty nationalities celebrate their heritage through music, dance and food. (412) 278–1267.

May. Pittsburgh Marathon and 10K, Point State Park, downtown. (412) 647–7866.

June. Three Rivers Arts Festival, Gateway Plaza and Point State Park, downtown. Artists market, free entertainment highlight this seventeen-day event. (412) 281–8723.

June. Mellon Jazz Festival, downtown. Ten days of jazz and outdoor concerts in the parks and plazas around town. (412) 234–3275.

August. Pittsburgh Three Rivers Regatta, Point State Park, downtown. Air and water shows fill two family-oriented weekends during this event, the world's largest inland regatta. (412) 338–8765.

November–January. Pittsburgh Zoo Holiday Lights Festival, Pittsburgh Zoo, One Wild Place. (412) 665–3639.

December. Holidays at the Carnegie, Carnegie Museums of Pittsburgh, Oakland. Extravagant holiday displays and seasonal concerts. (412) 622–3131.

December. Holidays at the Nationality Classrooms, University of Pittsburgh, Oakland. Twenty-four rooms that depict the city's diverse ethnicity are decorated for the holiday season. (412) 624–6000.

OTHER RECOMMENDED RESTAURANTS AND LODGINGS

Shadyside

Appletree Bed & Breakfast, 703 South Negley Avenue; (412) 661–0631. This B&B is conveniently located close to shops and dining possibilities as well as the

Carnegie Museums. Eight distinctive and beautifully decorated rooms all take the names of apple varieties. The Braeburn Apple Room features true handicapped accessibility. Rates: $130–$180, includes full breakfast.

The Shadyside Bed & Breakfast, 5516 Maple Heights Road; (412) 683–6501. This English Jacobean mansion, constructed at the turn of last century and furnished with antiques, sits on a hilltop overlooking Shadyside. Eight guest rooms, a guest kitchen for longer stays, and a billiard room for guests to enjoy. Rates: $130–$145, includes a deluxe continental breakfast.

Downtown

Westin William Penn, 530 William Penn Place; (412) 281–7100. This grand hotel is as special today as it was when it was first built in 1916. Chandeliers, soft music, and even a Starbucks grace the lobby. Rooms during the weekend can cost as little as $99 based on availability; special packages are often available.

The Pittsburgh Marriott, 112 Washington Place; (412) 471–4000 or (888) 456–6600. Houses the Spa Uptown and Steelhead Grill restaurant. Rates: $79–$99 or $114 including breakfast.

The Sheraton Hotel Station Square, 7 Station Square Drive; (412) 261–2000 or (800) 255–7488. A convenient location near shops and restaurants. The Bed & Breakfast package is $99; other weekend specials run as low as $109.

Mt. Washington

Le Mont, 1114 Grandview Avenue, near the incline; (412) 431–3100. Completely renovated and redecorated, this is a great choice for romantic dining and great views of the city. Entrees like flaming chateaubriand for two ($59.95) are perfect for special occasion evenings.

The Grandview Saloon, 1212 Grandview Avenue; (412) 431–1400. Casual—plastic chairs outdoors on the patio—but the burgers and views are super and the prices are reasonable.

North Side

James Street Restaurant, 422 Foreland Street; (412) 323–2222. Live New Orleans–style jazz and moderately priced cuisine. It's a few minutes from the Priory Inn.

FOR MORE INFORMATION

Greater Pittsburgh Convention and Visitors Bureau, Four Gateway Center, Pittsburgh, PA 15222; (800) 366–0093 or (412) 281–7711. Call (800) 927–8376 to reach the weekend package hot line.

Shadyside Chamber of Commerce, 5541 Walnut Street, Pittsburgh, PA 15232; (412) 682–1298.

Pennsylvania's Laurel Highlands

NATURE'S SPLENDOR

2 NIGHTS

Mountain crests and river gorges
Architectural gems • Pleasant pampering

The Laurel Highlands area, traversing the Laurel and Chestnut Ridges of the Allegheny Mountain range in southwestern Pennsylvania, attracts visitors as diverse as the activities it offers. It has been a popular summertime resort area for a century, but the mountains and deep river gorge offer a scenic backdrop for outdoor enthusiasts every season. Before trip planning to this region decide among those many options—skiing, white-water rafting, hiking and biking, golfing, antiquing, architectural tours, or decompressing at a luxurious spa. Of course, you can easily combine a few of your favorites, depending on the climate. The season you select will affect the range of available activities.

Tailor the trip to interests and budget, but whatever you select, the weekend promises to include sights you won't find anywhere else. To save on rentals, pack your own sporting gear. You'll be traversing the mountainous highlands once you exit the turnpike, about an hour past Pittsburgh, so allow a little extra time to maneuver the winding and curving unfamiliar routes.

DAY 1

Afternoon

The trip will take about three hours, so leave as time permits. Head toward the Pennsylvania line from I–80 east to I–76 east. It will become the turnpike as you enter Pennsylvania. Drive southeast to exit 8, then south on U.S. 119 to U.S. 40 east in

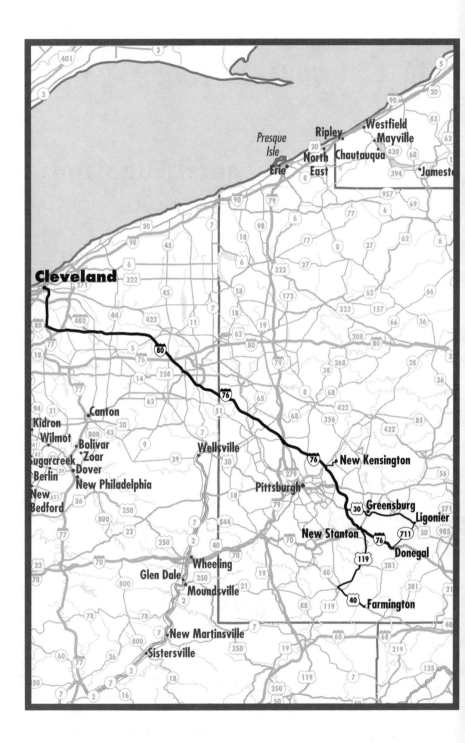

Uniontown. Continue toward **Farmington** to **Nemacolin Woodlands Resort and Spa** (1001 LaFayette Drive, Farmington; 800–422–2736). This first-class resort in the midst of the Laurel Highland Mountains on 1,500 acres of pristine countryside has won numerous accolades for its spa, golf, lodging, and culinary offerings.

Drive up to the doorman awaiting your arrival at the Chateau LaFayette, a European-style hotel patterned after the Ritz in Paris. The English Tudor lodge, the original on the property, is connected to the LaFayette and more closely resembles a country inn. It still has a bit of the flavor of its former use as a private hunting lodge.

Boutique shops along Heritage Court connect the more rustic lodge and the glittery hotel. Dubbed the "Heritage Trail" and resembling the Cumberland Trail, the make-believe street of yesteryear takes visitors back to pioneer days. You'll find resort apparel, galleries of original art and sculpture, several of the resort's restaurants, and a cigar shop, lauded among the best in the state.

A few of the resort amenities include the new spa facilities for head-to-toe pampering, as well as a full beauty center, indoor swimming, and exercise and juice bar facilities. There's also a ski lodge and school, a three-sided 50-foot climbing wall, two golf courses (one of them, The Links, is open year-round), horseback riding at the equestrian center, and trout fishing in the stocked pond. The resort's newest addition, the Shooting Academy, is a sporting clays course that rivals any other in the country. If you're traveling with the family, take advantage of the baby-sitting and planned activities for children and teens, and opt for casual dining at P.J's Ice Cream & Pizza Parlor or at the Caddy Shack on the Links Golf Course. There are also townhouses available for larger groups.

Check in and walk around the resort to get a feeling for what's close at hand before dinner. Time permitting, try one of the pools or drive to the equestrian center, ski lodge, or miniature golf course.

The executive chef has added healthy-lifestyle cuisine in the newest restaurant, adjacent to the world-class spa. More eclectic selections can be found in the other restaurants. If you are traveling during peak times, arrange dining plans when you make your reservations. Otherwise, you can wait until arrival.

After traveling, a good choice is the casual atmosphere at the **Caddy Shack,** open from April through December. Sandwiches, barbecue ribs, and pastas are among the moderately priced comfort foods.

After dinner, stop by **Diamond Lil's,** the high-energy nightclub, or next door at **The Tavern,** an English-style pub, for a game of pool.

LODGING: You're only steps away from your room and a good night's rest before an energetic day of activities and sightseeing tomorrow.

DAY 2

Morning

BREAKFAST: Enjoy breakfast in the lodge at the **Golden Trout.** There's a wide variety, but try an egg-white omelette with goat cheese and salsa garnish ($7.75) if you're in the mood for something light and healthy.

After breakfast, tour one of the Frank Lloyd Wright homes nearby. If this is your first time to the area, opt for the tour of **Fallingwater** (State Highway 381, Mill Run; 724–329–8501), one of the best examples of Wright's talent.

Located about fifteen minutes from the resort, Wright's creation, originally designed as a weekend home for Edgar J. Kaufmann, sits over the waterfalls of Bear Run. There is considerable walking involved: about a quarter-mile hike to reach the home from the visitor's center, and then many steps in the home once the one-and-a-half-hour guided tour begins. Transportation can be arranged for those unable to walk the rhododendron-lined trail. Seeing the home is well worth the effort even if all of the nooks and crannies of the upper levels can't be reached by some. A video explains the upper floors; foreign-language tapes are also available. Make advance reservations, especially important in peak times of July, August, and October during fall color. It is closed in January and February. Tickets are $12.00 on weekends, $8.00 Tuesday through Friday.

The building is currently being repaired but is still open to the public. Some structural strengthening began in 1999, but visitors on tour can see the architectural cantilevered sandstone "trays," exterior "rooms," plunge pools, carports, and other natural elements of Wright's focus. Also, nearly all of the originally designed furnishings and art, as well as wonderful works by other contemporary artists, remain at Fallingwater.

LUNCH: Have a light lunch in the cafe at the visitors center at Fallingwater and browse the gift shop, where Wright reproductions and books are in hefty supply. There are also interpretive nature walks and a tended child-care facility for youngsters under the nine-year-old age requirement for the home tours.

Afternoon

Nine miles away, architectural buffs will also want to tour **Frank Lloyd Wright's House on Kentuck Knob** (P.O. Box 305, Chalk Hill; 724–329–1901). To get there from Fallingwater take State Route 381 south to Ohiopyle. Cross a short bridge in the park and take an immediate right toward Cucumber Falls. Travel about three miles to the crossroads at the top of the hill, turning left onto Chalk

Hill Road. The home at Kentuck Knob will be about two miles down on your left.

During summer, water lilies cover the lake on the way, but other times, the scenery is also breathtaking. Remarkably, Wright designed Kentuck Knob when he was eighty-seven years old, at the same time that he was working on another commission, the Solomon R. Guggenheim Museum in New York City. This home, with triangular shapes and hexagonal spaces, features many of the architect's trademarks, such as the clerestory windows, skylights, and distinctive furnishings, but for some reason it remains relatively undiscovered by tourists. The current owners, Lord and Lady Palumbo of London, England, added a sculpture park. Among their holdings is a piece of the Berlin Wall, visible as you drive up to the house, and a Claus Oldenberg sculpture, *Apple Core.*

Meet at the greenhouse for the guided tour, which lasts about an hour. Admission is $15 per person on weekends, $10 Tuesday through Friday.

The drive back to the resort, like most of them in this area, is scenic. You might indulge in a spa treatment, play a round of golf, or choose another activity from the long list of possibilities. There are guided hikes and maps for self-guided ones, as well as an art tour at 3:00 P.M.

DINNER: There are a dozen dining and entertainment options at Nemacolin Woodlands Resort and Spa, but **Seasons** is a good choice, especially if you are new to "conscious cuisine" or are vegetarian. The chef's selections include regionally grown and organic ingredients whenever possible, and the meals are balanced for the best nutritional composition. The presentation adds an artistic component. Grilled vegetable lasagna ($16) and wok-seared sea bass with basmati rice ($21) are staples. Try the roasted banana sushi for dessert.

Nemacolin's lodge is a veritable museum. After a leisurely dinner, take a self-guided tour of the extensive art and sculpture collection.

LODGING: Nemacolin Woodlands Resort and Spa.

DAY 3

Morning

BREAKFAST: Sleep in and enjoy another of the lodge's amenities before the lavish Sunday brunch served in the French bistro, **Lautrec.** The decor reflects the restaurant's name—all French originals—as does the menu at other meals. The buffet is different from most. Items are custom created—no chafing dishes at this brunch. There are stations where omelettes and waffles are prepared and prime rib is sliced. Be sure to leave room for bumbleberry pie. Brunch is $32 per person.

The spa at Nemacolin Woodlands is part of the luxurious amenities visitors enjoy during a weekend reserved for rest and relaxation.

Take the scenic way back to the turnpike by following Route 381 north off U.S. 40. It cuts through Ohiopyle State Park, with scenic gorge overlooks. Cucumber Falls is just off the road.

To return to Cleveland travel Route 381 north to Normalville, then follow 381/711 to Champion, Pennsylvania. Turn left onto State Route 31 and watch for the entrance (exit 9) to the Donegal Turnpike (I–70/I–76). Follow I–76 west into Ohio.

THERE'S MORE

Whitewater rafting. The Youghiogheny River, shortened to "the Yough" (pronounced *yock*) by locals, is a highly ranked trout stream. It offers excellent flat water for canoeing, but is a favorite among white-water rafters as well. Different sections (from Class I to Class V) make it appropriate for varying skill levels and there's plenty of beautiful nature scenery for everyone. Ohiopyle State Park attracts 2.2 million visitors annually. Shuttles, equipment, and launch fee permits are often extra charges that will boost fees. Check with the guide companies for their unguided trips.

Wilderness Voyageurs, P.O. Box 97, Ohiopyle; (800) 272–4141. This company offers a wide variety of rafting trips for all levels on the Youghiogheny River. Trips range from three hours to overnight excursions. Bike rentals, starting at $3.00 per hour, and combination pedal and paddle activities ($29–$39) are also available. Rental canoes and variations of kayaks and rafts on the lower and middle portions of the river range in price based on the trip and craft. Some trips are appropriate for children as young as four years, while other trips have twelve-year age minimums.

White Water Adventurers, Inc., P.O. Box 31, Ohiopyle; (800) WWA–RAFT. This outfitter recommends the family adventure trip for ages five and older. Adult prices for the three- to five-hour trip are $22.95 Monday through Friday, $30.95 on Saturday, and $25.95 on Sunday. Children's rates are $17.95, $25.95, and $20.95. More challenging portions of the river are higher, depending upon season and day of week. A deli lunch is provided on both trips.

Mountain Streams, P.O. Box 106, Ohiopyle; (800) RAFT–NOW. Kids under twelve raft free; bicycle and boat rentals.

Youghiogheny Outfitters, P.O. Box 21, Ohiopyle; (800) 967–2387. Rents equipment for unguided trips. Individuals are responsible for acquiring their own launch times and permits from the Ohiopyle State Park Office, (724) 329–8591.

Laurel Highlands River Tours, P.O. Box 107, Ohiopyle; (800) 472–3846. Guided raft tours and guided fishing programs as well as instructional courses and team building events. Trips range from $22.95 to $76.95 for adults depending upon day of week and month.

Fort Necessity National Battlefield, One Washington Parkway, Farmington; (724) 329–5512. Stop here for a reconstructed version of Fort Necessity, site of the first battle of the French and Indian War. George Washington was defeated here, but the Mount Washington Tavern, an original stagecoach stop, still stands. Open daily 9:00 A.M. to 5:00 P.M. year-round. Admission is $2.00 for adults; children age sixteen and younger are free.

SOUTHEASTERN

Youghiogheny River Trail, 101 North Water Street, West Newton; (724) 872–5586. One of the Rails-to-Trails projects, this 67-mile crushed limestone multiuse path runs through Ohiopyle State Park from Confluence to Mc-Keesport.

Idlewild Park, Route 30, Ligonier; (800) 4–DAYFUN. This historic park offers family entertainment—amusement rides, Story Book Forest, water slides, kiddie rides, Mister Rogers' Neighborhood of Make-Believe—seven theme areas in all. Open Memorial Day through Labor Day. Closed on Mondays except holidays. One-price admission is $15.95, seniors $11.50, under two free. Second-day passes are available.

Skiing. Three ski areas make this scenic region a year-round destination. Mystic Mountain at Nemacolin Woodlands Resort and Spa, (1001 Lafayette Drive, Farmington; 800–422–2736) and Hidden Valley Four Seasons Resort (One Craighead Drive, Hidden Valley; 800–458–0175) have downhill slopes for skiing and snowboarding, trails for cross-country skiing. Seven Springs Mountain Resort (RR #1, Box 110, Champion; 800–452–2223) is the largest resort in the region; ten chairlifts and six tows take skiers to an elevation of nearly 3,000 feet. The resort includes a full-service lodge, ski school, snow tubing park, rental shop, child care, bowling alley, game rooms, fitness center, hot tubs, indoor swimming pool, restaurants, and live entertainment.

SPECIAL EVENTS

January. Antique Show and Sale, Mountain View Inn, Route 30, Greensburg. Just one of the activities hosted at this historic inn. (724) 834–5300.

August–September. Greater Pittsburgh Renaissance Festival, 2100 Mt. Pleasant Road, West Newton. (724) 872–1670. Held during weekends from mid-August through Labor Day. Jousts, sixteenth-century English foods, games, humor, and themed performances.

September. Flax Scutching Festival, 145 Fort Hill Road, Stahlstown. An unusual festival featuring the process of creating fiber clothing, for example, from the flax plant. French and Indian War reenactments, too. (724) 238–9244.

September. Ligonier Highland Games at Idlewild Park, the Mountain View Inn, and downtown Ligonier. Lots of Celtic entertainers and competitions, even a Scottish fair and dog exhibit. (412) 851–9900.

OTHER RECOMMENDED RESTAURANTS AND LODGINGS

Greensburg

Mountain View Inn, Route 30 East; (800) 537–8709. A mix of old and new, the original part of the inn was built in 1924 and has grown continually since the current owners took over in 1940. The older sections offer some of the largest accommodations (ask for the canopy bed in the Innkeepers Wing) but the newest Loyalhanna Wing has plenty of room and an airy feeling. Many different room configurations. Rates, based on single occupancy ($10 extra per person), range from $69 to $300 for the largest suite. All include a deluxe continental breakfast. Nice gardens, a gazebo, and outdoor pool. Antique furnishings throughout the common areas; a self-guided walking tour that explains the collection. Special events and big band dances throughout the year. Several dining rooms; the 1776 Tavern features large portions and moderate prices.

Ligonier

Ligoner Tavern, 137 West Main Street; (724) 238–4831. In the midst of a three-block shopping area downtown, this restaurant was originally the 1895 home of the town's first mayor. The menu features a wide variety, including many vegetarian items. Moderate.

Staci's Pastries, 127 West Main Street; (724) 238–9628. Great sticky buns.

Donegal

The Country Pie Shoppe Bakery and Restaurant, Route 31 East; bakery, (724) 593–7105; restaurant, (724) 593–7104. Homemade pies and cinnamon rolls are the house specialties. Moderate.

Farmington

Historic Summit Inn Resort, 2 Skyline Drive; (800) 433–8594. Open only seasonally, but a good choice if you're visiting between April and October. Historic 1907 inn, on the National Register of Historic Places, takes visitors back to the styles of the last century. Rates begin at $75, based on double occupancy. Menu is upscale but affordable American cuisine.

The Stone House Historic Restaurant and Inn, 3023 National Pike; (724) 329–8876. This 1822 wayside inn on the National Road is listed on the

National Register of Historic Places. Half of the fifteen rooms are new, but follow the historic guidelines, all have either four-poster or sleigh beds, no TVs or telephones. Rates: $105 for rooms with private baths, $95 for shared baths. Rates include continental breakfast. Weekend celebration package runs $159 for lodging, breakfast, $40 dinner allowance, and wine for two. Moderately priced dinners ($6–$18) feature American continental and Italian specialties, including homemade pastas, breads, desserts.

Champion

The Huber Haus Bed and Breakfast, 2381 Indian Head Road; (800) 584–3072. Walking trails and country setting. Three rooms with private baths and two with shared bath. Full breakfast served outdoors, if guests wish. The whole house can be rented for $1,500 for the weekend, other rates are $95–$100.

FOR MORE INFORMATION

Laurel Highlands Visitors Bureau, 120 East Main Street, Ligonier, PA 15658; (800) 333–5661; www.laurelhighlands.org.

SOUTHEASTERN

West Virginia's Panhandle
ALONG THE OHIO RIVER

2 NIGHTS

Homemade in West Virginia • Hard time • Victorian flair

When you're looking for a weekend that's off the beaten path, full of more hills than you'll find in Ohio and a few hairpin curves for variety, head south to West Virginia's northern panhandle. If you want to take full advantage of the mountainous scenery, plan the trip during mild climates and optimal driving conditions.

Most of the trip follows the Ohio River along West Virginia's State Route 2, maneuvering less traveled routes, like Proctor Creek Road. Instead of the Ohio River, this route follows the creek it's named for as it traverses toward lofty elevations, making sharp turns for spectacular vistas far above the narrow stream at its terminus. During winter, prudent plans would leave this jog off the itinerary and include the area's Victorian home tours and museum stops, adding a visit to Oglebay Resort during its colorful Winter Festival of Lights.

DAY 1

Morning

Leave by 9:00 A.M. for the two-hour trip south. Take I–77 south to Canton, then U.S. 30 east toward East Liverpool. Your travels along portions of the Lincoln Highway follow America's main streets past town halls in the small towns along the way. Cross the Ohio River at Chester, West Virginia, and take State Route 2 to **Newell.**

Afternoon

You'll want to be at the **Homer Laughlin China Co.** (Sixth and Hamilton Streets, Newell; 800–452–4462) by 12:30 P.M. That's when the last factory tour begins, showing how the popular Fiesta ware is produced. Even more popular than the factory tours is the Seconds Warehouse, with bin after bin of slightly imperfect pieces. Armed with lists and a dishcloth or rag, seasoned shoppers dust off each piece to check for flaws before making final selections, marked down to make the search worthwhile. The adjacent retail shop sells first-quality merchandise at substantial discounts and houses a company museum that traces the history of this classic style back more than 125 years.

With bargains in hand, continue south along State Route 2 to the river town of Wellsburg. This is where you'll be having dinner later tonight. However, before dinner, drive about 6 miles south of town on State Route 67 to historic **Bethany.** The Historic Bethany Information Center (Delta Tau Delta Founders House, Main Street; 304–829–7285) offers a self-guided walking or driving tour amid its quiet, tree-lined streets and on the campus of Bethany College. The information center is open weekdays from 8:30 A.M. to noon and from 1:00 to 4:00 P.M.

After your tour of Bethany, take State Route 67 back to **Wellsburg** for dinner.

DINNER: Drover's Inn, 1001 Washington Pike, Wellsburg; (314) 737–0188. Built in the mid-1800s, it served as the Fowlerstown post office and general store and provided overnight lodging even then. Now serving a home-cooked buffet ($7.50) and menu items, the restaurant attracts crowds on weekends, making reservations advisable. The specialty is hot wings, available in eight strengths and one- and two-pound portions ($3.75 and $5.75). The tavern on the lower level is a favorite of local college students.

After dinner, drive back to State Route 2. Continue south for 25 miles, through Wheeling to **Glen Dale.**

LODGING: The **Bonnie Dwaine Bed and Breakfast** (505 Wheeling Avenue, Glen Dale; 888–507–4569 or 304–845–7250) is on the right about ten minutes from Wheeling. The innkeepers will take you on a tour, after which you can look at before and after photos of this Victorian home. The work that went into remodeling and adding on to the original structure is inspirational, especially if you've ever considered rehabbing an old building.

Innkeeper Bonnie Dwaine, a retired home-ec teacher, is a talented seamstress. She created all the window treatments; her husband handled the painting. Each contributed family antiques and added something left behind by previous owners to each room.

Each of five guest rooms has a fireplace, air-conditioning, and a private bath with whirlpool. There's a self-serve pantry with snacks and beverages; a full gourmet candlelight breakfast is served on weekends. Other times, it's continental. The innkeepers believe in providing little surprises and using family heirloom china and crystal. There is a TV, private telephone, and Internet connection in each room.

DAY 2

Morning

BREAKFAST: Another special treat can be expected at the inn, perhaps breakfast bananas Foster before a hot entree.

After breakfast, set out for the hills where you'll discover the "beeman" and a knowledgeable vintage toy maker. Take State Route 2 south through Moundsville to **Proctor** (don't blink), turning left onto State Route 89 (Proctor Creek Road).

At the top of one of the many ridges, you'll find **Thistle Dew Farms** (R.D. 1, Box 122, Proctor; 800–854–6639). Owners Steve and Ellie Conlin set up their beekeeping business in an old two-room school house and are glad to share their honey knowledge, recipes, and tips with visitors during a tour of the production kitchen. Follow up with some taste-testing in the gift shop, picking up some beeswax hand lotion and lavender honey to take home.

Follow the winding road southeast for another 10 miles to the **Mountain Craft Shop** (American Ridge Road, Route 1, New Martinsville; 304–455–3570). It will be on the first paved road you come to. Here you'll find 81-year-old Dick Schnacke busy filling orders for his traditional American folk toys. From this modern hilltop craft shop, Schnacke sells reproduction toys to history museums throughout the country. They are individually created by craftspeople throughout the county according to his prototypes. Allow a little extra time here for playing with the vintage toys on display.

After the morning's scenic drive, travel west, returning to State Route 2. It's time to head back into **Wheeling** for lunch and a few of the city's unique offerings.

LUNCH: The **River City Ale Works** (1400 Main Street, Wheeling; 304–233–4555) serves very large portions at moderate prices. Homemade breads and pizza, desserts, and handcrafted beer account for its popularity.

Afternoon

Upstairs you'll find the **Wheeling Artisan Center** (304–232–1810). It's a great place to find crafts, edibles, and souvenirs made by local artisans.

The building, rehabbed from a former industrial site, dating back to the 1880s, now reveals a spacious look with exposed brick, skylights, and Swedish halogen lighting. Be sure to visit **Wymer's General Store Museum** on the upper level. Set up like an old-fashioned general store, Betty June Wymer's private collection of Wheeling memorabilia represents twenty-five years of collecting slices of Wheeling history. There's a $3.00 admission for the close-up look at local pottery, glass, vintage Marx toys, and other Wheeling-made items. Open Friday and Saturday 11:00 A.M. to 8:00 P.M., Sunday noon to 4:00 P.M., other times by appointment. Contemporary works, crafts, and souvenirs such as carvings made from West Virginia coal, are sold in the artisan gallery.

Before leaving downtown, stop at **West Virginia Independence Hall Museum,** around the corner at 1528 Market Street (304–238–1300). Originally, the 1839 sandstone edifice housed the U.S. Custom House; heated debates and the constitutional convention here led to the Restored Government of Virginia's split from Virginia, bringing about West Virginia's statehood. Along with original gas lights and memorabilia, changing and permanent exhibitions and a 20-minute video explain life during the Civil War. Admission is $3.00 for adults, $2.00 for students.

Drive north on Main Street to I–70. Take the interstate east to exit 2A and follow State Route 88 for about 2½ miles to reach **Oglebay Resort.** Depending on the season and your interests, choose among outdoor activities (three golf courses, strolls among the 1,650 acres of municipal parkland and gardens and Good Zoo) or indoors at the Carriage House Glass Museum and Factory and the Oglebay Mansion Museum. Once the summer farm home of Cleveland industrialist, Earl Oglebay, the home and grounds were bequeathed to Wheeling before his death and remain a local gem, no matter the season.

Self-guided tours at the glass museum provide excellent overviews of West Virginia glass production and opportunities to shop for Blenko, Pilgrim, Fenton, and other current day brands not close enough for a factory stop. Usually a working glass artist or demonstration takes place on the lower level. Admission is $3.25 for adults, $1.00 for children thirteen to seventeen.

The mansion is beautifully decorated at Christmastime. During the holidays, the huge G-gage electric train exhibit is worth a stop. Other seasons, each of a dozen rooms reflects an era of Wheeling history and an extensive collection of original Oglebay family belongings. Visitors cannot enter most rooms, but large picture windows provide visual access. Admission is $4.25 for adults, $2.00 for students thirteen to eighteen, and free for children twelve and under accompanied by an adult.

DINNER: Leave the park in time for dinner at the bottom of the hill at **Strafford Springs Restaurant** (Oglebay Drive; 304–233–5100). Listed on the National Register of Historic Places, the property was originally a country club. Now the caddy shack is a candy store, and small shops, including **Words & Music** (800–428–8410), a delightful place to find books and CDs, occupy the former pro shop. The clubhouse has turned into a comfortably casual restaurant with an extensively eclectic and moderately priced menu, including one for kids. Sandwiches, house specialties, and snacks are favorites in the adjoining Grill Room. The menu changes occasionally, but the chicken potpie ($10.95) and liver and onions ($12.95) are popular choices. Trays of homemade desserts accompany gourmet coffee drinks.

Stop in downtown Wheeling for a look at the suspension bridge while it is lit up. One of the best views is from the Best Western Wheeling Inn, at Tenth and Main Streets. You can stop for a drink or coffee on the terrace overlooking the bridge.

Call ahead for a schedule of events at **Capitol Music Hall** (1015 Main Street; 304–234–0050 or 800–624–5456). Country music, Broadway shows, and the Wheeling Symphony are among the offerings.

LODGING: It's a ten-minute drive back to the Bonnie Dwaine Bed & Breakfast.

DAY 3

Morning

BREAKFAST: Weekend breakfasts are too good to pass up at Bonnie Dwaine. You'll be unable to resist the steaming sticky buns hot from the oven.

Before leaving the area, drive south into **Moundsville** to do a little "hard time" at the former **West Virginia State Penitentiary** (818 Jefferson Avenue, Moundsville; 304–845–6200). It's oddly located in a residential neighborhood and remains an integral part of the community. The outstanding guided tour ($8.00 for adults and $5.00 for children six to ten) lasts one-and-a-half hours and includes interesting facts and memorabilia. You'll stop at the visitation areas at North Hall,

Wheeling's suspension bridge takes on a different look at night.

where the most dangerous inmates lived, and at the electric chair, in use until capital punishment was abolished in 1965.

Across the street is the **Grave Creek Mound Historic Site** (304–843–4128). It's open daily and is considered the largest Adena burial mound in the world, measuring 69 feet tall with a diameter of 295 feet. Open Monday through Saturday 10:00 A.M. to 4:30 P.M. and Sunday 1:00 to 5:00 P.M. Access to the mound closes at 4:00 P.M. Admission is $3.00 for adults and $2.00 for children ages six to sixteen.

LUNCH: Stop for a cup o' Joe and a huge cinnamon bun at **Café La News** in downtown Wheeling on the way to the interstate. The small coffee shop also features deli sandwiches for lunch. Prices are inexpensive and portions are large. Café La News is located in the McClure House, which recently became a Ramada Inn (Twelfth and Market Streets; 304–232–7170).

Afternoon

Follow signs to I–70, heading west to I–77 north in Cambridge, Ohio. You'll be home in less than three hours.

THERE'S MORE

Artworks in Oldtown, 747 Market Street, Wheeling; (304) 233–7540. Cooperative gallery displays works by local artists. Special presentations and gallery hop first Friday of each month from 5:00 to 8:00 P.M. Open Monday to Saturday 10:00 A.M. to 5:00 P.M., Sunday 1:00 to 5:00 P.M.

Kruger Street Toy & Train Museum, 144 Kruger Street, Wheeling; (877) 242–8133. Located in a Victorian schoolhouse, there's a little bit of everyone's past here. Classrooms showcase model trains, dollhouses and interactive train layouts. Hours vary by season. Admission is $8.00 for adults, $7.00 for seniors, $5.00 for children ten and older.

Eckhart House Tours, 810 Main Street, Wheeling; (888) 700–0118. Small tours through one to four of the area's most elegantly furnished and painstakingly restored homes give visitors a history of Wheeling's importance and wealth during the Industrial Revolution. Several of the properties are works in progress. Tours by guides in period costumes begin at 1:00 P.M. from May through October. Tours cost $3.00 for one house, $6.00 for two, $8.00 for three, and $10.00 for all four.

Wheeling Symphony, Capital Music Hall, 1025 Main Street, Suite 307, Wheeling; box office, (800) 395–9241. Classics, pops, and special concerts. Tickets range from $15 to $35.

Towngate Theatre & Cinema, 2118 Market Street, Wheeling; (88–TOWN-GATE). Part of the Oglebay Institute. Ten community theater productions annually and independent films shown twice monthly in a former church. Movie prices, $3.00 to $5.00; live theater, $10.00.

Good Zoo, Oglebay Resort and Conference Center; (800) 624–6988. Along with new animal exhibits, there are planetarium programs and a Discovery Lab. Adults are $4.50, children $3.50.

Wheeling Heritage Trails, Wheeling; (304) 234–3701. Take your bike, in-line skates, or walking shoes for 12 miles of scenic views of the Ohio River.

Shorter portions through Wheeling follow level asphalt multiuse paths. Handicapped-accessible parking areas and trails.

Challenger Learning Center, 316 Washington Avenue, Wheeling; (304) 243–4325. On the Wheeling Jesuit University campus is a hands-on space exploration experience. Participants in various youth and adult programs take roles of astronauts and mission controllers during realistic missions. The four-hour weekend Parent/Child Discovery Missions for middle school–age children and a parent cost $50.

Townhouse Gallery, 718 Main Street, Sistersville; (304) 652–1214. Jody Boyd, the director of this 1980s Victorian home gallery, works hard to fill artists' and residents' needs by offering traveling exhibits, juried shows, workshops, private lessons and receptions. Open Wednesday through Friday 10:00 A.M. to 2:00 P.M., Saturday and Sunday 1:00 to 5:00 P.M., other times by appointment.

SPECIAL EVENTS

March. Wheeling Celtic Celebration, Wheeling Artisan Center. Music and dance. Admission is $3.00 for ages twelve and up, Friday event is free. (800) 828–3097.

May. Elizabethtown Festival, former West Virginia Penitentiary, Moundsville. Market for West Virginia–made products, food, prison tours, arts and crafts, old-fashioned games, and contests. Admission: $3.00 for adults, $1.00 for children six to twelve. (304) 843–1170.

June. African-American Jubilee, Waterfront, Wheeling. (304) 233–4640.

July. July Fourth Wheeling Symphony Concert, Riverfront, Wheeling. Free. (800) 395–9241.

July–August. American Heritage Glass and Craft Festival, Oglebay Resort and Conference Center, Wheeling. (800) 624–6988.

October. Dungeon of Horrors, former West Virginia Penitentiary, Moundsville. Hour-long haunted tour, $8.00. (304) 845–6200.

November–January. Oglebay's Winter Festival of Lights, Oglebay Resort and Conference Center, Wheeling. (800) 624–6988.

November–January. City of Lights Driving Tour, downtown Wheeling. More than 1.5 million lights illuminate the downtown area. (800) 828–3097.

OTHER RECOMMENDED RESTAURANTS AND LODGINGS

New Martinsville

Quinet's Court Cafe, 217 Main Street; (304) 455–2110. Located across the street from the Wetzel County Court House, this cafe has taken over much of the historic building. As you might expect in a small town, it's a popular spot among locals, but the variety of its buffet (fifty items) and dessert bar is known throughout the Ohio Valley region. Homemade bread and rolls accompany the entrees; desserts vary—perhaps chocolate chip cookies still warm from the oven, bread pudding, or a favorite, Hawaiian Wedding Cake. All this for $5.95 at lunch and $8.95 at dinner. Open Monday to Saturday 6:00 A.M. to 8:00 P.M., Sunday 7:00 A.M. to 7:00 P.M.

Weirton

DeeJay's, 1229 Pennsylvania Avenue; (304) 478–1150. A favorite for ribs among locals and Pittsburgh professional sports players, who visit frequently. Moderate.

Sistersville

The Birch Tree, 717 Wells Street; (304) 652–1337. A surprisingly interesting menu for such a small town includes pasta, hand-cut steaks, fresh baked bread. Open Tuesday through Friday for lunch and dinner, Saturday for dinner only.

Historic Well's Inn, 316 Charles Street; (888) 688–4673. This 1894 inn was built for wealthy visitors of the booming oil companies (there were 190). Recent and ongoing refurbishments and moderately priced country cooking make it a delightful stop for lunch (11:00 A.M. to 2:00 P.M.) or dinner (4:00 to 9:00 P.M.). Open Sunday from noon to 9:00 P.M. for dinner only. Try the fresh cream of tomato soup. Original rooms all have private baths and are typical of early days. Rates begin at $69.

Wellsburg

Drover's Inn Restaurant, Tavern, and Lodge, 1001 Washington Pike; (304) 737–0188. A restored log house now hosts overnight guests with no desire for phones or TVs; there are private baths and gas fireplaces. Rates: $50, including continental breakfast.

Wheeling

Wilson Lodge at Oglebay Resort and Conference Center; (800) 624–6988. Standard room rates range from $79 to $140. Packages including breakfast and other admissions and amenities are offered. Cottages, ranging from $460 to $980 for two nights, include everything but your personal items and food.

Undo's Famiglia Ristorante, Route 2 South, Benwood; (304) 233–0560 or (800) 964–2929. Daily and early-bird specials, plus an extensive Italian menu (including pizza), all authentic and moderately priced.

FOR MORE INFORMATION

Wheeling Convention and Visitors Bureau, 1401 Main Street, Heritage Square, Wheeling, West Virginia 26003; (800) 828–3097; www.wheelingcvb.com.

Hancock County Convention and Visitors Bureau, P.O. Box 1215, New Cumberland, West Virginia, 26047; (877) 723–7114; www.hancockcvb.com.

West Virginia Division of Tourism, (800) CALL–WVA.

Moundsville Economic Development Office, 818 Jefferson Avenue, Moundsville, West Virginia, 26041; (304) 845–6200.

SOUTHERN
ESCAPES

Columbus

URBAN NEIGHBORHOODS

2 NIGHTS

Grand Grandview • The artsy Short North
Quaint German Village • Discovery District

Ohio's largest city has a neighborly feeling even in its urban areas. It's easy to explore them from a downtown base. Of course, there are megamalls, sports arenas, and Big Ten tourneys, as well as federal and state offices, but for this getaway weekend, you won't feel like you're in the all-American city. You'll be discovering the more off-the-beaten-path spots: New York–style loft accommodations, small cafes and bistros, and intimate galleries, along with a little-known house museum.

It will be a sophisticated yet fun weekend and it's just a few hours away. Hard to believe? It's possible—here's the plan.

DAY 1

Afternoon

It's a 147-mile drive from Cleveland to **Columbus.** By leaving after work on Friday you can count on arriving in Columbus for a late but leisurely dinner. To get there take I–71 south all the way to Columbus. Take the Spring Street exit (#109C), turn right onto Spring Street, right onto High Street, and right again at Nationwide Boulevard. You'll be staying and dining in the same complex, the second building on your right.

DINNER: Fifty-five on the Boulevard (55 East Nationwide Boulevard; 614–228–5555) is located in the same building as your accommodations for the

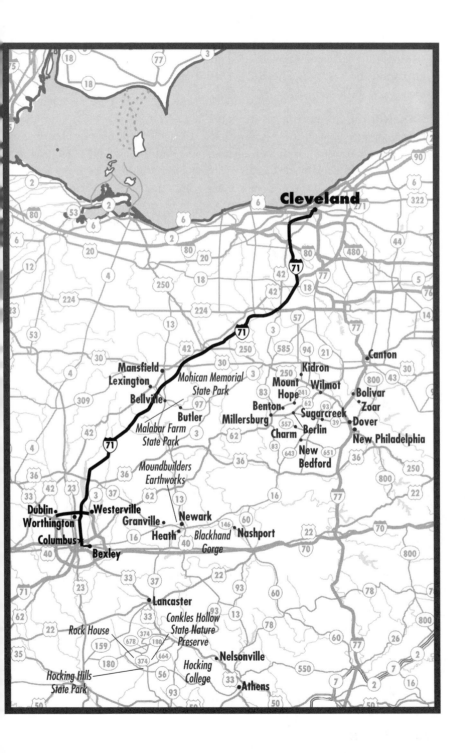

weekend. The restaurant (one of a local group) specializes in seafood, but also features steak and a great house salad. It's moderate to expensive, with a pleasantly romantic ambience.

LODGING: Upstairs from the restaurant is **The Lofts** (614–461–2663). Converted from a commercial warehouse dating back to 1882, the classy boutique hotel now sports forty-four rooms with high ceilings, some with exposed brick and heating vents. Ironically, many of the upscale contemporary furnishings are manufactured right here in Ohio, but the plush linens are imported and the atmosphere will remind you of New York's SoHo. Artwork from city library archives reflects Columbus's past—there's even a cell door from the old Ohio Penitentiary on display.

Guests can enjoy a hot-tub soak at the Crowne Plaza, connected to the Lofts. Rates ranging from $199 to $259 include breakfast and amenities at the Crowne Plaza.

DAY 2

Morning

BREAKFAST: The breakfast butler will arrive at your door when you specify and wheel in a trés deluxe continental breakfast, your choice of fresh fruit, pastries, cereals, and beverages.

Spend the morning in **German Village,** located 6 blocks south of the State Capitol and about 1 mile from the hotel. The narrow, uneven brick streets, some lined with residences and others with shops, have a European ambience bearing accents of wrought iron, flowers, and shuttered brick facades. Early German laborers settled here in the mid-1800s; you can learn their history from a short video at the **German Village Meeting Haus** (588 South Third Street; 614–221–8888). You'll find guided tours there or you can walk the area yourself. You'll discover gift shops and art galleries, restaurants, and even a park.

At the **Golden Hobby Shop** (630 South Third Street; 614–645–8329), operated by Columbus Recreation and Parks, each room of an old school now brims with handmade crafts created by local seniors. Head across the street to the thirty-two-room **Book Loft** (614–464–1774). You actually need a map to get through this maze of a bookstore, but once you find your favorite sections, you just may want to stay lost anyway.

Weather permitting, stop next door for coffee at **Cup O' Joe** (627 South Third Street; 614–221–1563), before walking south toward **Schiller Park,** about

6 blocks away. Walkers enjoy the flower-lined paths; during summer, free evening dramas are performed here.

Leave the village in time for lunch and more browsing in the **Short North.** The first stop is the **North Market** (59 Spruce Street; 614–463–9664). Originally the site of Columbus's first cemetery, it's now a lively mix of ethnic vendors selling fresh produce, cheeses, breads, wines, and most everything else you might hunger for. It's most busy on Saturday mornings, so don't wait too long to browse if you want to shop too. One bakery, the **Tapatio Bread Company** (614–224–1958) starts off with 1,000 loaves of bread, but usually closes early when they are all sold.

LUNCH: After exploring a few of the Short North's artsy shops along High Street, have lunch at **Dagwoodz** (660 North High Street; 614–228–5004). Prices are reasonable, portions are big, and the menu is interesting. The Dagwood sandwich piles up hand-sliced turkey, cappicola, Swiss cheese, peppered bacon, and banana peppers on house-baked bread served with a basil pesto mayo. It comes in two sizes, $6.95 and $8.95.

Afternoon

Finish roaming the Short North's galleries, artist cooperatives, and funky shops while walking off lunch. Don't miss **Riley Hawk Galleries,** 642 North High Street, for wonderful glass masters and **Fioriware Art Pottery,** 8 East Lincoln, for pottery dinnerware.

Another of the urban neighborhoods, **Grandview Heights,** is a mix of retail and residential properties. It has become one of the city's most popular neighborhoods. Just northwest of downtown, Grandview Avenue is the main street, with a few eateries and shops on perpendicular access streets. Although close to the Short North and downtown, it provides most of the necessary amenities like grocers, banks, and dry cleaners to make the location work for residents. No matter the season, the area's coffeehouses and restaurants bustle. Plan to arrive early enough to peek in a few of the shops, like **Adornments** (1306 Grandview Avenue; 614–486–7473), where "uniquities for the artful kind" prevail.

DINNER: Figlio's (1369 Grandview Avenue; 614–481–8850) will be your favorite if you love wood-fired pizza and unusual pasta dishes. The owners have their own selection: Peter & Laurie's Favorite Pizza topped with grilled chicken, fresh herbs, caramelized onions, Parmesan, tomatoes, Gorgonzola, and blue cheese ($9.50). The menu changes seasonally, but the Favorite is a staple.

After dinner try the late showing (around 10:00 P.M.) down the street at the historic art deco **Drexel Grandview Theatre** (1247 Grandview Avenue; 614–486–6114). You'll likely find a foreign flick you haven't seen.

If it's the first Saturday of the month, head back to the Short North for the Short North Gallery Hop. Neighborhood galleries and restaurants stay open late, and there's often outdoor entertainment.

LODGING: The Lofts.

DAY 3

Morning

BREAKFAST: For a grand Sunday Brunch, drive to the Hyatt on Capital Square, 75 East State Street, where a lavish spread awaits in the **Plaza Restaurant** (614–228–1234). It's $20.95 per person.

Before leaving Columbus, explore one more neighborhood, which has come to be known as the **Discovery District.** Located just east of downtown, the area offers some of the city's best treasures. Stop at the topiary garden in the **Old Deaf School Park** on the corner of East Town and Washington Streets (614–645–0197). The famous landscape painting *A Sunday Afternoon on the Island of la Grande Jatte* by Georges Seurat is in three-dimensional form here. The animals and people look their best from mid-July through November. If you're visiting other times, there's always something abloom at the **Franklin Park Conservatory and Botanical Garden,** a little further east at 1777 East Broad Street (614–645–8733).

Drive west on East Broad Street to Jefferson Avenue and the setting for many of James Thurber's stories. Sunday tours of the **Thurber House** (77 Jefferson Avenue; 614–464–1032) take visitors through the house where the famous humorist resided. Call ahead for a schedule of programs featuring current literary greats. There's also a little bookshop here. Open daily noon to 4:00 P.M. Self-guided tours are free. Sunday guided tours, on a drop-in basis, are $2.00 for adults, $1.50 for students and seniors.

A few blocks west is the **Columbus Museum of Art** (480 East Broad Street; 614–221–6801). The museum generally features a major exhibit as well as permanent displays. Open Tuesday to Sunday 10:00 A.M. to 5:30 P.M. Admission is $3.00 for adults, $2.00 for students and seniors, free for children under twelve.

To reach I–71 for your return trip, travel north to Long Street and then east to the interstate. Cleveland is two and a half hours north.

The topiary garden at the Old Deaf School Park blooms with Georges Seurat's A Sunday Afternoon on the Island of la Grande Jatte.

THERE'S MORE

There are more urban neighborhoods to explore and several small towns within 10 miles or so of downtown.

Brewery District, adjacent to German Village, employed many of the German settlers living nearby. There were seven breweries here until Prohibition put them out of business. Redevelopment has brought several back along with a winery and several upscale restaurants. During warm days, dining is alfresco and there's live entertainment.

Dublin, northwest of Columbus, offers a bit of the Irish. There are import shops, St. Patrick's Day festivities, and an Irish Festival each August. Try the Brazenhead Irish Pub, 56 North High Street, for authentic surroundings, ale, and music.

Westerville, a charming college town northeast of Columbus, is home to Otterbein College. Several B&Bs, quaint shops, eateries, and small museums can easily fill a weekend getaway. The Hanby House, an Underground Railroad station and home to African-American composer Benjamin Hanby ("My Darling Nellie Gray"), is one of the historic properties. Operated by the Ohio Historical Society, it's open for tours.

Bexley, east of Columbus, is home to another educational institution, Capital University. Stop at the Blackmore Library on campus for glimpse of history. There's a 2.8-ton section of the Berlin Wall on exhibit. Open during the academic year, the Schumacher Gallery on the library's third level hosts changing exhibits and is well worth the visit, but call ahead to verify hours; (614) 236–6411. Beautiful old homes, including Ohio's governor's mansion, line Bexley streets. Interesting boutiques, dining, and the Drexel (for foreign films) along East Main Street attract locals, students, and visitors.

SPECIAL EVENTS

June. Columbus Arts Festival, downtown riverfront. (800) 345–4FUN.

June. Vintage Columbus, Coffman Park, Dublin. Wine festival; live entertainment, food, and wine tasting. (800) 227–6972.

July. Red, White & Boom!, Downtown. Festival celebrating the Fourth of July. Daylong events, entertainment, and the largest fireworks display in the Midwest—synchronized to music. (614) 267–BOOM.

August. Dublin Irish Festival, Coffman Park, Dublin. (614) 761–6500.

August. Brewery District Festival, South Front Street. Food, beer, and entertainment. (614) 848–6507.

September. German Village Oktoberfest, between South Grant Street and East Livingston Avenue. (614) 224–4300.

OTHER RECOMMENDED RESTAURANTS AND LODGINGS

Downtown

Red Roof Inn Columbus Downtown, 111 Nationwide Boulevard; (614) 224–6539 or (800) THE–ROOF. Another restored warehouse property, this Red

Roof isn't like the ones along the interstate. Extra-roomy accommodations. Leisure king or doubles have recliners and include complimentary European-style continental breakfast. Weekend rate: $89.99.

Westin Great Southern, 310 South High Street; (614) 228–3800 or (800) 228–3000. This preserved Victorian-style hotel is on the National Register of Historic Places, but has all the amenities of an elegant new hotel and it's connected to the Southern Theatre. Weekend specials run as low as $109.

Fusion Restaurant, Crowne Plaza, 33 Nationwide Boulevard; (614) 461–4100 or (800) 465–4329. Adjacent to The Lofts. Open for breakfast and lunch. Fill up at the "Ultimate Feeding Station," a buffet running $8.95 for breakfast, $9.95 for lunch. Menu selections also available.

Short North

50 Lincoln Inn, 50 East Lincoln; (614) 299–5050 or (888) 299–5051. This unique B&B takes on an artsy appeal. Each of the eight guest rooms is decorated in the style of a famous artist—Ansel Adams, Picasso, Van Gogh. All have private baths; continental breakfast is included. Rates: $99 to $119.

German Village

G. Michael's Italian-American Bistro & Bar, 595 South Third Street; (614) 464–0575. Upscale but casual alfresco dining. Menu offers about a half dozen pasta choices and as many salads; unique entrees like the portobello mushroom Napoleon ($13.95). Moderate.

Grandview Heights

Shoku, 1312 Grandview Avenue; (614) 485–9490. Delightful pan-Asian restaurant open for lunch and dinner. Many menu choices: satays and tempuras, wraps, and sushi, as well as grilled, fried, and sushi bento boxes served with miso soup; house specialties served with Asian vegetables, rice, and salad. Sake list. Moderate.

Grandview Cafe, 1455 West Third Street; (614) 486–2233. The house specialty is fish and chips ($8.95) but the menu is eclectic, featuring a reasonably priced list of sandwiches at lunchtime.

FOR MORE INFORMATION

Dublin Convention and Visitors Bureau, 129 South High Street, Dublin, Ohio 43017; (800) 245–8387.

Westerville Convention and Visitors Bureau, 28 South State Street, Westerville, Ohio 43081; (800) 824–8461

Greater Columbus Convention and Visitors Bureau, 90 North High Street, Columbus, Ohio 43215; (800) 426–4624.

Short North Business Association (for Short North Arts District information), 40 West Third Avenue, Columbus, Ohio 43201-3209; (614) 421–1030.

SOUTHERN

Mansfield

A LITTLE BIT OF COUNTRY
NOT FAR FROM THE CITY

1 NIGHT

Painted ponies • Nature's bounty • Manicured gardens
The Hollywood connection • Behind bars

With a population just topping 50,000, Mansfield, Ohio, and its surrounding region is small by most standards, but big enough to fill the bill for a relaxing getaway. Unless you're visiting during a festival or event, you'll leave traffic jams and congestion behind, finding friendliness in town and pristine scenery in the surrounding countryside. It's a good place to experience a B&B. You'll find several in rural settings, some providing picnic lunches and gourmet dinners, if you inquire.

Lexington, a village to the south of Mansfield, put the area on the map among race car fans who watch or participate in national motorsports events at Mid-Ohio Sports Car Course. If your interests include the silver screen, you may already know more about Mansfield than you think, even if you've never stopped for a visit. It seems Hollywood discovered the area long ago and revisits most often when shooting movie prison scenes, so you may have visited vicariously while enjoying a flick, *Air Force One,* for example. As you explore the area, you'll soon discover destinations quite different from your usual cell-block view.

Activities include stops in the historic Carrousel District to watch master carvers restore or build the animals prancing around carousels all over the country. No trip would be complete without riding the town's own 1930s merry-go-round and exploring the shops nearby. Gardeners and nature lovers will enjoy one of the most prolific gems in the area, Kingwood Center, where more than 40,000

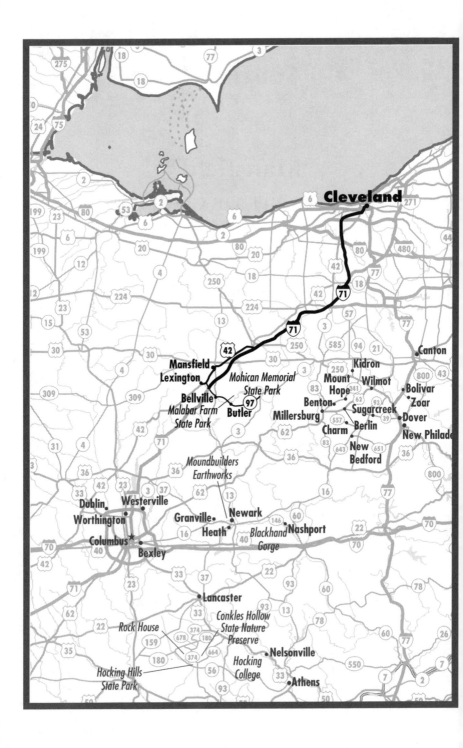

tulips welcome spring each year and usher in season after season of blossoming gardens.

You'll also visit the only park in the state's award-winning system to boast a working farm on the grounds. If bike riding or in-line skating are passions, bring them along for a leisurely ride along the **B&O Trail,** crossing the county for an 18-mile jaunt through the countryside.

The trip south to **Mansfield** is an easy hour-and-a-half drive down I–71 south to U.S. 30 west (exit 176). Drive 4.5 miles and turn left on North Main Street.

DAY 1

Morning

Arrive in town by midmorning, stopping first in the Carrousel District. Have some coffee and muffins at **Brunches Restaurant & Gourmet Coffee** (103 North Main Street; 419–526–2233) before browsing the shops nearby and taking a ride at **Richland Carrousel Park** (75 North Main Street; 419–522–4223). During warm weather, huge paneled doors surrounding the carousel open to let the music waft throughout the Historic Carrousel District. You'll spot the pirate cat and the sea horse—a half-fish, half-horse "hippocampus." They are two of the twenty-two menagerie animals and thirty horses that parade to the music of the Stinson Band organ. The carved and painted carousel is the first of its kind created since the Great Depression. Two brightly painted chariots provide handicapped accessibility, and two more horses swivel to accommodate a wheelchair. Rides are 60 cents each or two for $1.00.

Walk down the street a block to **Carousel Magic!** (44 West Fourth Street; 888–213–2829) to watch what's taking place in the workshop where craftsmen carve and paint carousel figures. Tours, costing $3.00 for adults, $1.00 for children, run thirty to forty-five minutes, Monday through Saturday 10:00 A.M. to 4:00 P.M. Out in front, the Gift Horse stocks carousel horse items.

Off the carousel theme, but within sound's reach, is the **Richland Academy of the Arts,** home of the new **Arts and Science Center** (75 North Walnut Street; 877–522–8224) featuring state-of-the-art hands-on activities that uniquely combine art and science. The center is open Monday through Thursday 10:00 A.M. to 7:00 P.M. and Sunday 1:00 to 5:00 P.M. Admission is $3.00 for adults, $2.00 for children.

Next, drive west along Park Avenue to one of the state's top stops for horticulture, **Kingwood Center** (900 Park Avenue West; 419–522–0211). Nearly fifty

Thousands of tulips welcome spring at Kingwood Center.

acres of landscaped grounds and formal gardens surround the historic mansion. The grounds dress in full blooming regalia from early spring, when the daffodils and crocuses first blossom, through summer, and into fall's vivid annual displays. Even the resident peacocks and waterfowl put on a colorful show. Early May is the best time for visiting, if you'd like to see what 40,000 tulips look like, but even in the dead of winter, the greenhouses are lush and the grounds offer a peaceful repose. The gardens open daily at 8:00 A.M., closing a half hour before sundown; greenhouses close a half hour earlier. Kingwood Hall is open for self-guided tours Tuesday through Saturday 9:00 A.M. to 5:00 P.M., Sunday 1:00 to 5:00 P.M.

LUNCH: When you exit Kingwood Center, turn left and drive south on Trimble Road to Lexington Avenue. Turn left again and drive to a small strip center just past Cook Road for lunch at **Paisley Park** (827 Lexington Avenue; 419–756–3357). Order your sandwich, soup, and salad at the counter from the menu board. Prices are moderate. Weather permitting, get it to go and enjoy a picnic at Malabar Farm State Park, your next stop.

Afternoon

Go back to the corner of Cook Road and Lexington Avenue and turn left. Take State Route 13 south to the first light and turn left at Hanley Road. After 2 miles, turn right at Washington Road South and left onto Pleasant Valley Road. Continue for 5 more miles into **Lucas** to **Malabar Farm State Park** (4050 Bromfield Road, Lucas; 419–892–2784).

The park pays tribute to Pulitzer Prize winner Louis Bromfield, who tended the property by implementing his conservationist philosophy and brought his famous movie-star guests to visit. His home recalls those earlier times, through the mid-1950s. It became a state park in 1976.

To gain a better idea of Louis Bromfield's popularity and his impact on society, stop at the gift shop adjacent to the Big House to sign up for a house tour. If you have to wait, try some of the homemade fudge, visit the working barn, take a wagon tour of the 914-acre estate ($1.00 for adults, free for children under 12), or stroll the grounds on your own.

Often special events, like maple-sugaring, Civil War encampments, and hearthside cooking take place during weekends. If you hike the trail up to Pugh Cabin, on the way to the sugar shack, you'll be in the opening scene of *The Shawshank Redemption*. Then it's on to beautiful trails leading to caves, spring waterfalls, and lush woods.

The guided tour of Bromfield's thirty-two-room "Big House" provides the scoop for another Hollywood connection—it's were Humphrey Bogart and Lauren Bacall were married. Tours lasting forty-five minutes begin on the hour. Admission is $3.00 for adults, $1.00 for children ten to eighteen. Open March through October, daily from 10:00 A.M. to 5:00 P.M., November and December, daily from 11:00 A.M. to 5:00 P.M., January and February, weekends only from 11:00 A.M. to 5:00 P.M.

Stop at your night's lodging by backtracking about 3 miles along Pleasant Valley Road to **Angelwoods Hideaway** (1983 Pleasant Valley Road, Lucas; 419–892–2929). There are six guest rooms with private baths, some with whirlpool tubs. One is handicapped accessible. Amenities include roses and chocolates on your pillow, evening snacks, and little gifts. Cabins are under construction, as is an on-site restaurant. Binoculars and birding books, an outdoor pool, and campfires and benches in the woods bring guests in touch with the natural surroundings. There are hiking trails throughout the forty-six acres; for a minimal donation, the innkeepers will arrange a picnic basket full of homemade goodies. Rates: $95–$140.

Check in and relax, perhaps in the hot tub, before dinner. The innkeeper has a collection of angels, hence the name of the inn, which you'll enjoy if you share her hobby.

DINNER: Angelwoods Hideaway. Dinner is included in your overnight rate. The innkeeper will ask your preferences and special dietary needs when you reserve your accommodations. Dinners are a preset menu including appetizers, soup, salad, main dishes, and dessert. Guests usually choose a video from the inn library, enjoy a swim, take an evening walk, or watch the bonfire out back before retiring.

LODGING: Angelwoods Hideaway.

DAY 2

Morning

BREAKFAST: The innkeepers serve a full country breakfast: always fresh fruit and perhaps quiche or blueberry pancakes. The baked oatmeal is a granola-tasting treat.

Save time for a hike on the trails surrounding the B&B (the innkeepers' dog can show you the way).

Stop for a tour of Mansfield's old **Ohio State Reformatory** (100 Reformatory Road; 419–522–2644). The Mansfield Preservation Society stopped the wrecking ball from destroying the remains of the castlelike structure, a local landmark since the late 1800s, and offers one-and-a-half-hour Sunday afternoon tours from 1:00 to 4:00 P.M. for $5.00. You can actually visit the "hole," the warden's office, and the east and west cell blocks. Trivia buffs take note: *The Guinness Book of World Records* says the west cell block, with six tiers, is the world's largest freestanding cell block. Sorry, no children under seven or pregnant women can tour because of the lead-based paint used in the old prison. Open mid-May through October. Tour reservations can be made ahead of time.

Turn right as you exit the prison to U.S. 30 west, following signs to State Route 309 and then Fourth Street. You'll see the sign for lunch as you approach the exit ramp.

LUNCH: El Campesino, 1971 West Fourth Street, Mansfield; (419) 529–5330. Whet your appetite for authentic Mexican cuisine. The family, from Mexico's western coast, serves up generous portions in both combination platters and dinners. La Mejor dinner includes a chicken chimichanga and beef taquito along with sides for $5.95.

After lunch browse the current exhibit at the **Mansfield Art Center** (700 Marion Avenue; 419–756–1700). To get there drive west (a left turn from the parking lot) on Fourth Street to Lexington-Springmill Road. Turn left (south) and drive about 3 miles to Millsboro Road. Turn left and continue another 2 miles. The art center is the modern white building on the right at Marion Avenue and Millsboro Road. This modern facility hosts a full exhibition schedule, often showcasing Ohio artists or works borrowed from major museums' collections. The outstanding gallery shop offers pieces by local artists as well as nationally acclaimed artists. Open Tuesday through Saturday 11:00 A.M. to 5:00 P.M. and Sunday noon to 5:00 P.M.

To reach I–71 north for your return trip, turn left out of the parking lot and right at the first street, Cline Avenue. At Lexington Avenue (U.S. 42) turn left and then right onto State Route 13 (Main Street), following signs for the interstate.

THERE'S MORE

The Richland B&O Bike Trail winds through the city. The paved 18-mile Rails-to-Trails project connects Mansfield to the south with the small towns of Lexington, Butler, and Bellville. You can exit I–71 at #165 and drive to any of several access points. Turn right (southeast) toward Bellville to find a parking lot and trail entry less than a mile away.

Oak Hill Cottage, 310 Springmill Street; (419) 524–1765. Mansfield's own house of seven gables, a little-known treasure full of chimneys, fireplaces and unique furnishings. The Richland County Historical Society offers Sunday tours of this 1847 Gothic structure from 2:00 to 5:00 P.M. Admission is $3.00 for adults, $1.00 for children twelve and under.

The Renaissance Theatre, 138 Park Avenue West. Worth a stop, even if there's no performance, just for a peek at the restoration. A grand movie palace from 1928 through the '40s, it began to decline over the next two decades, reaching a low as an X-rated theater, then closed in 1979. By the mid-80s community efforts reopened the newly renovated theater, aptly named the Renaissance. A new chandelier and original baroque designs shine today. For a schedule of upcoming performances call (419) 522–2726.

The Living Bible Museum, 500 Tingley Avenue; (800) 222–0139. This museum attracts visitors interested in touring dioramas and exhibits depicting New and Old Testament scenes. Woodcarvings, a rare bible collection, and folk art display are included in the guided tours. Admission is $4.50 for adults, $4.25 for seniors, and $3.50 for students six to eighteen for one display, but reduced fares are offered to see both.

Shopping. While browsing Mansfield's historic district, you'll find several shops to pique your interest: Carrousel Antiques, Ltd., 118 North Main Street, where forty dealers display; Main Street Books, 104 North Main Street; Home Collection, 105 North Main Street; City News–Suzy's Smoke Room, 100 North Main Street, for cigars and coffee; and Estate of the Arts Gallery, 109 North Main Street.

Mid-Ohio Sports Car Course, Steam Corners Road, Lexington; (419) 884–4000. Pack a picnic to enjoy on the grounds or purchase meals at one of several on-site eateries and join the crowds who come to watch the races. Call (800) MID–OHIO for tickets; prices vary according to the event.

SPECIAL EVENTS

March. Maple Syrup Festival, Malabar Farm State Park. (419) 892–2784.

August. Heart of the City Cruise-In. Downtown Mansfield becomes the scene for vintage cars. (800) 642–8282.

October. Haunted Prison Tours, Ohio Reformatory. (419) 522–2644.

November–December. Annual Holiday Fair, Mansfield Art Center. Soup kitchen provides lunch and the entire gallery space is arranged with art that is for sale. Artists are carefully selected for highest quality. (419) 756–1700.

November–December. Christmas at Malabar Farm State Park, Lucas. The Big House is decorated for the holidays. Tours include music, special events, and refreshments. (419) 892–2784.

November–December. Holiday Spectacular, presented by the Mansfield Symphony Orchestra and the Mansfield Symphony Chorus. Matinee and evening performances are held at the Renaissance Theatre. Call for prices, schedules of performances. (419) 522–2726.

November–December. Christmas at Kingwood Center. The mansion is carefully decorated with flowers grown and dried on-site. It's the place to gather ideas for the season. (419) 522–0211.

OTHER RECOMMENDED RESTAURANTS AND LODGINGS

Mansfield

The Skyway East, 2461 Emma Lane; (419) 589–9929. Located a half mile from I–71 at U.S. 30. Moderately priced extensive menu features American entrees.

Mama's Touch of Italy, 275 Park Avenue West; (419) 526–5099. Locals enjoy the lunch and dinner specials here—large portions and inexpensive prices. Often there are all-you-can-eat options.

Coney Island Diner, 98 North Main Street; (419) 526–2669. This downtown landmark is a regular stop for the downtown crowd; known for breakfast and coneys. Inexpensive; counter and booths.

Uncorked, 108 North Main Street; (419) 524–9463. Wines, beers, coffee, and desserts in one of the historic buildings in the Carrousel District. Guitarist on Friday evenings.

Baymont Inn & Suites, 120 Sander Avenue; (419) 774–0005 or (800) 301–0200. Rooms begin at $64.95, ambassador suites with two adjoining rooms are $94.95. Several weekend packages are also available. Continental breakfast is included.

Lexington

Buck's Bar & Grill, 192 East Main Street; (419) 884–2825. Popular with racing fans, this bar and grill keeps a racing theme on its menu (check out the burgers) and in decor. Moderate; large portions. Closed Sunday.

Checker Flag Grille and Pub, 275 East Main Street; (419) 884–9140. Also a popular stop for racing fans. Entrees as well as sandwiches; moderate.

White Fence Inn, 8842 Denman Road; (419) 884–2356. Rural atmosphere with a pond and farm animals; guest rooms are decorated on different themes; some have fireplaces. Delicious breakfasts. Rates are $71 for a room with a shared bath, $87 for a room with queen-size beds, $115 to $125 for king-size beds. Book well in advance during mid-Ohio race weekends.

Ramada Limited, I–71 at exit 165, State Route 97; (419) 886–7000 or (800) 272–6232. Indoor pool, convenient location, and reasonable prices. Rates start at $79 and include a continental breakfast.

FOR MORE INFORMATION

Mansfield and Richland County Convention and Visitors Bureau, 52 Park Avenue, West Mansfield 44902; (800) 642–8282; www.mansfieldtourism.org.

Ohio's Amish Counties

THE WORLD'S LARGEST
AMISH POPULATION

1 NIGHT

Hearty cooking • Backroads • Simple pastoral scenery

After driving along the interstate for an hour or so, a leisurely departure through the countryside will lead you to the largest Amish community in the world. You'll know you're heading the right direction when black buggies share the hilly roads, clotheslines full of solid colors stretch behind farmhouses, and you don't see any electrical lines running from the road. You've just entered the slow lanes of Holmes, Wayne, and Tuscarawas Counties.

Over the past decade, these narrow farm roads, connecting such communities as Kidron, Wilmot, Mt. Eaton, Sugarcreek, Charm, and Shreve, have become a mecca of tourist sights, nearly atop the list of Ohio's most visited destinations. If you really want to enjoy and understand the area, veer off the main thoroughfares, get "lost" on the back roads, and let the bucolic scenes and rural lifestyle of the Amish and Mennonite residents take you to another time and place.

DAY 1

Morning

Leave by mid- to late morning so that the 80-mile excursion begins in time to whet your appetite for a hearty Amish-style lunch. Travel south on I–77 27 miles to State Route 21 south. Go 9 miles and turn right on State Route 585, then left onto State Route 94, crossing U.S. 30 after 11 miles. A few miles later, turn right

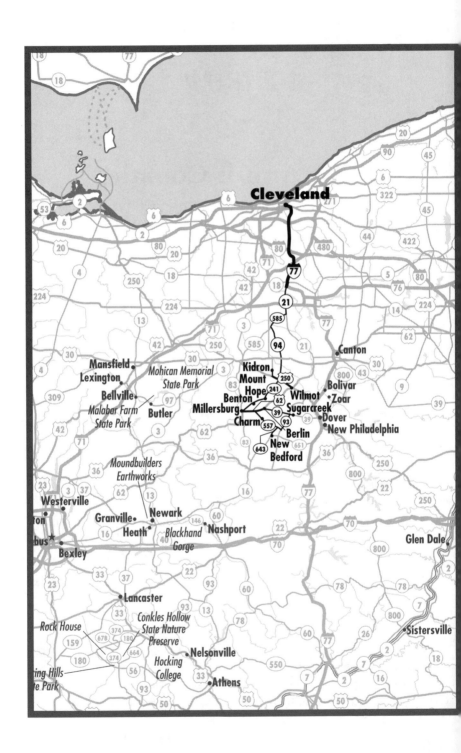

at Jericho, following the signs to **Lehman's** (One Lehman Circle, Kidron; 330–857–5757). Until the Y2K scare, this "nonelectric" general store catered to the simple needs of the locals and others by catalog, selling sadirons and gas refrigerators, juicers and canners, wooden spoons and iron kettles, and thousands of other handy and hard-to-find items. Now its catalog has a Web presence: www.lehmans.com. Not only will the aisles of merchandise intrigue "English" or non-Amish visitors, but the book section offers a good selection of how-to guides and literature about the Amish and Mennonite sects that settled here.

Across the street, stop in at the **Kidron-Sonnenberg Heritage Center** (13153 Emerson Road, Kidron). Here antiques, books, furniture, and textiles are displayed. There is also an extensive genealogy department. Admission is by donation. Open June through September on Thursday, Friday, and Saturday, from 11:00 A.M. to 3:00 P.M.

LUNCH: Pick up U.S. 250 just south of Kidron and follow it south about 7 miles to U.S. 62. Turn right and soon you'll see the **Amish Door Restaurant** (Apple Blossom Drive, Wilmot, on the left; 888–AMISH–DOOR or 330–359–5464). Take your choice of family-style meals or the individual menu. Owners say they serve between 500 and 1,000 pounds of mashed potatoes and close to 200 pies on a busy day. Favorites include roast beef, chicken, noodles, and bread stuffing. The restaurant serves large portions at reasonable prices and is open from 7:00 A.M. to 8:00 P.M. Monday through Saturday. There are several on-site shops and a bakery for perusing after lunch.

Afternoon

From the Amish Door continue to drive south on U.S. 62 to **Winesburg.** Turn right onto County Route 160, stopping at **Winesburg Collectibles** before a stroll down the street to **Eagle Song Studio** (330–359–5786). If you're longing for a hand-carved fireplace mantel or an interesting carved stone birdbath, you'll find unique ones here.

Continue your drive along County Route 160 into **Mt. Hope,** where you'll find a smaller version of Lehman's and other local shops, like **Homestead Furniture** (County Road 77; 800–893–3702, ext. 0210) and the **Lone Star Quilt Shop** in front. Continue a leisurely drive west on State Route 241 toward **Millersburg,** the seat of Holmes County. Turn left onto County Road 203, following the signs and curves to the Inn at Honey Run, your respite for the weekend. Don't be impatient as you carefully maneuver the narrow route; the award-winning contemporary inn at the end of your drive will be worth the road test.

This typically furnished Amish bedroom is part of a home tour available in Holmes County.

DINNER AND LODGING: The **Inn at Honey Run,** 6920 County Road 203, Millersburg; (800) 468–6639; www.innathoneyrun.com. After checking into your lodging, either a room in the lodge or in the "honeycombs" up the hill, take a walk along one of the marked trails through the woods or drive to the orchard on the end of the inn's 290 acres. Then just sit and soak up the views. All of the rooms are designed to bring a bit of nature into view with large windows, birding books, binoculars, and bird feeders within close range. Rates vary according to three seasonal schedules, ranging between $65 and $150 for the lodge, $99 and $160 for the honeycombs, and $150 and $225 for accommodations in the three guest-houses. There are twenty-five lodge guest rooms and twelve honeycombs.

Reserve a table for dinner at the inn. Entrees feature homemade breads and muffins, fresh fruit, and jams from the orchard. Selections might include locally farmed trout. On summer weekends, the chef tends an outdoor barbecue at the Mikhaus Cafe. If you don't save enough room for dessert, you can get a half order. Please note: Only nonalcoholic wine and beer are sold.

If you're looking for evening entertainment, videos are available for the VCRs in each room, a recent addition. There's also a game room in the inn and comfortable seating surrounding the fireplace. There is a full schedule of wintertime symposiums as well as "Fireside Sundays," a time for guests to share their favorite stories and experiences.

DAY 2

Morning

BREAKFAST: Breakfast is included in the guest rate. Those staying in the honeycombs may opt for a continental breakfast delivered to their door. Otherwise, breakfast is served in the dining room. The peaceful surroundings may lure you to sleep a little later than usual, but if you're an early riser, find a window or go out for a walk. The early morning light on the hills and the friendly sheep out in the pasture are inviting sights no matter the season.

Before heading into the heart of Amish Country drive over to the only Rails-to-Trails project that shares its multipurpose trail system with Amish buggies. Turn left out of the inn onto County Road 203 and then turn right onto State Route 241. In Benton, turn left onto County Road 189 to **Holmesville.** Turn left onto County Road 558 and then left onto State Route 83. Park at **Skip's Trail Depot** and take a relaxing walk along the trail, possibly seeing an Amish buggy or horsemen before returning. Eventually the path will run 29 miles, linking two ends of the county, but for now 10 miles between Holmesville and Millersburg are open.

From Skip's, follow State Route 83 back into **Millersburg.** Stop to browse in Millersburg, a quaint community with several antiques and collectibles shops worth exploring, including the **Antique Emporium** (113 West Jackson Street; 330–674–0510) and **Thoughts that Count** (88 West Jackson Street; 330–674–6900). History and antiques buffs will want to include a stop at a Queen Anne gem, the **Victorian House Museum** (484 Wooster Road; 888–201–0022). Admission is $3.00. Local collectors have filled twenty-eight rooms with antiques. Open May through October from 1:30 to 4:00 P.M. Tuesday through Sunday. If you're looking for an original or print of an Amish scene, stop at **Graebner Gallery** (136 West Jackson; 330–674–6755), where nationally recognized artist Diane Graebner sells her work.

LUNCH: Take State Route 39/U.S. 62 east toward **Berlin,** stopping at the **Dutch Harvest Restaurant** (5324 County Road 201, Berlin; 330–893–3333). It's on the corner of Route 201 and State Route 39. Here you can enjoy another hearty meal—perhaps an open face pot roast sandwich on homemade bread with a side of mashed potatoes—but leave room for the house specialty, "bag apple pie." Meals range from $3.99 to $10.99.

Afternoon

Drive through Berlin, pronounced with the accent on the first syllable. Berlin Furniture, on South Market Street, 1 mile south of Berlin, features the famous red "Berlin Flyer" wooden wagons in five sizes. You'll begin to notice the abundance of primitive-looking hickory rockers, each one handcrafted for an individual "sit."

As you leave Berlin, stop at the **Mennonite Information Center** (County Route 77, Behalt; 330–893–3192). A 360-degree mural painted by Heinz Gaugel, a local artist, depicts Amish and Mennonite history beginning with their Anabaptist roots in Switzerland. Admission is $5.50 for adults and $2.50 for children for the guided tour.

Travel east on State Route 39 to **Walnut Creek** on the way to **Yoder's Amish Home** (6050 State Route 515, Walnut Creek; 330–893–2541). You'll visit a traditional Amish home, the Dawdy House where the elders reside, and the barn, usually well stocked with farm animals. A short buggy rides provides another opportunity to talk to the Amish or Mennonites, but don't take their pictures. Their disapproval stems from religious teachings, as do their decisions to dress differently and live a simpler lifestyle.

For one of the most scenic "backroads" drives and an authentic look at the Amish countryside, drive the township roads between Walnut Creek and Charm. From Yoder's, turn right onto State Route 515. At State Route 39 turn left, then right onto Township Road 114, and then right onto Township Road 70. This will take you into the charming Amish community of **Charm,** located on State Route 557. It's a typical community, one where you might see quilters at work at **Miller's Dry Goods** (4500 State Route 557), but you won't find electricity—no high-tech cash registers and no telephones.

For the easiest route back, backtrack slightly by traveling southeast on State Route 557 to State Route 643 east and then onto State Route 93 north. At State Route 39 turn right (east) and drive through hilly Sugarcreek, reminiscent of the Swiss Alps and home to Amish Swiss cheesemakers. It's another good stopping point if you have time, before picking up I–77 north in Dover.

THERE'S MORE

The Shoppes at Buchanan Place, located north of Wooster on State Route 585; (330) 669–3911. The Shoppes provide a sampling of regionally produced craft items and other collectibles, bulk foods, and toys. Adjacent is **The Barn Restaurant** (877 West Main Street, Smithville; 330–699–2555). Constructed in the shape of a huge Amish style barn, this meat and potatoes restaurant features an extensive salad bar along with the hearty fare, including BBQ ribs and homemade breads and pies, reasonably priced with pleasant views of the countryside.

FJ Designs, 2163 Great Trails Drive, Wooster; (330) 264–1377. To collectors, this home of the Cat's Meow Village and its tiny black cat named Casper has put Wooster on the map. Tiny paw prints guide visitors along narrated visits through the manufacturing plant. Guided tours lasting about forty-five minutes are offered Monday through Friday at 10:00 A.M. and 1:00 P.M. Gift shop.

Coblentz Chocolate Company, 4917 State Route 515, Walnut Creek; (800) 338–9341. This chocolate factory conducts its "tours" through a glass window, but you can watch the process, June through October 9:00 A.M. to 6:00 P.M. and November to May from 9:00 A.M. to 5:00 P.M. Homemade fudge and other chocolates.

Schrock's Amish Farm and Home, 4363 State Route 39, Berlin; (330) 893–3232. Guided tours ($3.50 adults; $2.50 children) through an Amish home and the "grandfather's house" along with a video, a short buggy ride (same price as tour), petting animals in the barn ($1.50) are available. For all activities, including a storyteller and history room, the price is $7.00 for adults and $5.00 for children. Open Monday through Friday, 10:00 A.M. to 5:00 P.M.

SPECIAL EVENTS

May. Dandelion Mayfest, Breitenbach Wine Cellars, 5934 Olde Route 39, Dover. National Dandelion cook-off, live entertainment, children's activities, and dandelion foods (cheese bread, sausage, coffee, omelettes, dandelion flower muffins, and pizza). 5-K run. Free admission. (800) THE–WINE.

May. Holmes County Kidney Fund Auction, Mount Hope Auction Barn. (330) 674–6268.

August. Ohio Haiti Benefit Auction, Mount Hope. (330) 852–4855.

September. Ohio Swiss Festival, Sugarcreek. (330) 852–4113.

October. Charm Days, Charm. (330) 893–2251.

OTHER RECOMMENDED RESTAURANTS AND LODGINGS

Charm

The Charm Countryview Inn B&B, 4280 Township Road 356; (330) 893–3003. The views are great from the porch swing at this aptly-named inn is.

Wilmot

Hassman House B&B, 925 U.S. 62; (330) 359–7904. This antique-filled Victorian painted lady contrasts sharply with its pastoral setting. There are four rooms with private baths and air-conditioning. Guests are given breakfast vouchers for the Restaurant at the Amish Door nearby, except on Sundays when breakfast is served at the inn. Rates: $79–$119.

Inn at Amish Door, Apple Blossom Drive; (888) AMISH–DOOR. Each floor features a different local wood in the trim and decor. Indoor pool. Rates begin at $95 and include a continental breakfast.

New Bedford

A Valley View Inn, 32327 State Route 643; (800) 331–VIEW. Christian-owned B&B with ten guest rooms, full breakfasts. Overlooks an Amish community in the valley below. Rates: $80–$105.

FOR MORE INFORMATION

Tuscarawas Convention and Visitors Bureau, 125 McDonalds Drive SW, New Philadelphia, Ohio 44663; (330) 339–4353 or (800) 527–3387.

Wayne County Convention and Visitors Bureau, 428 West Liberty Street, Wooster, Ohio 44691; (330) 264–1800 or (800) 362–6474.

Holmes Country Chamber of Commerce and Tourism Bureau, 35 North Monroe Street, Millersburg, Ohio 44654; (330) 674–3975.

Canton/Stark County Convention and Visitors Bureau, 229 Wells Avenue NW, Canton, Ohio 44703; (330) 454–1439 or (800) 533–4302.

Hocking Hills
THE STATE PARK AND BEYOND

2 NIGHTS

Country inns • B&Bs • Cabins in the woods

No matter the season, just when you think you'd like to escape to a cabin in the woods and unwind, Hocking Hills comes to the rescue. There's no better place in Ohio to discover nature's beauty, but the scenery changes with the seasons. All in one area, you'll discover state nature preserves, parks, and forests, along with lesser-known walking paths, sometimes just beyond your door.

This Appalachian Mountains' foothills region beckons those who need a break from work stress, families who enjoy being together, and couples eager to rejuvenate their relationships. The three-hour drive takes you back millions of years to the formation of this magnificent scenery—waterfalls, gorges, wildflowers, and forests—perfect for hiking, walking, and picnicking. Along with too many trails to explore in just one weekend, visitors also have their choice of accommodations, from rustic cabins to those with more amenities than home, from B&Bs to modern motels. Hearty breakfasts abound, and dining can be do-it-yourself grilling or elegantly presented meals prepared by staff chefs.

DAY 1

Afternoon

Leave by early afternoon on Friday, to allow for some sightseeing and dinner in Lancaster. Follow I–71 south through Columbus, picking up I–70 east for about 4 miles to U.S. 33 south. Continue south on U.S. 33 for 25 miles.

As you approach **Lancaster,** follow the signs toward downtown. Turn left onto Wheeling Avenue, right onto Broad Street, and park at **Shaw's Restaurant & Inn** (123 North Broad Street; 740–654–1842 or 800–654–2477). Make dinner reservations for later and borrow a cassette recording, the *Square 13 Historic Walking Tour.* Staff will point you in the right direction for the forty-five-minute walk around several blocks just off downtown's square.

You'll pass interesting eighteenth-century architecture, including the **Georgian Museum** (105 East Wheeling Street; 740–654–9923). You'll easily recognize it by its five white Ionic pillars and its "widow's walk." Inside, you'll find local history exhibits and period furnishings.

Continuing along the tree-lined streets, where most homes are encircled by wrought iron gates, you'll come to the brick **Sherman House Museum** (137 East Main Street; 740–687–5891). It was the boyhood home of Civil War General William Tecumseh Sherman and his brother John, a prominent U.S. legislator and author of the Sherman Anti-Trust Act. The museums operate April through mid-December, Tuesday through Sunday, 1:00 to 4:00 P.M. Other times by appointment. Admission is $2.00 for adults and $1.00 for students ages six to sixteen.

Return the tape when you are finished and get ready to enjoy an upscale yet reasonably priced meal before continuing another half hour to the Hocking Hills region and your overnight accommodations.

DINNER: Shaw's Restaurant boasts of the chef's regional themes. The menu changes daily and there's even a calendar of events. You can plan your getaway to coincide with one of the special evenings, perhaps a wine tasting or seasonal theme. Dinners include delicious homemade cinnamon rolls. Prices range from $6.00 to $9.00 for lunch, from $11 to $25 for dinner including two side dishes, and under $10 for a light Sunday supper available from 3:00 to 9:00 P.M.

Continue on U.S. 33 south toward **Logan,** following signs to the Hocking Hills State Park. Turn right onto State Route 664 and continue about 10 miles to a left onto State Route 374. Just when you begin to worry that you're on the wrong road, you'll see your accommodations for this escape.

LODGING: The Inn at Cedar Falls, 21190 State Route 374, Logan; (800) 65–FALLS. You can stop in front of the 1840s log cabin that serves as a welcoming lobby, but it is actually the dining facility. Parking is across the road. Your choice of accommodations includes one of six cabins secluded in the woods or a Shaker-style guest room in the main lodge overlooking sixty acres. Whichever you choose, you won't find telephones or televisions. Rates range from $55 to $102 for the inn, and $110 to $240 for a cabin. Weekends require a two-night minimum stay.

Cabins tucked in the woods are popular overnight accommodations in the Hocking Hills.

DAY 2

Morning

BREAKFAST: Whether it's outdoors on the patio overlooking the gardens or indoors in the rustic log cabin facing the open kitchen, breakfast at the inn is a treat. Homemade granola and muffins are self-serve while you await one of the house specialties, perhaps baked cherry french toast with praline topping.

Order a picnic from the innkeeper (you can pick it up following the morning's activities), lace up your hiking boots, then head to the hills. Retrieve your car from the overnight parking lot and turn right, following the signs to Old Man's Cave parking. Old Man's Cave is located on State Route 664 south, 11 miles from the Hocking Hills Regional Welcome Center (near the intersection of U.S. 33 and 664 south). You can pick up a trail map and stop in the nature shop at the visitors' center before continuing.

It's especially important to stay on the well-defined trails throughout the park, forest, and nature preserves for safety's sake and to preserve the ecology. Wear appropriate gear, especially hiking boots during most seasons. Specially designed ice cleats are helpful during wintry hikes, and a hiking stick comes in handy. Bring water or snacks if you plan on hiking for hours. You'll find rest rooms near the parking lots and trailheads, in most cases.

Don't let these aforementioned precautions scare you. Hikes range in difficulty, but there's something for everyone, even if you're pushing a baby stroller. Perhaps the easiest trail in the system is the one leading to Ash Cave, considered by many to be the crown jewel of the entire Hocking Hills State Park. The trail and adjacent rest rooms are wheelchair accessible. It's a short path, measuring a quarter mile to the spectacular recess cave, which provided shelter for early inhabitants. During spring the path is lined with wildflowers; in winter, ice formations hang along the way to a frozen waterfall.

Look for the "Democracy Steps for Cedar Falls" along the Cedar Falls Trail. They were designed by Japanese artist Akio Hizume and installed in 1997. Interestingly grouped in three sets, they set the walker on a rhythmical path that is both physically relaxing and expressive of the artist's connection to nature.

For a more vigorous workout, opt for the 6-mile Grandma Gatewood Trail, beginning at the Upper Falls at Old Man's Cave. It connects the beautiful scenery of Old Man's Cave, Cedar Falls, and Ash Cave.

LUNCH: Drive back to the Inn at Cedar Falls and pick up your picnic lunch. The staff refers to them as brown bag lunches, but they are anything but ordinary. A sandwich, sides, and fruit run $6.50–$7.50. If you are visiting between April and October, continue toward U.S. 33 for an afternoon of canoeing at **Hocking Valley Canoe Livery and Fun Center** (31251 Chieftain Drive, Logan; 800–686–0386). (At other times, choose among the alternatives at the end of the chapter or curl up with a good book in front of the toasty fire in your cabin or at the inn.) If you're famished, enjoy lunch at a picnic site before you begin. If you prefer to take your lunch with you, you'll find many great stops along the way as you traverse the Hocking River.

Afternoon

Choose from various lengths and types of canoe trips and modes of transportation. Canoes, kayaks (both double and single), and rafts are available. If you're a novice, arrange for a canoeing workshop to learn the safe and fun aspects of being out on the water. The length of regular trips range from two hours to three days (there's primitive camping along the way). A two-hour canoe trip costs $21; a canoe holds two adults and two children.

The Fun Center features a driving range, miniature golf (adults $4.50, children $3.50), and go-carts ($5.00 for five minutes). Combination packages for $20 include the two-hour canoe-trip, two rounds of miniature golf, two go-cart rides, and either a bungee trampoline or a bucket of balls for the driving range.

DINNER: The menu is arranged ahead of time, so check with the innkeeper if you have special requests. A full gourmet meal, accompanied by a wine and beer list, is served at the single seating. Prices are $21 weekdays and $30 on the weekends. The open kitchen allows for some interaction with the chef. It's a bit incongruous to enjoy such gourmet meals in a log cabin, but it happens here every evening.

Nightlife is limited in Hocking Hills. Occasionally an interpreted night hike is offered. If one is available, try not to miss it—the woods take on a magical atmosphere, often iridescent in color. Check with the innkeeper or call the park, (740) 385–6841.

LODGING: The Inn at Cedar Falls.

DAY 3

Morning

BREAKFAST: Choose a different room to enjoy your gourmet breakfast in, perhaps the most recent addition to the log home, a public area on the other side of the kitchen. It's furnished with some handcrafted pieces and a fireplace for a rustic feel.

Before leaving the area, make sure to visit **Conkle's Hollow State Nature Preserve** (State Route 374, Logan; 614–265–6453). The walk is particularly scenic here and there is a short, newly constructed boardwalk to make it easily accessible. The 200-foot cliff face of blackhand sandstone is impressive, whether you choose the lower hike or the rim trail. The Gorge Trail is a half mile; the rim paths are 2 miles.

LUNCH: From the preserve continue driving north for 5 miles until you reach U.S. 33. Take it west about 45 miles to I–270 north. Travel 17 miles to the **Easton** exit, where Easton Town Center awaits for a lunch, entertainment, or shopping detour. You'll find some shops and restaurants here that are unavailable anywhere else in Ohio, like the **Ocean Club** (614–416–2582) for lunch and the **Cheese-cake Factory** (614–418–7600) for dessert. There are also several coffeehouses, if you're looking for something light.

Afternoon

From Easton, continue north on I–270, following signs for I–71 north to Cleveland. You're about two-and-a-half hours from home.

THERE'S MORE

Stone Valley Ranch, 31606 Fairview Road, Logan; (740) 380–1701 or (800) 688–5196. Offers trail rides for $17 per person and private off-trail riding at $25 per hour. Plan your visit during a full moon for the moonlight rides that include refreshments and hot dogs cooked over a bonfire.

"Adventures in Learning." Self-enrichment workshops are offered throughout the year at various sites. Poetry reading, photography workshops, basketry, and jewelry making are but a few offerings, usually lasting several hours and costing very little. Call the Hocking County Tourism Association (740–385–9706) for a schedule.

Rockclimbing and rappelling, the Hocking State Forest off Big Pine Road in Spring Hollow. The only area site for these sports. Call (740) 385–4402 for information.

SPECIAL EVENTS

January. Annual Winter Hike, Hocking Hills State Park. Continuous starts from Old Man's Cave to Ash Cave with shuttles to your car. Hot refreshments for a donation, but the 6-mile hike is free and attracts thousands. (740) 385–6841.

April. Wildflowers and Waterfalls Hike, Hocking Hills State Park. Participants meet at the welcome center at Old Man's Cave. (740) 385–6841.

May. Spring Arts & Crafts Show, Hocking Hills State Park Lodge. Sponsored by the Hocking Hills Artists and Craftsmen's Association. (740) 385–8245.

June. Downtown Summer Cruise-In, downtown Logan. (740) 385–6836.

September. Annual Hocking Hills Indian Run. Truly a cross-country event along forest trails, across streams, and traversing hills. 5K, 10K, 20K, and 60K courses. $25 standard registration. Sponsored by the Hocking County Tourism Association; (740) 385–9706.

October. Halloween Campout, Hocking Hills State Park. (740) 385–6841.

OTHER RECOMMENDED RESTAURANTS AND LODGINGS

AmeriHost Inn, 12819 State Route 664, Logan; (800) 459–4678. Reasonably priced rooms, indoor pool, and complimentary breakfast.

Glenlaurel Inn and Cottages, 14940 Mount Olive Road, Rockbridge; (800) 809–REST. Choose a luxurious room at the inn or a cottage suite. Dinners are set to a Celtic theme, complete with bagpipe music and Robert Burns's poetry. Reservations are required for the prix fixe menu that runs $34 per person during the week and $44 on Saturday evening.

Bear Run Inn B&B, 8260 Bear Run Road, Logan; (740) 385–8007. Offers both cabins and bed-and-breakfast rooms surrounded by 400 acres. Rates range from $70 to $130 and include a full breakfast. Three- and four-bedroom cabins begin at $280 and require a two-night minimum stay.

Crockett's Run, 9710 Bauer Road, Logan; (800) 472–8115. Luxury lodges that sleep sixteen to twenty people are the perfect size for family reunions; smaller cabins sleep up to six adults. Primitive campgrounds in a beautiful setting near the Buckeye Trail and other hiking trails are on the property. Cabin rates are $153 during the week and $170 on weekends.

Resort at Blackjack Crossing, 19601 State Route 664, Logan; (800) 504–9993. Wooded cabins with hot tubs (a popular amenity locally) and an unusual extra in this area, an in-ground swimming pool. Cabins have grills and kitchens.

The Brass Ring Restaurant and Lounge, 14405 Country Club Lane, Logan; (740) 385–8966. Serves up daily chef's specials of pasta and infusion entrees along with other innovative dishes. Prices range from $10 to $17 for dinners, less for lounge food. Also open for lunch.

Graham's Colonial Inn, 922 West Hunter Street, Logan; (740) 385–7214. This local favorite is most famous for what isn't on the menu: the free book each customer chooses on the way out. Once the leftovers from a literacy grant obtained by the owner, now customers help keep the shelves stocked so the tradition can continue. It is also known for prime rib ($13.99 and $17.99).

Great Expectations, 179 South Market Street, Logan; (740) 380–9177. Relax in this cozy Victorian home turned book loft and gift shop, then dine on grilled panini sandwiches in the little eatery in the back room. Sandwiches average $3.79.

FOR MORE INFORMATION

Hocking County Tourism Association, 13178 State Route 664 South, Logan, Ohio 43138; (740) 385–9706.

Fairfield County Visitors and Convention Bureau, One North Broad, Lancaster, Ohio 43130; (800) 626–1296.

Athens, Ohio

THE ARTS

Uptown and home grown • Appalachian inspiration

If you're thinking of traveling south to Athens, Ohio, for an overnight of art and entertainment, you've a good idea, unless it's Halloween weekend. That's when the college crowd from all over Ohio converges on the streets encircling Ohio University for the most notorious party in the state—it's definitely the time for adults to stay home and pass out candy.

During other times, and especially when classes are in session, your visit will be met with the vitality you'd expect in a college community. Ongoing university performances, recitals, exhibits, and annual events complement the music and entertainment scene you'll discover off-campus in Uptown. Athens brims with artists, both visual and performing. There's beautiful hilly scenery and an abundance of natural space. Locals say that it's the perfect place for creative types to develop their craft. If you venture beyond the city limits, you'll likely meet some of them and discover unique shops along the way.

The enthusiasm and vibrancy of university life spill over to the community and to guests opting for a down-home getaway in the heart of Appalachia. Reflecting today's trends, most everything is casual here.

DAY 1

Morning

Take the scenic route for the 175-mile drive to **Athens.** Leave early in the morning to reach the Athens region by 1:00 P.M. or so. Travel I–77 south from Cleve-

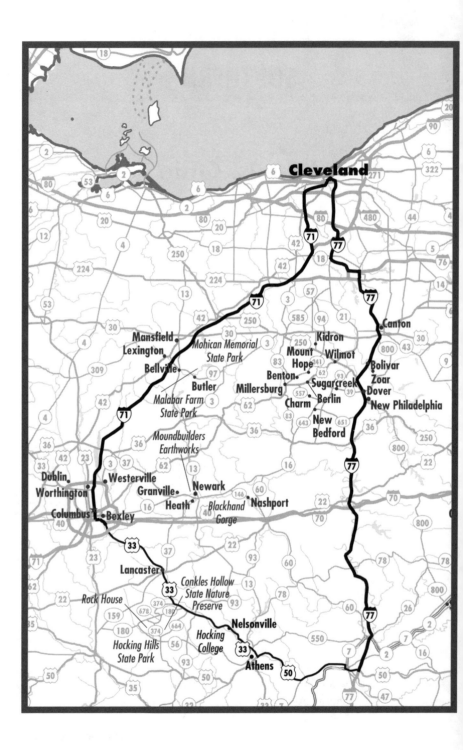

land, picking up State Route 7 east of Marietta. Continue south, following U.S. 50 when it veers northeast. Take State Route 682 north/Athens exit (also marked for Ohio University). Turn right at the bottom of the exit ramp onto Richland Avenue and left onto Shafer Street at the next block, then right onto West Union Street. Albert's is located two blocks ahead on the left side in a large brick building housing many university offices.

LUNCH: Albert's Cafe and Confections (158 West Union, Athens; 740–594–2233) offers American fare—sandwiches, soups, salads and gourmet coffee, candy, and ice cream—at moderate prices.

Afternoon

Visit some of the nearby galleries where local craftspeople sell their work. You'll find examples at **Court Street Collection** (64 North Court Street; 740–593–8261), **Lamborn's Studio** (19 West State Street; 800–224–5567), and **Mountain Leather and General Store** (25 South Court Street; 740–592–8261) for starters. If you skipped dessert, **Perk's Coffee House** (740–594–PERK), on the corner of Court and Union Streets, is a good place to regroup and enjoy a cappuccino or sinful dessert.

The next stop is the **Kennedy Museum of Art** at Lin Hall (740–593–1304). It's located in an area known as the Ridges, a name that has stuck for the parklike hilltop portion of Ohio University. From uptown turn right onto State Route 682 and then left at the entrance to the Ridges, less than a quarter mile. Drive to the museum at the top of the hill. This nineteenth-century architectural gem was formerly the Athens Asylum for the Insane, caring for as many as 1,800 patients in its heyday. Its twentieth-century renovation still contains elements of its days as a mental hospital. Somehow the black and white tiled floors, open spaces, high ceilings, and Victorian woodwork make a perfect backdrop for the permanent collection of Southwestern Native American tapestries and changing exhibits. Admission is free. Open Tuesday through Friday noon to 5:00 P.M. (until 8 P.M. on Thursday), Saturday and Sunday 1:00 to 5:00 P.M.

Another unusual site for art shows is the **Dairy Barn Cultural Arts Center** (8000 Dairy Barn Lane, Athens; 740–592–4981). It too had a former life—as a milking facility. It was saved from the wrecking ball, preserved, and adapted, and now houses great exhibits, including the biennial *Quilt National* (next scheduled for 2001). It's open Tuesday through Sunday 11:00 A.M. to 5:00 P.M., until 8:00 P.M. on Thursday.

The Kennedy Museum of art sits high on a hill overlooking the Ohio University campus.

DINNER: You may have already noticed the **Casa Nueva Restaurant and Cantina** (4 West State Street; 740–592–2016). This eatery, a worker-owned cooperative, serves locally harvested and created organic products and nearly everything is made from scratch. The restaurant serves Mexican and eclectic "world cuisine"—the organic coffee is harvested by Mayan farmers—and eighty beers from all over the world. Inexpensive to moderate.

Stay for the cantina's live entertainment, which could be jazz or bluegrass. Before retiring to the inn, sample a handcrafted brew or draft root beer at **O'Hooley's Irish Pub & Microbrewery** (24 West Union; 740–592–9686).

LODGING: Renovations have changed the look of the guest rooms at the **Ohio University Inn** (331 Richland Avenue; 740–593–6661). There is an outdoor pool and full-service dining in Cutler's Restaurant and The Bunch of Grapes Tavern. There's also a fitness center and business center and rooms have coffee makers. Rates range from $82 to $99 but increase slightly during special weekends at the University.

ESCAPE FIVE

SOUTHERN

DAY 2

Morning

BREAKFAST: Take your choice of a light breakfast or the reasonably priced Sunday brunch at the inn. Then head for some exercise on the **Hockhocking Adena Bikeway,** on the old Columbus and Hocking Valley Railroad bed. The 16.4-mile paved trail connects Athens and **Nelsonville,** running through the Wayne National Forest.

If you brought walking shoes, your bike, or in-line skates, you may be able to make the entire trip. Otherwise, stroll a segment, return to your car, and follow signs to the **Hocking Valley Scenic Railroad** (U.S. Route 33 and Hocking Valley Drive, Nelsonville; 740–753–9531 or 800–967–7834). The railroad operates on a segment of track for rides at noon and 2:30 P.M. weekends from Memorial Day to the end of October. There are also Santa trains from late November through December. The 12-mile jaunt to Haydenville costs $7.50 for adults and $4.75 for children; a longer ride to Logan is $10.50 and $7.25. Both stop at **Robbins Crossing** (3301 Hocking Parkway, Nelsonville; 740–753–3591). This nineteenth-century interpretive village, operated by students at Hocking College, will take you back to earlier days in southern Ohio before you come back to the twenty-first century and your highway/freeway ride home.

LUNCH: Continue west on U.S. 33 to **Lancaster,** stopping at **Four Seasons Bakery and Deli** (135 West Main Street, Lancaster; 470–654–2253). Turn right onto Main Street from U.S. 33. You'll find street parking nearby and the restaurant on your left. Overstuffed deli sandwiches are the specialty, but soups, salads, delicious pastries, and ice cream round out the menu. Gourmet coffees and teas are also available. Moderately priced.

Continue your trip on U.S. 33 northwest toward Columbus, picking up I–70 west and then I–71 north back to Cleveland.

THERE'S MORE

Ohio University events. Music, plays, movies, lectures and guest speakers fill the venues around Ohio University most evenings when school is in session. Contact the University's Haning Hall ticket office (614–593–1780) or the Athens County Convention and Visitors Bureau (800–878–9767) for schedules and ticket information.

SOUTHERN

The Foothills School of American Crafts, 11 State Street, Amesville; (740) 448–2053. Located in a rural setting on State Route 550 in the midst of Appalachia, instructors are teaching locals to develop their talents and take advantage of the resources around them. There's an ongoing exhibit of student and professional work. No admission for exhibits, only for classes. Open by chance, so call for an appointment.

Stuart's Opera House, on the square in downtown Nelsonville; (740) 753–1924. The cultural cornerstone of Nelsonville. Productions by the Berean Community Players and the Ohio University Athenian Players take center stage in this restored Victorian theater, but tours of the historic building can also be arranged.

Rocky Shoe and Boots Factory and Outlet Store, 39 Canal Street, Nelsonville; (800) 421–5151. Heavy-duty work boots and hiking boots at discount prices. Factory tours are available if you call ahead.

Fur Peace Ranch Guitar Camp, P.O. Box 389, Pomeroy, Ohio 45769; (740) 992–6228. A music school and performance center providing a fall series of events, including gourmet dinners and concerts. Events are $25 per person, except for the fall holiday fair, which has a $2.00 admission charge.

The Big Chimney Baking Co., 8776 Mine Road, Canaanville; (614) 592–4147. A big assortment freshly baked breads and pastries.

SPECIAL EVENTS

April–May. International Film and Video Festival, Ohio University. (740) 593–1330.

May. International Street Fair, Uptown Athens. (740) 593–4330.

August. International King Midget Jamboree, Uptown Athens. Free. (800) 878–9767.

August. Parade of the Hills Festival, Public Square, Nelsonville. (740) 753–3051.

September. Barn Raisin,' Dairy Barn Southeastern Ohio Cultural Arts Center, Athens. Outdoor arts festival. (740) 592–4981.

October. Paul Bunyan Festival, Hocking College Campus, Nelsonville. Forestry trade show. Admission is $5.00 for adults, $3.00 for seniors and $2.00 for students. (740) 593–3591.

OTHER RECOMMENDED RESTAURANTS AND LODGINGS

Nelsonville

Ramada Inn, U.S. 33 and State Route 691; (740) 753–3531. A full-service motel with unique dining facilities. Hocking College operates the fine-dining Foxfire Restaurant as well as the Garden Terrace for more casual options. There is often locally outstanding live entertainment too. Rates: $67 to $100.

Old Towne Bed & Breakfast, 240 Jefferson Street; (740) 753–1773. Reasonably priced accommodations, some with kitchenettes, near the center of Nelsonville. The hospitable innkeeper serves breakfast in the coffee shop downstairs. Rates: $59 to $125.

Coffee Cup, U.S. 33; (740) 753–3336. Local landmark for home-cooked food, notebook-size menu. Inexpensive and casual.

Athens

Seven Sauces, 66 North Court Street; (740) 592–5555. Opens for dinner at 5:00 P.M. Pastas, seafood, steak, and chicken. Innovative and upscale; moderately expensive by Athens standards, but considered very reasonable if you're from a larger city.

AmeriHost, 20 Home Street; (740) 594–3000 or (800) 434–5800. Indoor pool, complimentary continental breakfast. Rates: $67 to $100.

Glouster

Burr Oak Resort and Conference Center, 10660 Burr Oak Lodge Road, State Route 2, Box 159; (740) 767–2112. A full-service lodge and thirty fully furnished two-bedroom cabins, 15 miles northeast of Athens. Part of the award-winning Ohio state parks system. Hiking trails, themed weekend specials, indoor swimming pool. From April through October, rooms range from $72 to $107, cabins from $130 to $155.

FOR MORE INFORMATION

Athens Area Chamber of Commerce, 5 North Court Street, Athens, Ohio 45701; (740) 594–2251.

Athens County Convention and Visitors Bureau, 667 East State Street, Athens, Ohio 45701; (800) 878–9767.

Granville, Ohio

NEW ENGLAND'S CHARM
IN CENTRAL OHIO

1 NIGHT

Native American sites • Family fun • Victorian underwear

Spending a weekend in the Newark region of Ohio sounds like the city mouse visiting the country mouse, and in some respects it is. You won't find bustling nightlife or New York shops, but do expect some terrific scenery, original tastes, diverse overnight accommodations, and even a few great shopping finds. New England charm, created by shuttered buildings, wide brick streets, and treed lawns, beckons travelers to enjoy a quiet overnight here.

Granville and Newark in Licking County are two towns that make enjoyable getaways with or without children. If you decide to take children, perhaps inviting the grandkids, choose activities that will hold your youngsters' attention. Include a swimming pool and bike trail to burn off energy, a few museums for the educational component, and an underwear discussion for laughs. Add a ghost story or Native American tale and a healthy-size portion of hearty cuisine in simple flavors, and you have a weekend getaway that will make everyone happy.

You might want to extend your stay to two nights rather than returning home the next day. By doing so, you'll have ample time to enjoy the natural surroundings as well as your accommodations at a more leisurely pace.

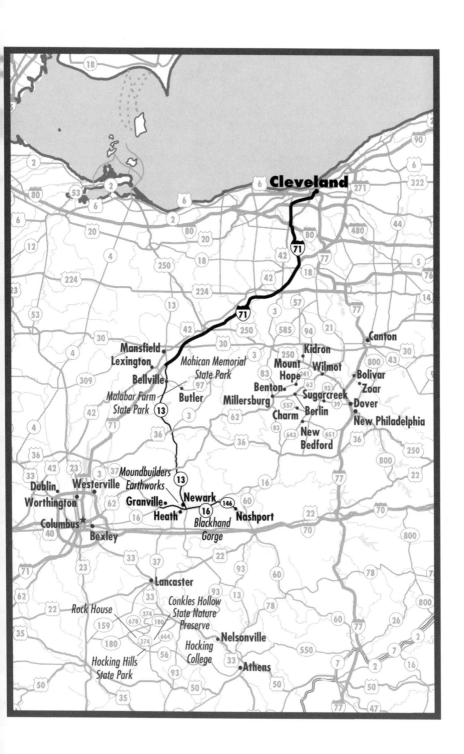

SOUTHERN

DAY 1

Morning

No matter your passengers' profile, leave early enough for lunch when you get to the region. Allow two and a half hours for the 130-mile trip. Follow I–71 south to State Route 13 south in Mansfield, traveling through Mt. Vernon and into **Newark.**

Your first stop is **Moundbuilders State Memorial** (800–600–7174), located on the south side of Newark off Route 79 between Parkview Drive and Cooper Street. Moundbuilders offers a look into the relics left behind by Ohio's early residents, the Hopewells. Stop in at the museum to gain a better understanding of the people who lived here 2,000 years ago and built the mounds in nearly every county in the state. The National Historic Landmark operated by the Ohio Historical Society is open mid-May through Labor Day, Wednesday through Saturday from 9:30 A.M. to 5:00 P.M., and year-round on Sunday from noon to 5:00 P.M. The cost is $3.00 for adults, $1.25 for children.

Next, it's on to the **Institute of Industrial Technology** (55 South First Street; 740–349–9277), located in a restored 1881 steam engine factory in downtown Newark. The first-floor displays illustrate some of the current technology used in the Newark area; upstairs, visitors stroll down the *Streets of Yesteryear,* one of the original COSI exhibits recently donated to this center. Volunteers interpret weaving, candlemaking, and other crafts of the day. In the rear of the building, there's a working glass studio from the National Heisey Glass Museum. Glassblowers demonstrate their art, and scheduled programs, like the paperweight creating class, give novices the rare opportunity to experience the art of glassblowing for themselves. Museum admission is $4.00 for adults, $3.00 for seniors, and $1.00 for children. There are more special events on selected Saturdays throughout the year.

Art-glass enthusiasts will want to include a stop at the **National Heisey Glass Museum,** in Veterans Park at Sixth and Church Streets (614–345–2932). The glass patterns were locally produced between 1896 and 1957. The distinctive pieces, some of which traveled the United States in railroad dining cars, are all on display. The attractive museum is open Tuesday through Saturday 10:00 A.M. to 4:00 P.M. and Sunday 1:00 to 4:00 P.M.

LUNCH: Stop for lunch at **Miller's Essenplatz** (1058 East Main Street; 740–345–7900). Located 2 miles east of State Route 13, it's a locally owned Amish-style restaurant featuring sandwiches and dinners along with homemade breads and desserts. Hot roast beef, pork, or turkey sandwiches served with mashed potatoes or dressing and another side dish of your choice costs $7.95 and will more than fill you up. A more reasonable half portion is offered for a dollar less.

Afternoon

Take State Route 16 west to **Granville,** home of Denison University and a host of shops, museums, eateries, and inns.

The Victorian underwear program at the **Granville Lifestyle Museum** (121 South Main Street; 614–587–0373) is sure to entertain everyone in the group. The home museum displays an outstanding collection of hats, photos, and items used by the owners, Hubert and Oese Robinson. Visitors can easily imagine them still living in the 1870 Victorian—it's just the way they left it. Open Sunday 1:00 to 4:30 P.M. or by appointment; there is usually a hands-on children's craft or activity following the tour. You can swing on the porch swing or visit the garden whenever the gate is open. Admission is $1.50 for adults, free for children under twelve.

The **Granville Historical Museum** (115 East Broadway; 740–587–0373) displays furnishings brought by the earliest settlers from New England. You'll see the resemblance of a New England town inside the home museum and throughout town. Open Friday through Sunday from 1:00 to 4:00 P.M.

Among the shops in Granville is **Foot Loose** (121 South Prospect Street; 740–321–1198). It's a good spot for discovering men's and women's vintage clothing and accessories.

DINNER: Stop for dinner at the **Granville Inn** (314 East Broadway; 740–587–3333). Fireplaces provide a cozy atmosphere and the food is delicious. Be sure to try the frosted raisin bread, a house specialty. Dinners range from $15 to $28.

After dinner, peek in the **Buxton Inn** across the street. Stories about a resident ghost flourish in this one-time stagecoach stop, but most guests never meet her. Although the innkeepers don't advertise her existence, perhaps you'll catch a tale if you order dessert and coffee here.

From the Granville Inn parking lot, turn left onto Broadway. Turn right onto Cherry Valley Road. Continue, crossing State Route 16. The Cherry Valley Lodge is a quarter mile on the left.

LODGING: The **Cherry Valley Lodge,** 2299 Cherry Valley Road; (800) 788–8008. The lodge has a restful quality, with stone fireplaces and comfortable furnishings, and an outdoor courtyard and pool. If you're toting children, the inn provides extra services. You'll find a special amenities package of baby products in your room and can request a baby swing, rocker, electrical outlet safety caps, special pool toys for the indoor and outdoor pools, and complimentary duck food for the courtyard inhabitants. There's a game room, gummy bear on the kids' menu, family videos, and more for older kids. Loaner bikes, with or without baby seats, for use on the paved bike path make a bike ride possible even if you didn't bring your own. Depending on season, standard rooms range between $138 and $169 for two. There is no charge for children and suites are also available. Call ahead for weekend, holiday, and seasonal specials.

DAY 2

Morning

BREAKFAST: Cherry Valley Lodge. Some weekend packages include breakfast, but standard room rates do not. Brunch is ordered, not buffet style here.

Allow time for a bike ride on the Thomas J. Evans Bike Path. Avid riders will want to bring equipment from home and ride various portions or all of the 36 miles. One of the most scenic portions is a 4-mile segment cutting through the Black Hand State Nature Preserve east of the lodge.

Before leaving the area, drive into **Newark** and head south on State Route 13 for a stop at **Dawes Arboretum** (7770 Jacksontown Road Southeast; 800–44–DAWES). Even during winter, when neutral earth shades subdue the Japanese Garden, it is beautiful and peaceful. It's on the 2½-mile auto tour for visitors who would like an overview of the park without traversing the many trails. There are maps for walkers and hikers too. Be sure to notice the grove of Ohio Buckeye trees planted in the shape of the number 17, in honor of Ohio being the seventeenth state to enter the Union. The grounds are open daily from dawn to dusk. Free.

LUNCH: When you finish at the park, head north on State Route 13 to begin your return trip home. **Ye Olde Mill** (State Route 13, Utica; 800–589–5000), where Velvet Ice Cream is manufactured, serves great ice-cream concoctions as well as a full menu. It closes at the end of October for the winter.

Continue north on State Route 13 to I–71 north. The return trip will take about two and a half hours.

THERE'S MORE

Robbins-Hunter Museum, Avery Downer House, 221 East Broadway, Granville; (740) 587–0410. Dating from the mid-1800s, this Greek Revival–style mansion displays period furnishings and decorative arts. Open from April

Ye Olde Mill in Utica is the place to stop for a picnic or a Velvet ice cream concoction.

through December, Tuesday through Sunday 1:00 to 4:00 P.M. or by special appointment.

Dillon Lake Water Sports Shop, 6275 Clay-Littick Drive, Nashport; (800) 640–7964. Offers a scenic way to see Blackhand Gorge: from canoe or kayak. Trips range in length from one and a half to six hours; $11 to $22 per person. Children six to twelve are half price; children under five are free.

Buckeye Central Scenic Railroad, 5501 National Road Southeast, Hebron; (740) 928–3827. Scenic railroad excursions are scheduled regularly from May through October. Additional holiday trains around Halloween, Memorial Day, and July 4, and Santa trains on weekends at 1:00 and 3:00 P.M.

Willow Hill Vineyards Winery, 5460 Loudon Street, Granville; (740) 587–4622. Call ahead for wine tasting on the deck overlooking surrounding hills and arbor.

OTHER RECOMMENDED RESTAURANTS AND LODGINGS

Granville

The Buxton Inn, 313 East Broadway; (740) 587–0001. Originally a stagecoach stop, the original inn and several adjacent buildings have been transformed into lovely B&B-style rooms, some with fireplaces and ghost stories about "the woman in blue." There's a light and airy atrium where breakfast is served. The twenty-five uniquely furnished guest rooms range from $70 to $80. Moderately priced lunch, dinner, and Sunday brunch are served to the public; reservations required.

The Granville Inn, 314 East Broadway; (614) 587–3333. Thirty uniquely decorated guest rooms; many have been newly refurbished. Rates: $78 to $138.

Brews Cafe and Brews Too, 128 East Broadway; (740) 587–0249. Moderately priced pub food—burgers, wood-fired pizzas, and daily entree specials—and a large selection of beers.

Victoria's Olde Tyme Deli and Cafe, 134 East Broadway; (740) 587–0322. Serves lunch (soups, salads, and quiche) from 11:30 A.M. to 5:00 P.M., pizza and pasta after 5:00 P.M., and desserts and coffee all the time (11:30 A.M. to 9:00 P.M. weekdays, 10:00 A.M. to 9:00 P.M. Saturday and Sunday). Sunday brunch from 10:00 A.M. to 1:00 P.M. Moderate.

Newark

Pitzer-Cooper House B&B, 6019 White Chapel Road Southeast; (800) 833–9536. This restored 1858 residence located a mile from Dawes Arboretum has two guest rooms with private baths, one that shares a bath. Rates: $90, including breakfast.

Thornville

Herb 'n' Ewe's Garden Cafe, 11755 National Road; (740) 323–2264. What began as an herb garden enterprise now features lunches and dinners delicately flavored with the garden's herbs. Entrees can be ordered a la carte, but the best value is the full meal, which includes appetizer, entree, dessert, and beverage. Lunches are moderate to expensive—$12.95 for pan roasted roughy, $14.95 for "supreme chicken Francese." By reservation only. The Garden Cafe serves daily from 11:00 A.M. to 3:00 P.M., Friday and Saturday dinner from 6:30 to

8:30 P.M., and Sunday 11:00 A.M. to 6:00 P.M. Stop to watch the soap-making process in the new herbal soap factory on the premises.

Hebron

AmeriHost Inn, 122 Arrowhead Boulevard, State Routes 79 and 40; (800) 434–5800. New hotel with indoor pool and complimentary continental breakfast. Rates: $69 to $79; whirlpool suites are $99 for two.

SPECIAL EVENTS

March. Maple Sugaring Days, Dawes Arboretum, Newark. (800) 44–DAWES.

May. May Day Celebration, Herb 'n' Ewe. (740) 323–2264.

May. Old-Fashioned Ice Cream Festival, Ye Olde Mill, Utica. Free. (800) 589–5000.

September. Buckeye Tree Festival, Ye Olde Mill, Utica. Free. (800) 589–5000.

December. Candlelight walking tours, holiday open houses and craft shows dot the area. Obtain a current calendar with dates and times from the Licking County Visitors Bureau; (800) 589–8224.

FOR MORE INFORMATION

Licking County Convention and Visitors Bureau, 50 West Locust Street, Newark, Ohio 43058-0702; (800) 589–8224.

SOUTHERN

Zoar and More

SETTLING IN OHIO

1 NIGHT

Living history • Buttons and carvers • Little Switzerland

Enjoying a good German meal is reason enough to visit Zoar, a tiny community south of Cleveland in Tuscarawas County, but views of the village from the hilly crest will tempt you to spend more time and explore the unique town below.

One of the most unusual aspects of the twelve-block historic district is that it remains part of the community. Some of the structures have been restored as private residences, businesses, shops, bed-and-breakfasts, and an inn, which may or may not reflect the original use. Others, like the ones maintained by the Ohio Historical Society, take visitors right back to 1817 when German separatists created their communal settlement here. Spend time visiting the living history site, browsing the quaint shops, and exploring the surrounding towns and Amish area before leaving.

Businesses are open year-round, but to take advantage of the Zoar Village State Memorial tours, plan your getaway during warmer months, when spring, summer, or fall chores are taking place in the village and the town is most scenic. Spend the night in one of the unique B&Bs. Ghosts of the past come alive during the candlelight dinner, but they won't interrupt your sleep.

DAY 1

Leave by midmorning, arriving in Zoar in time for lunch. Travel south through Canton on I-77, taking exit 93 in Bolivar and traveling southeast along State Route 212 to **Zoar.** The 75-mile trip will take about an hour and a half.

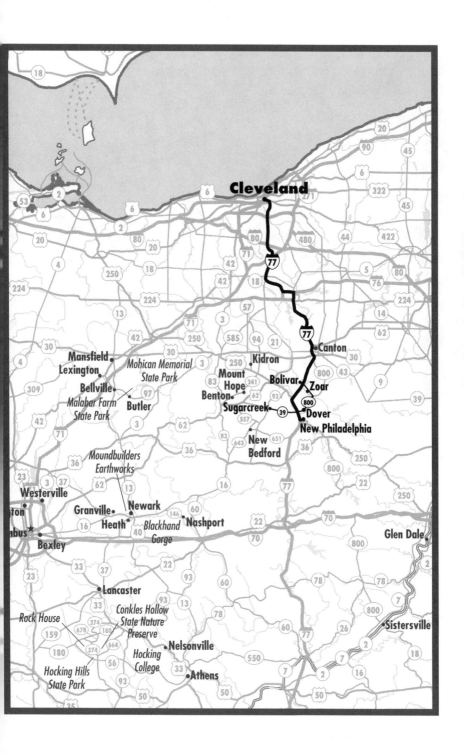

The community of Zoar still reflects the pristine quality of an early nineteenth-century German settlement.

LUNCH: Sample the German fare at the **Zoar Tavern & Inn** (Main Street, Zoar; 888–874–2170), built in 1831. Spatzels and cabbage accompany many of the German schnitzels and sausages, and bread pudding tops the list of homemade desserts. The moderately priced menu has entrees and sandwiches, and a children's menu is available. Reservations are accepted.

Afternoon

Tour the buildings of the **Zoar Village State Memorial,** 221 West Third Street, operated by the Ohio Historical Society (800–262–6195). Admission to the Bimeler Museum is free; tours cost $5.00 for adults, $1.25 for children. Hours vary with the seasons and it is closed for public tours during winter. Interpreters will show you around four of the buildings before sending you on a self-guided excursion, but if you call ahead to visit during seasonal programs, activities and demonstrations will bring the lessons to life.

Be sure to visit the "Magazine Complex," consisting of the dining room, kitchen, and laundry of Number One House, where the group's founder, Joseph Baumeler, lived. The magazine (which means storehouse) for the entire community and the dairy/springhouse were recently restored to help visitors understand the communal life of Zoar.

From its early days, the separatist movement was known for its hospitality, attracting visitors eager to share in the prosperity of the families' abundant agricultural bounty. Food preparation techniques are still a main part of the tour; German culinary practices are demonstrated in the kitchen and dining room, built in 1835. One of the interesting features is the "kettle-oven," a brick firebox with a cast-iron top. You might find kettles of *Schwarzbrotsuppe mit Bratwuerstchen* (black bread soup with bratwurst), *Gartnerinsuppe* (gardener's wife soup), or perhaps an earthenware crock full of *Marinierte-Birnen,* or pickled pears, on the reproduction stove patterned after the original found in the kitchen.

After the tour, stop in at the shops scattered throughout the village. Most sell antiques, collectibles, and gifts including primitive furnishings and candles crafted in Zoar.

DINNER AND LODGING: There are about a half dozen bed-and-breakfasts in Zoar, each with its own original character, but tonight you'll be staying in an 1817 log cabin. **The Inn at Cowger House #9** (197 Fourth Street; 800–874–3542), is owned by the village's former mayor, Ed Cowger, and his wife, Mary. They offer guests ten rooms, divided among three buildings, including an 1833 post-and-beam construction and a modern Amish style B&B with several handicapped-accessible rooms.

The 1817 log cabin, where candlelight dinners are served, is most rustic and cramped, but truly an unusual experience. Freshen up before dinner and meet at the log cabin for the 7:00 P.M. common seating. Arrange dinner and your choice of four entrees when you make your lodging reservation; space is limited to twenty people. Rates range from $70 to $159 including taxes; dinner is an extra $25 per person.

DAY 2

Morning

BREAKFAST: A full country breakfast is complimentary with your B&B lodging. On Sunday, it's served at 9:30. Afterward, take the scenic route south along State Route 212, following the Tuscarawas River. Turn right on State Route 800 and continue south to Dover. Turn left on Front Street to Tuscarawas Avenue. Turn right and drive 8 blocks to Karl Avenue for another unusual stop, **Warther's Carvings and Gardens** (331 Karl Avenue; 330–343–7513). The museum, behind the Warther family's brick home, pays homage to the creative talent of patriarch Ernest "Mooney" Warther and contains the current-day workshop of the family's knife manufacturing business. Usually a relative is on hand to explain Warther's intricate wood, ebony, and ivory carvings, including his steam locomotive engine and Lincoln's funeral train displays. Stop to view Frieda Warther's button collection, the gardens, and their Indian arrowheads. Admission is $7.00 for adults, $3.00 for children six to seventeen.

To contrast the simple Warther homestead, drive to the nearby **J. E. Reeves Victorian Home and Carriage House Museum** (325 East Iron Street; 800–815–2794). The museum shows off the lifestyle of the county's first millionaire, Jeremiah E. Reeves. Rooms are not cordoned off, so visitors can take a close-up look into the seventeen-room Italianate mansion, where 95 percent of the original furnishings remain. Edison's carbon filament bulbs still shine and century-old tapestries look brand-new. Guided tours here are $5.00 for adults, $2.00 for children.

LUNCH: Stop downtown at **Dover Station** (221 West Third Street; 330–364–7788). Don't be put off by the small-town atmosphere—locals enjoy the reasonably priced daily specials and homestyle fare.

From Dover Station follow Third Street west to Tuscarawas Avenue. Turn right (north) to Slingluff, and turn left (west). The I–77 north entrance ramp will be on your right just ahead.

THERE'S MORE

Fort Laurens State Memorial, 11067 Ft. Laurens Road, Bolivar; (330) 874–4292. Commemorates the only fort built in the state by the American Continental Army. A tomb dedicated to heroes of the American Revolution is also on the property. Admission is $3.00 for adults, $1.25 for children. Park and museum are open from April to October.

Schoenbrunn State Memorial, 1914 Delaware Drive Southeast, New Philadelphia; (800) 752–2711. Visitors can rent a cassette for a self-guided tour of this 1772 village, the first Christian settlement in Ohio. It was founded by David Zeisberger, a Moravian missionary who wanted to convert the Delaware Indians, but was abandoned during the Revolutionary War. Often volunteers demonstrate period activities at the eighteen cabins in the reconstructed village. Admission is $5.00 for adults, $1.25 for children. Open April to October.

Trumpet in the Land, Schoenbrunn Amphitheatre, New Philadelphia; box office: (330) 339–1132. Follow up your tour of the nearby historic sites with an outdoor drama depicting the massacre of Christian Indians in Gnadenhutten in 1782. Shows run from June through August, Monday through Saturday. Adult tickets are $13.00, children, $6.00. Backstage tours and ticket specials are available. The actual site of the massacre is located at the Gnadenhutten Memorial and Museum, Gnadenhutten, Ohio; (740) 254–4143.

Eiler Candy Shop, 225 West Third Street, Dover; (330) 343–3411. Sells homemade fudge and more. Open daily except Sunday from 10:30 A.M. to 6:00 P.M.

Chuckle's Antique Store, 229 West Third Street, Dover; (330) 343–1874. Treat yourself to a phosphate at the sixty-year-old soda fountain.

Sugarcreek, the "Little Switzerland of Ohio." Located 10 miles west of Zoar, the town developed when Swiss immigrants settled in the hilly countryside reminiscent of their homeland. The architectural gingerbread, colorful murals, and "Swiss" everything provide a glimpse into the Swiss and Amish heritage of the region.

SPECIAL EVENTS

May. Canal Dover Festival, downtown Dover. Street fair, beer garden, entertainment, and food. (330) 364–6678.

August. Zoar Harvest Festival. Civil War encampment, food, entertainment, and antiques. (330) 339–2646.

October. Wonders in Wood, Dover Middle School. Carvers' festival. (330) 339–6676.

October. Apfelfest, Zoar. Food festival. (330) 339–2646.

October. Ohio Swiss Festival, downtown Sugarcreek. Tuscarawas's biggest event. Swiss heritage festival with games, music, Swiss cheese judging and polka music. (330) 852–4113.

December. Christmas in Zoar. Candlelit walks, encampment, art show, and crafts. (330) 339–2646.

OTHER RECOMMENDED RESTAURANTS AND LODGINGS

Zoar

Zoar Tavern and Inn, One Main Street; (888) 874–2170. Overnight guests can choose from five guest rooms. Rooms are small but quaint, with hand-hewn beams, brick and stone walls, and antiques. Rates: $70–$95, including continental breakfast. Not handicapped accessible.

Dover

Olde World Bed & Breakfast, 2982 State Route 516 Northwest; (800) 447–1273. Completely restored Victorian B&B (the building stood empty for twenty years before current owners rehabbed it). Each of the five guest rooms follows a decorating theme—Parisian, alpine, Victorian. Full breakfast is served; lunch, dinner, and teas by reservation. Rates: $60–$100, depending on season and room selection. Often packages and special discounts are offered.

Whispering Hills Bed & Breakfast Retreat, 5388 Boy Scout Road Northeast; (888) 745–0846. Great hilltop views from outdoor decks, hot tubs, observation tower. Five guest rooms, private baths. Rates: $65–$135. Dinner can be arranged when you make your reservations.

New Philadelphia

Schoenbrunn Inn by Christopher, 1186 West High Avenue; (800) 929–7799. Some handicapped-accessible rooms. Complimentary deluxe continental breakfast, indoor pool. Rates run as low as $49.95 for two-night winter season stays, but usually weekend prices range from $62.95 to $72.95 per night, depending on season. Pets are permitted for an additional $10 per night.

Pro's Table, 878 East High Avenue; (330) 339–4212. A moderately priced restaurant with a golfing theme.

Uncle Primo's, 435 Minnich Avenue Northwest; (330) 364–2026. Pasta, steaks, and seafood; moderate. Make reservations here—it gets crowded.

FOR MORE INFORMATION

Tuscarawas County Convention and Visitors Bureau, P.O. Box 926, New Philadelphia, Ohio 44663; (800) 527–3387.

SOUTHWESTERN
ESCAPES

Indianapolis, Indiana
MORE THAN THE SPEEDWAY CITY

2 NIGHTS

Living history • Family fun • Memorials • Culture

Making the lengthy freeway trip to Indianapolis may seem rather bland to motorists, but the results are anything but boring. If you haven't visited Indianapolis in the last five years or so, you're in for a pleasant surprise. The gleaming downtown skyline is teeming with professional sports arenas, monuments, and museums. The focus of the city's rebirth, Circle Centre Mall, houses more than one hundred shops, eateries, and entertainment opportunities, along with the Artsgarden, a mecca for the visual and performing arts.

It's a perfect adult getaway, but too kid-friendly to leave your children behind. Most of Indianapolis's attractions can be enjoyed by adults and children, albeit on different levels. The decision is a tough one, but with either option, you'll be surprised at the friendly yet upscale feel of the city, melded with remnants of the past and plans for a growing future.

Adults may want to add a few hours of shopping or additional time in the museums, perhaps lingering a little longer at a restaurant, but otherwise, the itineraries are pretty much the same for all ages.

Don't plan your weekend during big race weekends (the Indy 500 in May and the Brickyard 400 in August), when you'll have to pay higher hotel prices and battle the crowds.

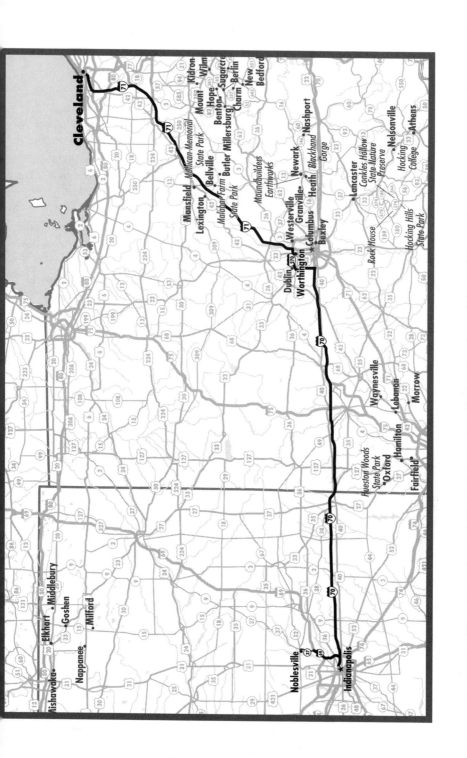

SOUTHWESTERN

DAY 1

Morning

BREAKFAST: Leave early on Friday morning, by 8:00 A.M. if possible. There's a 300-mile, five-hour trip ahead with only one pit stop for breakfast. Head south on I–71 toward Columbus and connect to I–270 west just north of the city. If you'd like a hearty breakfast and some fresh Java for reinforcements, exit I–270 at U.S. 23 and head south toward **Worthington,** bearing right on U.S. 23. Turn right into Worthington Mall where you'll find **First Watch** (614–431–9040) just inside the main entrance. Known for its large portions and breakfast specialties, you won't go wrong with any selection. If you prefer a quick bite, try **Bruegger's** for coffee and carry-out bagels.

Back on the I–270 leads you around Columbus's outskirts and onto I–70 heading west. Stay on this route until you come to Indianapolis's outerbelt, I–465. Follow it north around the city, but be ready to exit at Allisonville Road, the exit past the I–69 exchange. Head north for several miles into the affluent and fast growing suburban community of **Fishers.**

Afternoon

The first real stop is ahead at **Conner Prairie** (13400 Allisonville Road, Fishers; 317–776–6000). This living history museum takes visitors back to the early 1800s when William Conner first arrived and set up a trading post. Prairietown, the village-style museum restored through the philanthropy of Eli Lilly, is now owned by Earlham College and provides upscale dining, a venue for the Indianapolis Symphony Orchestra's summer concerts, and a wide variety of educational programs.

LUNCH: Enjoy a late lunch at **Persimmons** (317–776–6008) before exploring the museum. This fine-dining restaurant at Conner Prairie serves up innovative selections drawn from Native American, African-American, European, and regional areas. The wood-fired pizzas, salads, and sandwiches are all delectable. Moderate.

This history adventure combines the renovated beauty of an indoor exhibit center with "Prairietown," a forty-building village that draws participants into activities of the time through interactive and first-person exhibits. Get an overview of first-person characterizations by first attending the short video shown every half hour throughout the day.

There are hands-on areas as well as events that staff call "immersion history" settings—you will be expected to get right into character and participate. Become a fugitive slave, following the Underground Railroad as one might have in the 1800s, during the "Follow the North Star" presentation. It's a powerfully moving experience. Less difficult to digest is preparing an authentic hearthside supper and then feasting on the fruits of your labor by candlelight. Don't forget the home tour of the William Conner Estate, an 1823 Federal style brick home, the first of its kind in the county. The museum and outdoor village are open April through November, Tuesday through Saturday, from 9:30 A.M. to 5:00 P.M., and Sunday from 11:30 A.M. to 5:00 P.M. Admission to the grounds and museum is $10.00 for adults, $9.00 for seniors, and $6.00 for children five to twelve.

When you finish at Conner Prairie, if time permits, spend a few more hours in this suburban region before heading into the city. Drive a few miles north into **Noblesville**'s Historic District and explore the antiques shops. Stop at the old-fashioned soda fountain at **Alexander's on the Square** (864 Logan Street; 317–773–9177), or grab a latte at **Noble Coffee and Tea Co. Ltd.** (933 Logan Street; 317–773–0339). Peruse **Lake and Lodge Outfitters** (917 Conner Street; 317–773–4777) for the best selection of rustic furniture and items with a nautical theme.

Head south on Allisonville Road, turning left onto 116th Street. Continue for 5 miles to a right turn onto Brooks School Road. Turn left on Fall Creek Road and drive to the water's edge for dinner overlooking the Geist Reservoir.

DINNER: Along with great views, you'll find pastas, steaks, and seafood at **The Blue Heron** (11699 Fall Creek Road, Fishers; 317–845–8899). There's also a variety of sandwiches, salads, soups, and a children's menu, all moderately priced. The atmosphere is casual, filled with boaters in the summer and cozy fireplaces in the winter.

Pick up I–69 south in Fishers and head toward **Indianapolis.** After the interstate ends, continue on State Route 37 for about 15 miles. Turn left onto Meridian Street and drive to Monument Circle. Bear right and then take a right turn onto Market Street. It dead-ends at the State Capitol; turn left on Capitol Avenue, left on Georgia Street, and then right on Illinois Street.

LODGING: The **Canterbury Hotel,** 123 South Illinois Street, Indianapolis; (800) 538–8186. This elegant small hotel, listed as a National Historic Landmark, takes you back to the opulence of the 1920s with glittering chandeliers, marble, and Chippendale furnishings—perfect for a romantic getaway. There is valet parking, which is complimentary with several weekend packages ranging from $150 to $255 on all but race and sporting event weekends. The specials offer rate reductions and amenities like massages, dinner, and horse-drawn carriage rides.

DAY 2

Morning

BREAKFAST: Your room rate includes a continental breakfast served in the hotel's atrium, so take advantage of this convenience before heading out to explore the city. Then it's time to visit the **Indianapolis Motor Speedway.** Drive north on Illinois Street and turn left on Sixteenth Street. It won't take you long to glance at the displays of cars and trophies in the **Hall of Fame Museum** (4790 West Sixteenth Street; 317–481–8500), leaving time for a track tour for an additional $3.00 per person. Admission to the museum is $3.00 for adults, $1.00 for children ages six to fifteen. Do take your camera for a photo op in a racing car.

Your next stop is the **White River Gardens** (1200 West Washington Street; 317–630–2010), the new sister affiliation of the Indianapolis Zoo. This botanical paradise offers a relaxing interlude for nature lovers and gardening enthusiasts alike. Ongoing shows take place indoors under glass; outdoors, visitors can stroll the innovative "inspiration" gardens for ideas to take back home, and visit other areas, like the wedding garden and soothing water gardens. One popular spot is the train garden, complete with a miniature train making its way through the garden's topography. You can even bring your sick plants in for a consultation, if they are healthy enough to withstand the trip. Admission to the gardens is $6.00 for adults, $4.00 for youths and seniors.

When you finish here, continue through the adjacent Indianapolis Zoo before lunch. Zoo prices are $9.75 for adults, $7.00 for seniors, and $6.00 for children ages three to twelve. Admission is reduced from November through February.

LUNCH: Drive back downtown for a leisurely lunch near the hotel. One favorite choice is **Palomino Euro Bistro** (Circle Centre, 49 West Maryland Street; 317–974–0400). Not only does the menu include a wide assortment of inventive and uniquely prepared lunch and dinner choices, but you'll also find a schedule of upcoming events and "happenings" around town. The "Chop Chop Salad" is a luncheon specialty consisting of diced meats and cheeses tossed with fresh basil and balsamic vinaigrette. Many items are under $10 at lunchtime and average around $15 for dinner. This is a casual but sophisticated choice so if you're on a family excursion, you may prefer to purchase to-go lunches at the Circle Centre

Just a few minutes from downtown Indianapolis, the Eiteljorg Museum of American Indians and Western Art will take you far from your current destination.

food court and carry them to the **Artsgarden** (317–631–3301), overlooking Illinois and Washington Streets. It's an indoor glass enclosure seven stories above street level that connects the mall with hotels and offices. You'll likely find some free entertainment and an exhibit to browse afterward.

Afternoon

Unless you opt to spend the afternoon shopping and perusing Circle Centre, where Nordstrom, FAO Schwarz, and about one hundred other shops await, follow Washington Street west until you spot the distinctive southwestern honey-colored stone architecture of the **Eiteljorg Museum of American Indians and Western Art** (500 West Washington Street; 317–636–9378). The contemporary structure appears quite incongruent in its midwestern setting, but the stone was actually quarried in Minnesota. The founder of the museum, Harrison Eiteljorg, was born in Indianapolis long before he became enamored with art of the West and began his collection and philanthropy.

The exhibition takes interested visitors beyond its walls with works from the Southwest, Plains, and north into Canada via totems from the Northwest Coastal region. You'll also spot works by Remington, O'Keeffe, and members of the original Taos, New Mexico, artists' colony.

Throughout the year, special exhibits and workshops augment the permanent collection. There's even an annual "Some Like It Hot!" chili cook-off. The museum is open Tuesday through Saturday 10:00 A.M. to 5:00 P.M., Sunday noon to 5:00 P.M. It is also open on Mondays from June through August. Admission is $5.00 for adults, $2.00 for full-time students and children five to seventeen, and $4.00 for seniors.

Stop at the Visitor Information Center in the Pam Am Plaza located across from the RCA Dome on Capital Avenue and Georgia Street, for Indy artwork and souvenirs as well as visitor brochures. A 3-D light map of the city provides an easy frame of reference for locating the remaining sights on your list.

DINNER: Make reservations ahead of time at **St. Elmo Steak House,** right next to your hotel at 127 South Illinois (317–635–0636). It's been a local landmark since 1902 and still has a reputation for great steaks and seafood. Especially noteworthy are the shrimp cocktails, famous for the abundance of horseradish in the cocktail sauce—you can watch them being prepared in the window before you enter. It's pricey—$24 for the least expensive entree at last check—but dinners come with choice of navy bean soup or tomato juice and choice of potato.

Unless you purchased tickets for a concert or performance, take a romantic horse-drawn carriage tour around town. You can make advance reservations with **Yellow Rose Carriages** (317–634–3400). If you're in the mood for some laughs or entertainment, stop at **Howl at the Moon** (317–951–2045) or one of the other nightspots at the World Mardi Gras Entertainment Complex on the fourth level of Circle Centre, 49 West Maryland Avenue.

LODGING: The Canterbury Hotel.

DAY 3

Morning

Have coffee and the continental breakfast at the hotel, but save room for a late morning brunch before departing Indianapolis. Spend the morning on foot taking a walking tour of the memorials, including the **Soldiers' and Sailors' Mon-**

ument, a few blocks away at Monument Circle. Visit the new **Civil War Museum** on the lower level.

Also be sure to take in the **Medal of Honor Memorial,** located on the north side of downtown's Central Canal in White River State Park. The modern glass panels pay tribute to recipients of the Medal of Honor. At dusk each day you can hear their recorded stories of the military conflicts in which they fought. Contact Indianapolis City Center at (317) 237–5211 for walking tour information.

BRUNCH: Check out of the Canterbury Hotel and follow Illinois Street to **La Peep Restaurant** (301 North Illinois Street; 317–237–3447). This restaurant consistently gets local awards for preparing the best omelettes in town. On weekends they open at 7:00 A.M. and close by 2:30 P.M.

Afternoon

If you are toting children, make one more stop at the **Children's Museum of Indianapolis,** down the street from La Peep at Thirtieth and Meridian Streets (800–208–KIDS). There are hundreds of creative hands-on activities for children of all ages (even infants) to enjoy, more than 100,000 artifacts, and five levels of exhibit space. Children can climb in an authentic Indy car, move nearly weightless "rocks" in the construction area, sing along with performers, go on an archaeological dig, or explore the arts, history, and science—all the while being entertained. Admission is $8.00 for adults, $3.50 for ages two to seventeen, and $7.00 for seniors, with extra charges for the CineDome and carousel ride. Hours are 10:00 A.M. to 5:00 P.M. daily, until 8:00 P.M. on the first Thursday of each month; closed Thanksgiving, Christmas, Easter, and Mondays from Labor Day through February.

Leave by mid-afternoon and head back to Cleveland via I–70 and I–71, reversing the route for your return trip. If you'd like to break up the five-hour trip home, take exit 121 off I–71 to **Polaris,** about twenty minutes from Columbus. Bear right and turn right at the first street.

DINNER: Polaris Grill, 1835 Polaris Parkway, Polaris; (614) 431–5598. This informal restaurant offers an eclectic menu of entrees, including pasta, pizza, and its trademark salad. Moderate.

THERE'S MORE

Indiana Transportation Museum, located in Forest Park in Noblesville; (317) 773–6000. Excursion rides aboard diesel-powered locomotives and an electric trolley; the museum's artifacts provide the historical background. There are picnic grounds, dinner excursions, and special programs and rides planned throughout the year. The Fairtrain takes folks to the Indiana State Fair each August. Museum admission is $3.00 adults, $2.00 for children. Train fares vary depending on itinerary. The Atlanta Express costs $7.00 for adults and $5.00 for children and makes a 22-mile round-trip run between Hobbs Station in Noblesville and Atlanta, Indiana. The Atlanta Express operates weekends, April through July and September through October, departing Hobbs Station at 1:30 P.M. and returning at 3:30 P.M. When you get to Atlanta, a town so small there's not even a traffic light, buy a root beer float for $1.00 for the trip back.

Indianapolis Symphony Orchestra, 45 Monument Circle; (800) 366–8457. Performs more than 200 concerts, including its Marsh Symphony on the Prairie at Conner Prairie, plus jazz, ballet, and musical cabaret-style theatrical performances. Its regular home is Hilbert Circle Theatre downtown. The Broadway Series and other live performances take place at the Murat Centre (502 North New Jersey; 317–231–0000) and there's a brimming schedule of guest artists and community gigs throughout Indianapolis. Contact Ticket-Central at the Indianapolis Artsgarden (317–624–2563) for information.

Indianapolis City Market, 222 East Market Street; (317) 634–9266. This 1886 historic landmark features food stalls and products from around the world, along with a farmers' market during summer. With an Old World market feeling, it's just the place for finding out-of-the-ordinary ingredients and for sampling the variety of products at lunchtime. Live music during Friday shopping sprees adds to the bustle.

James Whitcomb Riley Museum Home, 528 Lockerbie Street; (317) 631–5885. Stop here for a tour of this historic home filled with mementos and personal items belonging to Indiana's famous poet. He lived here for twenty-three years while creating much of his poetry. Tours are $3.00 adults, $.50 for children, and $2.00 for seniors. Open Tuesday to Saturday from 10:00 A.M. to 4:00 P.M., Sunday noon to 4:00 P.M. The surrounding Lockerbie Square is a historic district worth perusing too.

President Benjamin Harrison Home, 1230 North Delaware Street; (317) 631–1898. Located in the Old Northside Neighborhood area, this Italianate mansion that once belonged to Indiana's only elected president is listed on the National Register of Historic Places. Guided tours point out many pieces belonging to Harrison, the twenty-third president of the United States. Open

Monday to Saturday 10:00 A.M. to 3:30 P.M., Sunday 12:30 to 3:30 P.M. Admission is $5.00 for adults, $1.00 for children, $4.00 for groups and seniors.

Duckpin Bowling. You can try your hand amid the '20s decor at Action Duck-pin Bowl (325 South College; 317–632–2878), or the '50s atmosphere at Atomic Duckpin Bowl, in the restored Fountain Square Theatre Building (1105 East Prospect Street; 317–686–6006). This activity costs $18.00 per lane plus $2.00 for shoe rental. Alleys are open Monday to Saturday 11:00 A.M. to about 10:00 P.M. (until 1:00 A.M. on weekends) and Sunday noon to 6:00 P.M.

SPECIAL EVENTS

May. Indianapolis 500 and the 500 Festival; (317) 481–8500 and (317) 237–3400, respectively. Activities surrounding the Indy 500 Race at the Motor Speedway. Events, including a parade and community-wide activities, run throughout the month.

June. Indian Market, Eiteljorg Museum of American Indians and Western Art. The largest in the Midwest. Demonstrations, dancing, storytelling, and family activities. (317) 636–9378.

July. Kroger Circlefest. Celebrates Monument Circle with family events, local and national entertainers, and food.

July. Glorious Fourth, Conner Prairie. A celebration that takes visitors back to Civil War years. Patriotic hat making, political debates, vintage baseball games, and other family-centered events. (800) 866–1836.

September. Penrod Art Festival, Indianapolis Museum of Art. The state's largest art festival. (317) 630–4000.

OTHER RECOMMENDED RESTAURANTS AND LODGINGS

Indianapolis

Crowne Plaza Hotel at Union Station, 123 West Louisiana Street; (317) 631–2221. Centrally located, near the RCA Dome and the Indiana Convention Center, but unique because thirteen original Pullman cars from train stations have been converted into twenty-six individually decorated hotel rooms, each named after a personality of the era.

The Courtyard by Marriott, 501 West Washington Street; (317) 687–0029. Close to Victory Field Baseball Park, home of the Indianapolis Indians (the Cincinnati Reds' farm team), and museums. Rates range from $79 to $139 but can go higher during special events and sells out quickly during summer weekends.

The Omni Severin Hotel, 40 West Jackson Place; (317) 634–6664 or (800) THE–OMNI. The Omni is a AAA, four-diamond historic 1913 hotel, upscale and newly renovated. Health club and indoor pool; gourmet coffee shop and full-service restaurant. Rates: $185 to $205 weekdays; often much lower on weekends.

Embassy Suites Hotel Downtown (110 West Washington Street; 317–236–1800 or 800–EMBASSY), Hyatt Regency Indianapolis (One South Capitol Avenue; 317–632–1234 or 800–233–1234), Radisson Hotel City Center Indianapolis (31 West Ohio Street; 317–635–200 or 800–333–3333) and the Westin Indianapolis (50 South Capitol; 317–262–8100 or 800–WESTIN–1) are all connected to Circle Centre or the Indiana Convention Center by skywalks. The Indianapolis Reservation Service (800–556–INDY) can help make reservations.

Dunaways, 351 South East Street; (317) 638–7663. In the former Oxygen building, it utilizes the theme "Like a breath of fresh air" on the rooftop. The decor takes on the art deco looks of its past use. Homemade pastas a specialty. Open for lunch and dinner, 11:00 A.M. to 10:30 P.M. Expensive.

The Cozy Restaurant & Lounge Nite Club, 20 North Pennsylvania Street; (317) 638–2100. Everything from sandwiches to fine dining, pool tables to live entertainment. There seems to be something for everyone here.

Rathskeller Restaurant, 401 East Michigan Avenue; (317) 636–0396. Located in the historic Athenaeum Building, in the charming Old Northside neighborhood, this authentic German restaurant features ethnic specialties like beef roll-ups known as rouladen that are served with hearty side dishes in an Old World atmosphere. Choose from an extensive list of imported beers and homemade desserts. Lunches and dinners, moderate. Add a performance at The American Cabaret Theatre (800–375–8887) in the same building for evening entertainment.

Stone Soup Inn, 1304 North Central Avenue; (317) 639–9550. Six unique guest rooms, ranging from $75 to $125 provide a quiet ambience close to downtown in the Old Northside neighborhood, a charming area undergoing revitalization. The Mission and Victorian style B&B offers a full breakfast, snack pantry, and friendly staff eager to suggest nearby activities. A sister property, the Looking Glass Inn, offers similar amenities around the corner at 1319 North New Jersey Avenue.

Fishers

The Frederick-Talbot Inn, 13805 Allisonville Road; (317) 578–3600 or (800) 566–BEDS. Located across from Conner Prairie. Ten rooms with private baths. A cookie jar of homebaked goodies, complimentary beverages, and a delicious breakfast buffet served in the main house's sunroom offer a relaxing repose. Rates: $99–$179.

Ritter's Custard, 10400 Allisonville Road; (317) 578–7212. This rich frozen custard is the real high fat, high caloric stuff memories are made of. Please note, it is open the end of March through the first part of November, Sunday through Thursday from 11:00 A.M. to 10:00 P.M. and on the weekends until 11:00 P.M.

FOR MORE INFORMATION

Hamilton County Convention and Visitors Bureau, 11601 Municipal Drive, Fishers, Indiana 46038; (800) 776–TOUR.

Indianapolis Convention and Visitors Association, One RCA Dome, Suite 100, Indianapolis, Indiana 46225; www.indy.org; (800) 556–INDY.

SOUTHWESTERN

Oxford and Hamilton, Ohio

SMALL TOWN CHARM AND SURPRISES

2 NIGHTS

Historic districts • Hiking paths • Foods from everywhere

With a state park system as grand and acclaimed as Ohio's, it's not difficult to find one close to nearly every regional getaway. Eight of the seventy-three state parks offer full-service lodge accommodations; Hueston Woods State Park, situated close to the Indiana border just north of Oxford, Ohio, in College Corner, is one the oldest and most popular. Here you'll find boat rentals and launch ramps, fishing, a sandy swimming beach, an eighteen-hole golf course, naturalist programs, miles of hiking trails, and seasonal activities, as well as several more indoor options when the weather doesn't cooperate.

These are just the park activities. There's more to do beyond these scenic 4,000-plus acres. Within a short drive, you'll discover some quirky, historical, entertaining, and educational activities.

DAY 1

Afternoon

The 250-mile drive to College Corner will take almost five hours, mostly along the interstate. Leave by midafternoon, taking I–71 south for the first half of the trip.

DINNER: As you near **Columbus,** exit I–71 at I–270 west. Take the first exit and drive north on High Street (U.S. 23). Turn right onto Vantage Drive and bear right

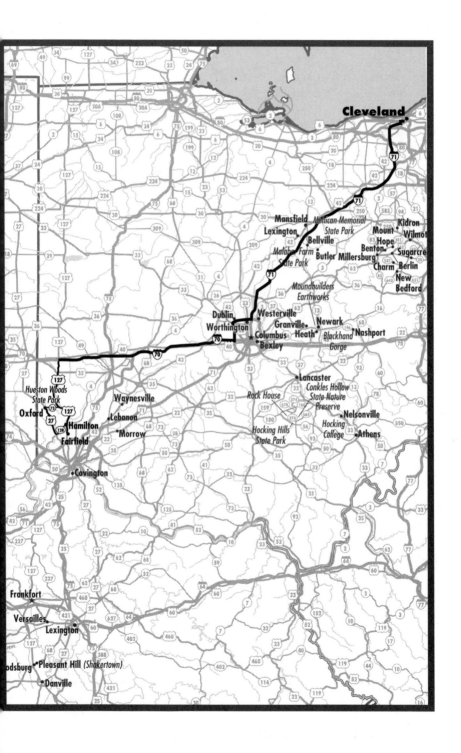

to **Voilà** (55 Hutchinson Avenue, Columbus; 614–846–5555). This locally owned restaurant specializes in casual French fare. Moderate to expensive.

Return to I–270 traveling west to I–70. Take I–70 west 82 miles to State Route 127 exit and turn left (south). Drive through Eaton to Camden, turning right (west) onto State Route 725 toward **College Corner.** Continue about 6 miles, turning left onto State Route 732 to the park entrance on the right.

LODGING: Hueston Woods Resort and Conference Center, RR #1, College Corner; (513) 523–6381. For reservations call (800) AT–A–PARK.

After check-in, explore the rustic lodge, decorated with murals of the Miami Indians who once lived in this area, and try out the pool or restaurant before retiring. Weekend rates range from $106 for a standard double to $209 for a suite. Various weekend packages, some including meals and special activities, are offered throughout the year.

The cabins are reopening in 2001 after an extensive "facelift." They've been redecorated and refurnished; fireplaces and cable TV have been added. Weekend rates are $125 for one bedroom, $140 for two bedrooms, $575–$725 if you stay all week.

Only one cabin is ADA compliant; four lodge rooms meet handicapped-accessible standards.

DAY 2

Morning

BREAKFAST: Have breakfast in the dining room, choosing a window table overlooking the lake. The breakfast buffet, available 7:00 to 11:00 A.M., costs about $6.00 per person. If you're an early riser, choose one of the many hiking paths and set out to discover a bit of the park's natural beauty.

From the lodge, take State Route 732 south into Oxford, turning left onto State Route 27 (High Street). At State Route 73 turn left (east) and drive 5 miles. Turn right onto State Route 177 through Hamilton, taking a right onto State Route 4 to **Jungle Jim's International Farmers Market** (5440 Dixie Highway, Fairfield; 513–829–1919). You're in for a treat, no matter your interest in shopping. Here you'll find the largest wine (and probably beer) selection in the state, along with wonderful bakery and produce departments. That's all before getting to the "European Village" of international foods and aisles of unusual and imported items. Singing Elvis keeps kids entertained. Maybe you'd just like to hang out in an extensive humidor, where cigar prices are generally discounted 20

Visitors can view outdoor sculptures from their cars as they drive through Pyramid Hill, a unique sculpture park in Hamilton.

percent. Footprints painted on the floor will keep you on the right path—that's how easy it is to get lost. The best part is that no matter what you're looking for, Jungle Jim's most likely has it.

If the weather cooperates, consider buying picnic ingredients to enjoy at your next stop, a unique outdoor sculpture garden and park in **Hamilton** known as **Pyramid Hill,** State Route 128, Hamilton; (513) 868–8336. The trip to get there may sound complicated because of one-way streets but it's not as difficult as it sounds. Take State Route 4 north. Turn left on High Street, left on Second Street, and right on Court Street. Turn left onto Front Street, following it to Neilan Boulevard, then driving along the Great Miami River and crossing it on the Columbia Bridge. Immediately after the bridge turn left onto State Route 128. Pyramid Hill is a mile on the right.

There's a $3.00 adult admission at the gate. From there, visitors can drive, hike, or arrange for a guided tour aboard a minibus to view thirty-five permanent installations in the 265-acre sculpture park. It's unique to Ohio and one of only three such parks in the United States. Most of the art pieces are contemporary, but there are a few from other periods. Several sculptors visited to assist in choosing the site for their work, so it's really a museum without walls that thoroughly incorporates the natural space surrounding the art. There is also a historic nineteenth-century pioneer home, an arboretum, miles of hiking trails, and picnic grounds on the property. Outdoor seasonal events and concerts as well an annual holiday light show during winter attract those looking for even more than the tranquility of the park.

LUNCH: Enjoy your picnic or stop at the park's tearoom where salads, soups, sandwiches, house specials, beer and wine, and a children's menu are available in light, cheery surroundings overlooking the sculpture garden. Prices are moderate.

Afternoon

Hamilton has several sites that are listed on the National Register of Historic Places, including Dayton Lane, where leading industrialists lived at during the nineteenth and twentieth centuries, the Rossville Historic District, German Village, and downtown. Don't miss taking a walk on the 3.5-mile **Hamilton Bikeway** along the Great Miami River past the Fitton Center for the Creative Arts, the reconstructed log cabin, and the adjacent Soldiers, Sailors, and Pioneers Monument.

Head back to **Oxford** via State Route 128 to U.S. 27 north, which leads right into town. Take time to visit the **McGuffey Museum,** corner of Oak and Spring Streets. It's a home built by William Holmes McGuffey while he was a professor at Miami University, where he created his famous McGuffey Eclectic Readers. In this home museum, the sign in front of the display reads, "Please touch the McGuffey books." Open Saturday and Sunday 2:00 to 4:00 P.M.; closed in August.

DINNER: A favorite among locals and visitors alike is **Kona Bistro & Coffee Bar** (31 West High Street; 513–523–0686). The restaurant has only nineteen tables inside, with extra patio dining during summer, so reservations are recommended. The owners and chef are Miami University grads with advanced degrees in restaurant management so you shouldn't be surprised by the service-oriented wait staff, creative kitchen and reasonable prices. There's a whole menu of coffee served with and without liqueurs, and always a soup and coffee du jour. Entrees, like salmon with lime and ginger served with linguine and steamed broccoli ($9.95), are served after 5:00 P.M.

For after-dinner entertainment, check out the university venues and hotlines: Sports, (513) 529–3924; Concert Board Hotline, (513) 529–5999; Performing Arts Series Box Office, (513) 529–3200; Shriver Center Box Office, (513) 529–1847, Center for the Performing Arts, (513) 529–2247. Several local hot spots along High Street book live bands on weekends.

LODGING: Return to Hueston Woods, only a ten-minute drive from Oxford, for the evening. The front desk offers video rentals.

DAY 3

Morning

BREAKFAST: Hueston Woods Resort. Take an early morning hike or reserve a tee time (513–523–8081), if you're a golfer. Green fees are only $24.40 for eighteen holes on weekends and holidays; $17.50 weekdays. (There are reduced rates after 4:00 P.M.) Otherwise, enjoy some more of the lodge's amenities, leaving for home by midmorning. Head back to Cleveland via State Route 127 and I–70, stopping at the half-way point in **Columbus** for a lunch break.

LUNCH: If you only want a sandwich or pastry and coffee, try **Panera Bread** (130 Hutchinson Avenue; 614–438–0200). In the mood for burger, shake, and good fries? There's a **Johnny Rockets** next door (150 Hutchinson Avenue; 614–846–7461). And next to that, there are big portions of Mexican fare at **Chipotle Mexican Grill** (154 Hutchinson Avenue; 614–433–0221).
After lunch, follow I–71 into Cleveland.

THERE'S MORE

Governor Bebb Preserve, 1979 Bebb Park Lane, Okeana; (877) PARK–FUN. One of the Butler County Metroparks, located midway between Hamilton and Oxford. The park has a village of reconstructed log cabins taken from the surrounding area to depict nineteenth-century life. On weekends the buildings, including the log house birth home of William Bebb, who was Ohio's nineteenth governor from 1846 to 1848, is interpreted by the park ranger and costumed volunteers. The only fee is a parking permit, $2.00 for the day or $5.00 for the season. The park is open daily until dusk year-round; buildings are open from 1:00 to 5:00 P.M. on weekends from Memorial Day to Labor Day.

Miami University Oxford Campus, Oxford; (513) 529–1809. Robert Frost described this campus as the most beautiful he had seen. There are several interesting self-guided walking tours. There's a one-hour trip past significant university buildings; other tours lead through formal gardens, the Western Campus (originally the home of Western College for Women) where stone bridges abound, and Central Campus; each takes one to one and a half hours. Maps are available at Shriver Hall. More than 1,000 acres of natural areas, called the Bachelor Reserve, offers hiking trails for university programs but are open to the public. The Art Museum on Patterson Avenue (513–529–2232) is open Tuesday through Sunday 11:00 A.M. to 5:00 P.M. Permanent collections and traveling exhibits are on view.

Lane-Hooven House, 319 North Third Street, Hamilton; (513) 863–1389. The unusual Victorian Gothic octagonal brick exterior beckons a closer look into the rich decor. It houses the Hamilton Community Foundation offices but is open to the public Monday through Friday 9:00 A.M. to 4:00 P.M. Across the street, in similar style, is the Lane Library, said to be the first free library west of the Alleghenies.

The Pioneer Farm and House Museum. Located adjacent to Hueston Woods and operated by the Oxford Museum Association, it is a representation of typical farm life in the mid-1800s. Open Memorial Day through Labor Day, Saturday and Sunday, from noon to 4:00 P.M. Call (513) 523–8005 to arrange a guided tour. Self-guided tours are free.

SPECIAL EVENTS

May. History Lives in Butler County, eleven historical sites throughout the county. Demonstrations of early crafts. (513) 867–5835.

June. Main Street Pioneer Jamboree, along Great Miami River. Storytellers, crafts, demonstrations, food. (513) 844–6246.

July. Annual Antique and Classic Car Parade, downtown Hamilton. Part of the Hamilton-Fairfield Antique and Classic Car Festival. Hundreds of vintage cars line the streets for this local event to make the town and festivalgoers take a look back in time. (513) 863–2334.

September. Pioneer Days Festival, Governor Bebb Preserve. (513) 867–5835.

November–December. Downtown Lighting Ceremony and Annual Main Street Music Fest. (513) 844–6246.

OTHER RECOMMENDED RESTAURANTS AND LODGINGS

Hamilton

White Rose Bed & Breakfast, 116 Buckeye Street; (513) 863–6818. A small B&B with only three guest rooms and two baths, but the congenial hostess offers gracious and friendly hospitality and a delicious breakfast. Conveniently located in German Village; bikes are available for the bike path. Rates: $65–$70.

The Rossville Inn, 117 South B Street; (888) 892–0871. This charming three guest room B&B dates to pre–Civil War. Elaborate gourmet breakfasts, hand stenciling, antiques, and high ceilings create a relaxing getaway in one of Hamilton's historic districts. All rooms have private baths. Rates: $90–$100.

Hamiltonian Hotel, One Riverfront Plaza; (800) 522–5570. Located in one of Hamilton's historic districts, this 1859 Greek Revival fits right in with its high ceilings, four-poster beds, and billiard room. There are also modern niceties, such as a steam shower in the king-size suite. Gourmet breakfast and snacks are included in the $75–$100 rates.

Oxford

The White Garden Bed & Breakfast, 6194 Brown Road; (800) 324–4925. This new Victorian structure is out in the country, not far from Hueston Woods, and is named for the all white flower gardens encircling the home's wraparound porches. It's obvious that the innkeeper, "the Martha Stewart of Oxford," loves cooking, decorating, and antiques shopping. Sunday brunch is an event. Rates: $75–$125.

Marcum Conference Center & Inn, 100 North Patterson; (513) 529–6911. Located on the campus, this 92-room complex offers a variety of rooms ranging from $70 to $95. Continental breakfast is included.

The Alexander House and the Governors Room Restaurant, 22 North College Avenue; (513) 523–1200. Five rooms with private baths just a block from High Street. Room rates are $90–$125, including breakfast. The gourmet restaurant is open for lunch and dinner Tuesday through Saturday and for Sunday brunch. Moderate to expensive.

FOR MORE INFORMATION

Greater Hamilton Convention and Visitors Bureau, One Riverfront Plaza, Hamilton, Ohio 45011; (513) 884–8080 or (800) 311–5353; www.hamilton-cvb.com.

Oxford Chamber of Commerce, 118 West High Street, Oxford, Ohio 45056; (513) 523–5200.

Lebanon and Waynesville

AN OHIO RECREATION AND
ANTIQUES CAPITAL

2 NIGHTS

Biking • Hiking • Canoeing • Shopping
Browsing • Bargain hunting

If you're searching for R&R blended with some "natural" excursions tinged with elements of history, then a weekend in Warren County south of Dayton should be among your plans.

Whether you opt for a bed-and-breakfast or an overnight in Ohio's oldest inn, whether you're an antiques buff or simply interested in walking in the woods, you'll be at home in Waynesville, called the Antique Capital of the Midwest, and in Lebanon, where more shops, a scenic railroad, and several outstanding museums await. For six weeks before fall, you can even step back to Merry Old England during the Ohio Renaissance Festival in nearby Harveysburg.

After sampling the activities, you may have to plan a repeat trip to see all you couldn't fit in one getaway.

DAY 1

Afternoon

The 200-mile drive down I–71 will take about three hours. To reach Lebanon in time to browse before dinner, get an early afternoon start. Follow I–71 south to exit 36 (Morrow–Lebanon) and follow the signs west into **Lebanon.** From Main Street, turn right on Broadway. The street is lined with more than a dozen spe-

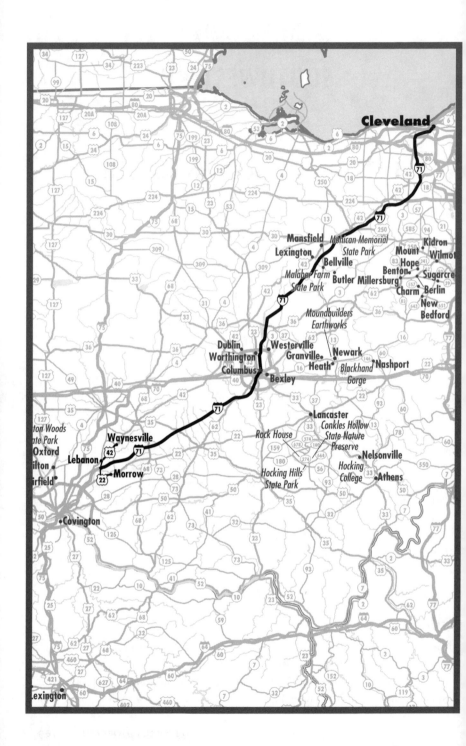

cialty shops and nearly two dozen antiques shops—all fun to browse.

If you are hungry, grab a sandwich or a shake at **Village Ice Cream Parlor & Restaurant** (22 South Broadway; 513–932–6918).

If you prefer museums to shopping, head over to the **Warren County Historical Society Museum** (105 South Broadway; 513–932–1817). It is one of the outstanding museums of its kind. You'll find a village green encircled by shops and nineteenth-century memorabilia. Upstairs, a Shaker exhibit features remnants from the Shaker community that settled just outside of town. Open Tuesday through Saturday 9:00 A.M. to 4:00 P.M., Sunday noon to 4:00 P.M.; closed on holidays. Admission is $3.00 for adults and $1.00 for students.

If time permits, take a scenic one-hour excursion on the **Turtle Creek Valley Railroad,** just down the street at 198 South Broadway (513–398–8584). Special themed rides are planned each month and schedules vary. Rates are $10.00 for adults, $9.00 for seniors, and $6.00 for children three to twelve. Next door there's a candy shop, the **Golden Turtle Chocolate Factory** (513–932–1990), for creamy chocolate indulgences.

DINNER: The Golden Lamb Inn (27 South Broadway; 513–932–5056) is practically a museum itself. Make dinner reservations at this hallmark Ohio inn, but allow a few minutes beforehand to peruse the hallways, peeking into open rooms and displays. Rooms are named for notable guests and are decorated with antiques. Entrees, moderately priced, often include period-style selections, and roasted turkey with all the trimmings is a mainstay no matter the season. There is also a gift shop on the lower level.

After dinner, walk down to **Doc's Smoke Shop** (12 West Mulberry Street; 513–932–9939) if you enjoy cigar smoke and live music.

LODGING: Drive north on State Route 42 and turn right onto Hatfield Road. The **Hatfield Inn** (2563 Hatfield Road; 513–932–3193 or 888–247–9736) is about ten minutes away from town. Each room of this renovated farmhouse, the boyhood home of the owner, features hand-stenciling and combines nuances of earlier times with modern luxuries. Wheelchair accessible rooms available. Rates are $75 per night, based on double occupancy; $60 for singles. Walk the grounds, sit by the pond out front, soak in the hot tub, or relax on the porch before turning in.

DAY 2

Morning

BREAKFAST: The Hatfield Inn serves a delicious and hearty breakfast, prepared in the open kitchen.

Drive into **Waynesville** (follow State Route 42 north about 6 miles) and park in the center of town amid seventy antiques and gift shops, all within a five-block area. Most open their doors by 10:00 A.M. and carry a general variety of antiques, but some do specialize in china or primitives, for example. If you need help organizing your shopping itinerary, stop at the Waynesville Area Chamber of Commerce on Main Street for assistance and a map. You can also pick up a self-guided walking tour brochure and learn the history of this quaint stagecoach stop.

LUNCH: On a pleasant day, dine outdoors on the porch of the **Hammel House Inn** (121 South Main Street; 513–897–2333), an original resting spot for those arriving by stagecoach as early as 1799. Lunch indoors is surrounded by an antique ambience. Soups, salads, sandwiches, and a fresh quiche of the day are among menu selections, all moderately priced.

Afternoon

Follow State Route 42 south into Lebanon and pick up State Route 123 going east. Cross I–71 and turn left onto State Route 350 and follow the curvy road for a real step back into America's history at **Fort Ancient State Memorial** (6123 State Route 350, Oregonia; 513–932–4421 or 800–283–8904). The new state-of-the-art museum managed by the Ohio Historical Society depicts the earliest settlers, prehistoric Indian groups who lived here nearly 15,000 years ago. You'll discover hands-on activities as well as informative dioramas and kiosks and even an outdoor garden brimming with historic and prehistoric varieties in season.

After you visit the museum, walk the grounds of the Hopewell Indians prehistoric hilltop enclosure. These earthen walls, created one basketful at a time, would fill dump trucks lined up the entire length of your journey between here and Cleveland. This National Historic Landmark is also a good place for picnicking. Do walk to the overlook for picturesque views overlooking the Little Miami River. From this point, you can also walk the trail.

The museum and the outdoor site are open 10:00 A.M. to 5:00 P.M. daily from March to Memorial Day and from September to November. From Memorial Day to Labor Day, the museum is open from 10:00 A.M. to 7:00 P.M. and the park is open until 8:00 P.M.

It's a twenty-minute ride to dinner. From Fort Ancient, turn left onto State Route 350 and continue until it dead-ends on State Route 123 at the I–71 junction. Turn right onto State Route 123 and proceed one mile to Stubbs Mill Road. Turn left and follow this winding, country road until it dead-ends. Turn left and look for Valley Vineyards on the left.

DINNER: The attire is casual and the service is pretty much do-it-yourself at **Valley Vineyards Winery** (2276 East U.S. 22/3, Morrow; 513–899–2485). On Friday and Saturday evenings, the winery offers steak cookouts. The meal includes a bottle of local wine, a decision that usually calls for some tasting beforehand. Then guests select and season their own steaks, taking them to outdoor grills during warm weather and to the enclosed deck other times. Accompaniments, including salad and baked potatoes, are served buffet style; homemade pies round out the meal. Dinners are $38 for two, including the wine. Reservations are highly recommended—people drive for miles for the wine and steaks as well as for the cellar tours.

LODGING: The Hatfield Inn.

DAY 3

Morning

BREAKFAST: Weekend breakfasts at the Hatfield Inn are usually extravagant. Choices might include biscuits and gravy and other items served buffet style. Eat hearty before a morning of outdoor activity: canoeing or kayaking the Little Miami River.

You'll begin your leisurely journey down the Little Miami Scenic River at **Morgan's Fort Ancient Canoe Livery** location on the Little Miami (Ohio Route 350 at the river; 800–EW–CANOE). To get there follow U.S. 42 south from the B&B to State Route 123 in Lebanon, turning left and continuing south. Then turn left onto State Route 350 (as you did to get to the Fort Ancient Museum). Continue to the river and the office, where you can select a trip of 3 to 18 miles, lasting between one hour and five to seven hours, depending on your energy and time constraints. Prices range from $18 per canoe for the 3-mile trip and $33 for the 18-mile trip. Float trips are specially arranged for groups and include a narrated nature tour with bits of folklore, history and ecology of the river. Lunch along the way can also be planned.

LUNCH: For lunch after a river trip, stop at **Best Café** (17 East Mulberry; 513–932–4400) in downtown Lebanon. Lunch prices are moderate with a good selection and antique furnishings. After lunch, drive east on State Route 123 to pick up I–71 and continue your ride back to Cleveland.

THERE'S MORE

The **Glendower State Memorial,** 105 Cincinnati Avenue, Lebanon. This home museum is located in an 1836 Greek Revival just outside of Lebanon. It's open for tours Wednesday through Saturday noon to 4:00 P.M., Sunday 1:00 to 4:00 P.M. from June through Labor Day and some fall weekends. Admission is $3.00 for adults and $1.00 for children.

Workshops of David T. Smith, 3600 Shawhan Road, Morrow; (513) 932–2472. Outstanding studio and showroom of reproduction furniture and Turtle Creek Pottery crafted on site.

Caesar's Creek Pioneer Village, 3999 Pioneer Village Road, Waynesville; (513) 897–1120. Reconstructed village focuses on life in pioneer times. Volunteers make crafts and tend the gardens and hearth.

LaComedia, 765 West Central Avenue, Springboro; (800) 677–9505. A buffet dinner before a live theatrical performance. Ticket prices range from $33 to $45 per person, including dinner, production, and taxes. Matinees and evening shows Wednesday through Sunday.

Biking, Hiking, In-Line Skating. Enjoy the outdoors on the Little Miami Scenic Trail, a 70-mile path leading through the most narrow of all Ohio state parks. No matter your age or physical condition, there are plenty of opportunities for enjoying the trail. If you don't want to transport your own bicycle or in-line skates, rentals are available at the Corwin Peddler (513–987–3536), on the Little Miami Scenic Trail at the staging area in the center of Corwin. Bike rentals range from $6.00 for one hour to $10.00 for all day use. You can also rent tandems, trailers, and 3-wheel varieties as well as skates.

SPECIAL EVENTS

August–October. Ohio Renaissance Festival, State Route 73, Harveysburg. (513) 897–7000.

Visit England during Shakespeare's day at the Ohio Renaissance Festival in Harveysburg.

October. Ohio Sauerkraut Festival, Main Street, Waynesville. (513) 897–8855.

November–December. Christmas in Olde Springboro Village, Main Street, State Routes 741 and 73. (513) 748–0074.

November–December. Christmas in the Village, Waynesville. (513) 897–8855.

November–December. Train Rides with Santa, Turtle Creek Valley Railway, Lebanon. (513) 398–8584.

OTHER RECOMMENDED RESTAURANTS AND LODGINGS

Waynesville

Hammel House Inn, 121 South Main Street; (513) 897–3779. Began as a stage-coach stop in 1822, but now five guest rooms upstairs provide a convenient location amid the town's antique shops. Rates: $75–$85, including breakfast.

Der Dutchman, 230 North U.S. 42; (513) 897–4716. Amish-style meals; hearty portions at reasonable prices. Closed Sunday.

Lebanon

Artist's Cottage Bed & Breakfast, 458 East Warren Street; (513) 932–5932. Stay in the former studio of the resident artist. Cozy overnight accommodations include wood-burning fireplace and breakfast on a table created with the artist's hand-painted tiles.

The Golden Lamb, 27 South Broadway; (513) 932–5065. Each of the eighteen guest rooms is uniquely decorated (some more lavishly than others) and named for a famous guest. The Charles Dickens Room, one of the fancier choices, runs $90 during the week, $100 on weekends. It is furnished with a replica of the original Lincoln bed found in the White House. If you are particular, it's best to ask for a room description when inquiring.

Corwin

Menker's Bikeway Cafe, 819 Corwin Avenue; (513) 897–0220. The casual ambience welcomes visitors from the trail. Sandwiches, pizza, entrees, and a children's menu are all reasonably priced.

FOR MORE INFORMATION

Waynesville Chamber of Commerce, Main Street, Waynesville, Ohio 45068; (513) 897–8855; www.waynesville.com.

Warren County Convention and Visitors Bureau, 1073 Oregonia Road, Lebanon, Ohio 45036; (800) 791–4386.

SOUTHWESTERN

Kentucky's Bluegrass

EXPECT THE UNEXPECTED

2 NIGHTS

*Tea for two • Green pastures and white fences
City of firsts • The Shaker lifestyle*

Kentucky is a long drive through Ohio for northern travelers, but worth the trip if you're looking for a southern sampler with a unique itinerary, perhaps the most eclectic and unexpected you'll find within these pages. There's something for your every whim, providing you're in the mood for variety. These southern destinations will surely give you a taste of down-home hospitality.

This getaway will put close to 700 miles on your odometer by your return. You may yearn for a horse, even if you aren't a horse lover, and you'll want to fill your car with antiques, kitschy crafts or skillfully created art, and perhaps a bottle of locally distilled bourbon. Along the way, you'll experience the magnificent, opulent, and pastoral bluegrass scenery. Even if you come back empty-handed, there will be plenty of experiences to relate—guaranteed.

DAY 1

Morning

Leave early, by 8:00 A.M. if possible, for the 340-mile, four-and-a-half-hour drive through the state via I–71 south. If you're destined to take a short break, do so at the Jeffersonville Outlets at exit 69, about three hours into the trip. There's a food court and ample room to stretch your legs before continuing down the highway toward Cincinnati.

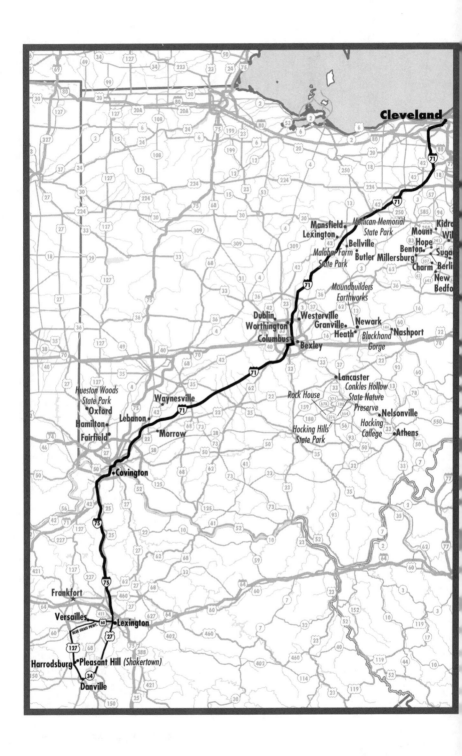

In Cincinnati, continue on the interstate south, connecting with I–75 before entering Kentucky. Once over the Brent Spence Bridge, take exit 192 (Fifth Street) and you're in **Covington,** where you'll find the best views of Cincinnati, along with the historic flavors of the community's heritage. Follow signs to historic **MainStrasse Village,** an old German neighborhood where walking, shopping, and lunch await.

LUNCH: Dee Felice (529 Main Street, Covington; 859–261–2365) serves Cajun specialties and regional favorites and features an extensive salad bar. Prices are moderate.

Afternoon

By early afternoon, continue your drive on I–75 south to the **Kentucky Horse Park** at exit 120, an hour from Covington. The park closes at 6:00 P.M. from Memorial Day to Labor Day and at 5:00 P.M. the rest of the year, but even a few hours is enough time to become acquainted with horse history via the International Museum of the Horse, a self-guided farm tour, and at least one of several shows offered throughout the day. During warm seasons, nominally priced carriage rides shorten the walk. Plan to watch the *Hall of Champions* for an introduction to several of the industry's wealthiest retired winners, and the interesting and colorful *Parade of Breeds* presentation, shows repeated throughout the day if you visit between May and October. The visit wouldn't be complete without stopping at the Man o' War Memorial where the racing champion is buried, encircled by the tombs of many of his progeny.

From the park, take I–75 south (it joins I–64 east at exit 118) to Newtown Pike (exit 115). Travel south to New Circle Road, also called Highway 4, and travel west to U.S. 60 west to the Bluegrass Parkway. Take the parkway to the U.S. 127 exit. Follow U.S. 127 south to **Harrodsburg.** The Beaumont Inn will be on the left.

DINNER: After winding through a short residential district, you'll see the **Beaumont Inn** atop the hill at 638 Beaumont Inn Drive, Harrodsburg (800–352–3992). Originally a girls' school, the brick Greek Revival later became a college. Check in, confirm your dinner reservations, and take a nickel tour of the inn before exploring the grounds. Outdoors, the ginkgo, catalpa, wild cherry, hackberry trees, and grapevines are identified. Indoors, the inn's history is showcased museum style. Dinner at the Beaumont Inn is peaceful and plentiful, featuring Southern specialties like old-fashioned yellow-legged fried chicken and Kentucky cured country ham. Vegetables and sides are passed family-style so you

White fences and beautiful horses flourish in Kentucky's Bluegrass region.

can overindulge in the signature corn pudding, but save room for a slice of General Robert E. Lee orange-lemon cake or prune cake with bourbon sauce. Prices are moderate.

There's a lovely walking tour for after-dinner entertainment, but hopefully you'll have energy enough to venture to the outdoor drama *The Legend of Daniel Boone* at the **James Harrod Amphitheater,** 400 West Lexington Street, next to Old Fort Harrod State Park (800–852–6663). It's performed June through August at 8:30 P.M. Tickets are $12.00 for adults, $10.00 for seniors, and $6.00 for children. The outdoor theater is handicapped accessible.

LODGING: The Beaumont Inn, 638 Beaumont Inn Drive, Harrodsburg; (859) 734–3381 or (800) 352–3992. The Inn has grown from its main structure that began as a girls' boarding school, to a small complex including The Bell Cottage ($82 to $95), the Greystone House ($97 to $115), and Goddard Hall ($82 to $99). Each room is uniquely decorated with antiques or reproductions. The inn ($77 to

$115) dates from 1845 and showcases its past through antique collections and memorabilia throughout. An outdoor pool and air-conditioning provide modern touches with a gift shop and public restaurant.

DAY 2

Morning

BREAKFAST: A deluxe continental breakfast, complete with cheese grits and biscuits and gravy is included with the room rate; a more extensive hot buffet costs an additional $5.00. Either choice will more than satisfy your hunger pangs.

After breakfast, it's time to start exploring the historically rich region of Harrodsburg, the first permanent English settlement west of the Alleghenies; Danville, home of Centre College and many Fortune 500 industries; and Perryville, site of the Civil War's bloodiest battle.

Stop at the **Old Fort Harrod State Park,** at the corner of U.S. 127 and U.S. 68, where current-day craftspeople portray life in the 1770s when Captain James Harrod made settlement here. The stockade and fort replicas have recently undergone renovations. There's an interesting pioneer cemetery, the oldest west of the Alleghenies. The site is open year-round from 9:00 A.M. to 5:00 P.M. daily except Thanksgiving, Christmas week, and Mondays in January. Fees are $3.50 for adults and $2.00 for children six to twelve.

Less than 10 miles south on U.S. 68 is **Perryville,** a town of 600 residents on the Chaplin River. Civil War buffs will want to stop at the battlefield where the north and south surprised each other in what later became known as the bloodiest battle of the Civil War and one that pushed the Confederacy out of Kentucky.

LUNCH: A more genteel reason for coming to this little village is for the surprise you'll find at **Elmwood Inn,** 205 East Fourth Street, where "proper afternoon tea" is served on Saturday at 11:00 A.M., 1:00 P.M., and 3:00 P.M., Thursday and Friday at 1:00 and 3:00 P.M. You'd be hard-pressed to find a more pleasing tea in England, let alone anywhere else in the United States. The owners, authors of three books about tea and purveyors themselves, lead an annual excursion to the U.K. in search of memorable traditional experiences and in so doing, create the best in their historic brick home. You'll be served a four-course selection of delectable goodies, accompanied by the tea of your choice. Fresh flowers, linens, and china and a changing exhibit of original artwork complete the luxurious ambience. Cost is $15 per person; reservations are necessary. Phone (800) 765–2139; www.elmwoodinn.com.

Afternoon

Drive east on U.S. 150 to **Danville,** dubbed the City of Firsts. It's the home of both Centre College, the first college in the west, and the state's first county courthouse, built in 1785. And it's here that the first successful abdominal surgery in the world took place in 1809. At the **McDowell House** (125 South Second Street; 859–236–2804), you'll discover the details behind Dr. Ephraim McDowell's first surgery, taking a look at period artifacts and visiting an incredible collection of medical instruments and apothecary supplies in the adjacent Apothecary Shop. Open 10:00 A.M. to noon and 1:00 to 4:00 P.M. Monday to Saturday, 2:00 to 4:00 P.M. on Sunday; closed on Monday from November to March. Tours cost $5.00 for adults, $3.00 for seniors, $2.00 for students, and $1.00 for children under twelve.

Visit the Constitution Square State Historic Site across the street.

As you depart Danville, drive north toward **Harrodsburg** on State Route 33 for 13 miles to the **Shaker Village of Pleasant Hill** (3501 Lexington Road, Harrodsburg; 800–734–5611). This living history site provides an in-depth look at Shaker life as it was lived here during the late 1700s and early 1800s. Thirty-three buildings with costumed crafters not only explain the village's industry but portray the communal philosophy, religion, and teachings here.

From April through November, the village quietly bustles with Shaker craft and trade demonstrations, including sheep shearing, chair making, and cooking. Special events are scheduled during other seasons. Museum interpreters relive daily Shaker activities from the 1830s, when 500 residents lived here in the various buildings. The lifestyle is interesting, but the pastoral setting alone is worth the trip.

Time and season permitting, take a one-hour Kentucky River excursion aboard the stern-wheeler *Dixie Belle* after checking in and making dinner reservations at the Trustees' Office. It operates May through October at 10:00 A.M., noon, 3:00 and 4:00 P.M., plus a 6:00 P.M. trip from Memorial Day through Labor Day. Tickets are $6.00 for adults, $4.00 for ages twelve to seventeen, and $3.00 for children three to eleven. Family tickets ($25) are also available.

DINNER: An abundant dinner, part of which is served family style, is in store. Along with Shaker and southern specialties are home-baked rolls and desserts. Try the Shaker lemon pie, if you like an intense flavor. The menu is moderate, especially considering the hearty portions.

An after-dinner stroll, perhaps down the 1837 turnpike or along the 1826 Shaker Landing Road will burn up a few of the calories. During the summer, popular guided evening walks, at $2.00 per person, are led through the village. Various topics—perhaps an in-depth discussion of Shaker history, the community today, or nature—are presented Wednesday through Saturday evenings.

LODGING: Rooms for overnight accommodations within the village, scattered among fourteen buildings where the Shakers once worked and lived, provide visitors with a true experience of "living history." Decorated with reproduction furnishings reflecting the straight, simple lines of the Shaker style and accented with handwoven rugs, spreads, curtains, pegs, and rails, visitors can easily reflect on the early settlement.

Rooms are huge, often with trundle beds, and all have private baths and televisions for modern guests. Small houses are perfect for a family weekend. The largest house, North Lot Dwelling, rents for $190 and sleeps ten. Other rates range from $66 to $190 depending on location and room configuration, based on double occupancy.

DAY 3

Morning

BREAKFAST: Sleep in late to enjoy the pastoral serenity of Shaker Village and then arrive in the dining room for the hearty breakfast buffet ($7.50 for adults and $3.00 for children three to nine). The usual breakfast entrees plus grits, fruit, and hot breads make it special.

After breakfast leave Pleasant Hill for the two-hour drive to **Newport.** Take U.S. 68 west to U.S. 127 north. Then travel the Bluegrass Parkway to the North Circle 4 turnoff on the outskirts of Lexington. Follow signs to Newtown Pike (exit 9B) and head north on I–75. Past Erlanger, Kentucky, take I–275 east to I–471.

LUNCH: In Newport, follow signs to the **Newport Aquarium** (One Aquarium Way; 859–261–7444). Stop to stretch your legs and have lunch in the on-site cafe before heading back to Ohio by traveling north on I–75 to I–71 north. The rest of the trip will take about four hours.

THERE'S MORE

Mary Todd Lincoln House, 578 West Main Street, Lexington; (859) 233–9999. Open for guided tours mid-March through December.

Walking Tours. Stop at the Covington's Riverside Drive–Licking River Historic Area near Covington Landing, for a walk amid pre–Civil War homes and tree-lined streets. You'll notice life-size bronze sculptures along the way. The East Row Historic District in Newport is another spot for a walking tour. Shaded streets here boast Victorian homes. Walk along a portion of the Daniel Beard National Boy Scout Trail at Riverboat Row on the Ohio River near the aquarium in Newport. Contact the Northern Kentucky Visitors Center (800–354–9718) for walking tours.

BB Riverboats, Covington Landing; (800) 261–8586. Call ahead for schedule, pricing, and reservations for day-trips and sightseeing cruises. Breakfast, lunch, dinner, and Sunday brunch buffet meals are served on others. Prices vary depending on length and meal options.

Pioneer Playhouse, 840 Stanford Road, Danville; (859) 236–2747. An outdoor dinner theater that presents a five-play schedule of off-Broadway performances seasonally amid the backdrop of a re-created nineteenth-century village. Reserved seats for dinner and the performance are $20.00 for adults, $6.50 for children under six. For theater tickets only, adults are $12.00 and children are $3.50. Dinner is corn pudding, green beans, and barbecued chicken.

Horse Farm Tours. Venture past the fencing and visit one of the beautiful country estates in the Bluegrass belt. There are some 450 working horse farms in the region, with about 150 in the Lexington area. Visitors must arrange for a visit beforehand because the working farms can only accommodate a few visitors at a time. Contact the Lexington Convention and Visitors Bureau (800–845–3959) for a brochure explaining how to arrange a tour and the etiquette that goes along with the experience.

Labrot & Graham Distillers, 7855 McCracken Pike, Versailles; (859) 879–1939. Provides complimentary guided tours of its copper pots and sour mash bourbon distillery that operates as it did in the early 1800s. It has the distinction of being Kentucky's smallest, oldest, and "slowest." Located in a picturesque rural setting, the recently renovated visitor center has a gift shop where you can purchase the bourbon-laced chocolates sampled on the tour as well as the "Woodford Reserve" distilled here.

SPECIAL EVENTS

June. Historic Fort Harrod Heritage Festival, Harrodsburg. (859) 734–3314.

June. Great American Brass Band Festival, Centre College, Danville. (800) 755–0076.

August. Pioneer Days, Harrodsburg. (859) 734–2365.

August. Pleasant Hill Craft Fair, Shaker Village of Pleasant Hill, 3501 Lexington Road, Harrodsburg. Reduced $5.00 admission includes craft fair and village tour. (800) 734–5611.

September. 19th-Century County Fair, Shaker Village of Pleasant Hill, Harrodsburg. (800) 734–5611.

September. Oktoberfest, Main Strasse Village. (859) 491–0458.

September. Historic Constitution Square Festival, Danville. (859) 239–7089.

October. Battle of Perryville Commemorative Weekend, Perryville. (800) 755–0076.

December. "Come Home to Christmas" Historic Holiday Homes Tour, Harrodsburg. $10 admission. (485) 734–5985.

OTHER RECOMMENDED RESTAURANTS AND LODGINGS

Covington

Clarion Hotel Riverview, 668 West Fifth Street; (800) 292–2079. Recently renovated. Offers getaway packages, but weekend rates are generally reasonable—$99 for Kentucky view, $109 for river view.

Embassy Suites River Center, 10 East River Center Boulevard; (859) 261–8400. Good location; full-service. Least expensive rack rate is $149 for two persons. •

Downtown RiverCenter Marriott, 10 West RiverCenter Boulevard; (859) 261–2900. A good location offering full-service amenities. Watch for special promotions, like the $89 holiday rate.

Lexington

Sam's Restaurant, 1973 Lexington Road, Georgetown; (502) 863–5872. This used to be a truck stop and is still open twenty-four hours. It's five minutes from the Kentucky Horse Farm. Offerings, served by friendly women in the style of southern diners, also typify the South: chicken-fried steak, Kentucky Hot Brown sandwiches and hamburger steak, and excellent slabs of homemade pie for dessert. Inexpensive.

Danville

Old Crow Inn, 471 Stanford Road; (859) 236–1808. Three rooms, private baths. Rates: $75–$90. Full breakfast in a 220-year-old stone manor house. Innkeepers also run a pottery and candlemaking studio and shop, The Elements Pottery & Crafts.

Nonesuch

Irish Acres Gallery of Antiques, 4205 Ford's Mill Road, Versailles; (859) 873–7235. The address may say Versailles, but this schoolhouse turned antiques mecca is really in Nonesuch and aptly placed. It's unlikely that you've ever seen a place like it. On the lower level, a five-course luncheon is served under twinkling lights. The menu changes every two weeks, but might feature delectables like goat cheese puffs, chicken rolls Madeira, and a nonesuch kiss (a baked meringue shell filled with coffee ice cream, hot fudge sauce, sliced almonds, and whipped cream); $13.95 includes beverage.

FOR MORE INFORMATION

Shaker Village of Pleasant Hill, 3501 Lexington Road, Harrodsburg, Kentucky 40330; (800) 734–5611.

Kentucky Department of Travel, 500 Mero Street, Suite 2200, Frankfort, Kentucky 40601; (800) 225–TRIP.

Harrodsburg/Mercer County Tourist Commission, P.O. Box 283, 103 South Main, Harrodsburg, Kentucky 40330; (800) 355–9192.

Danville–Boyle County Convention and Visitors Bureau, 304 South Fourth Street, Danville, Kentucky 40422; (800) 755–0076.

Lexington Convention and Visitors Bureau, 301 East Vine Street, Lexington, Kentucky 40507-1513; (800) 848–1224.

Northern Kentucky Convention and Visitors Bureau, 50 East RiverCenter Boulevard, Suite 100, Covington, Kentucky 41011; (800) STAY–NKY.

WESTERN
ESCAPES

Northern Indiana's Amish Country

ELKHART COUNTY'S QUIET TREASURES

2 NIGHTS

Woodworkers • quilters
Homestyle cooking • Gourmet dining
Amish buggies • Bicycle trails

It takes several hours to reach the peaceful countryside of northern Indiana's Elkhart County, but you'll soon discover unsurpassed scenery and solitude and a splendid weekend, especially well suited for a restful and relaxing departure from everyday stress.

Although many visitors come to northern Indiana to experience the Amish communities, there are other activities and opportunities to learn more about our neighboring state. Guided audio tours lead motorists through the countryside in search of fine furniture and along the Heritage Trail, a loop tying the smaller communities together. The gently rolling and nearly flat elevations and sparsely traveled byways make this area easily accessible to bicycling enthusiasts. Naturalists appreciate the pastoral scenery along the way. Interspersed, you'll find wonderful dining and lodging options along with unique shops where local craftspeople display and sell their wares.

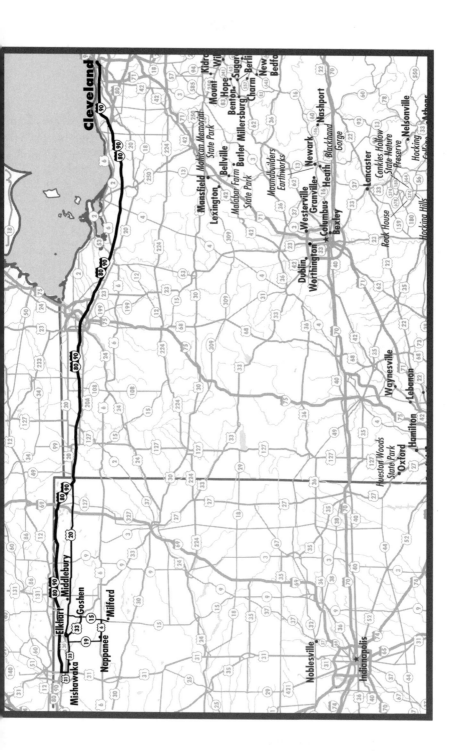

DAY 1

Morning

The drive to northwestern Indiana is about 235 miles and is going to take about four hours, so leave as early as possible. Travel across Ohio and Indiana via I–80/I–90. You'll reach Indiana in just under three hours. Exit I–80 at I–69 south.

LUNCH: Your first stop is for both lunch and scenery at the **Pokagon State Park,** State Route 127, just off I–69 south. Enjoy lunch overlooking Lake James at the **Potawatomi Inn and Restaurant** (219–833–1077 or 877–768–2928). A full luncheon buffet is served from 11:30 A.M. until 2:00 P.M. for $6.95. Take a scenic drive or walk after lunch before continuing. During winter, you might want to make a longer stop at the only refrigerated toboggan run in the Midwest—it's here in the park.

Afternoon

Instead of getting back on the turnpike, continue south on State Route 127 for 6 miles, turning west when you reach U.S. 20. You will drive through several small towns along this scenic route, and once you reach Lagrange you'll be in the heart of Amish farming communities.

Follow U.S. 20 west for 36 miles to a left turn onto State Route 13. Turn right onto State Route 4, and then left onto County Route 37 in **Goshen.**

LODGING: All of a sudden, the dormers of the **Checkerberry Inn** (62644 County Road 37, Goshen; 219–642–4445) pop into view amid Amish neighbors off to the right. It's less than an hour from your last stop. The inn, highly regarded for its luxurious and tranquil ambience and fine cuisine, beckons you to begin the renewal process as soon as you unpack or even before. Enjoy some time at the inn and let sightseeing go for the next day.

During warm seasons, an in-ground pool, tennis, and a croquet green await. Other times, visit the library, in its own wing off the eleven-room main inn. Each of the guest rooms is decorated differently. Susan Graff, half of the husband–wife ownership team, is particularly skillful in her decorating techniques. She blends only a touch of the inn's Amish location with light and airy schemes more typical of the Caribbean or perhaps the English countryside. You'll find an eclectic mix of lively and bright patterns, dark woods, light wicker, primitives, and her original boldly colored paintings throughout. A simple row of brimmed Amish straw hats hung over the bed may provide the only clue that you're in Amish country, but you'll surely know you're somewhere special. Rates range from $130 to $375.

DINNER: Reservations for dinner at the inn are a must. The restaurant is open to the public as well as guests, so make reservations when you book your accommodations. Dinner choices change each day, depending on what the chef wishes to create, but you'll find elegantly served entrees to fit your mood. Expensive, but worth it.

DAY 2

Morning

BREAKFAST: A continental plus, with emphasis on the plus, is provided at the inn. After breakfast get ready to explore the Amish communities in northern Indiana.

If you enjoy listening to audiotapes while driving, pick up either the Heritage Trail Auto tape tour and/or the Furniture Crafters Audio Driving tour at the Elkhart County Visitors Center, at exit 92 on I–80/I–90 in Elkhart. You'll need to leave a $10 deposit, refundable when you return with the tapes. CDs are expected soon but the deposit will be higher. Staff will help you get started or modify your trip as time permits, but the longer you spend, the more off-the-beaten-path you can drive and the more you'll learn about the Amish settlements in Elkhart, Bristol, Middlebury, Goshen, Nappanee and Wakarusa. The Heritage Trail is 100 miles in length; the Furniture Crafters Tour, 85 miles.

The Furniture Crafters trip will lead you to the **Old Bag Factory** (110 Chicago Avenue, Goshen; 219–534–2502). The factory originally manufactured soap, then mesh potato and onion bags and the tiny strips wrapped in Hershey Kisses. Then it became the terminus for Goshen's trolley system. The tracks run alongside the quaint edifice. Now local craftspeople sell their pottery, quilts, fine furniture, and other handmade items, as well as antiques and gifts.

LUNCH: Stop at the **Trolley Cafe,** on the lower level of the Bag Factory (219–534–3881). Soups, salads, and sandwiches are inexpensive yet satisfying.

Afternoon

The Heritage Trail audio driving tour has some easy breaking points. The entire route—with stops in Middlebury, Shipshewana, and Goshen—is outlined in red on the map supplied in the Northern Indiana Visitors' Guide. The second tape takes you through **Nappanee,** your last stop of the day.

Follow the audiotapes, but alter your route as necessary to make **Amish Acres** (1600 West Market Street, Nappanee; 800–800–4942) your last stop for the day. The complex—an 80-acre farm with lifestyle buildings scattered about—is listed on the National Register of Historic Places. The red Round Barn Theatre is its distinctive landmark. You never know what activities to expect, but there are generally farm chores in progress and crafters sharing their talents. Amish home tours and buggy rides are regularly scheduled. The house/farm tour and film is $6.95 for adults, $2.95 for children; a buggy ride is $3.95 for adults and $1.95 for children. The farm and shops are open March through December, 10:00 A.M. to 5:00 P.M. Theater productions run from April through December at 2:00 and 8:00 P.M.

DINNER: The Cow Shed, the Soda Shop & Fudgery, and the Bakery are all there to tempt you before dinner, but hold out for the Threshers Dinner. It's a family-style meal of Amish favorites, like hearth bread baked on the premises in the Amish kitchen, pot roast, ham, turkey and chicken with all the trimmings, and of course, homemade pie for dessert. It costs $14.95 for adults and $5.95 for children.

Stroll the grounds to work off a little of that hearty meal before finding your seat at the **Round Barn Theatre** for the evening's entertainment: a production of *Plain & Fancy* or one of the other Broadway musicals scheduled April through December. The regional theater company has performed in this reconstructed 1911 barn for more than a decade. Evening curtain is 8:00 P.M., matinees begin at 2:00 P.M. Ticket prices range from $20 to $25 for adults and $6.00 for children, but discounts are available to those who've ordered the Threshers Dinner.

LODGING: The drive back to the Checkerberry Inn will take about a half hour.

DAY 3

Morning

BREAKFAST: Get out early for a sight you won't want to miss. The Amish farms neighboring the inn take on a peaceful and quiet solitude as the morning sun burns off the early fog. Back inside the cheery inn it's breakfast time. Choose some of the homemade granola.

If weather permits, spend the morning recreating. Bicyclists, with bikes and gear in tow, will find five marked routes sharing the less traveled roads with Amish buggies. The gently rolling hills and nearly level roads make even designing your own itinerary easy enough.

From the inn, travel into Goshen via State Route 4. Goshen earned the distinction of being a "Bicycle Friendly Community" but walkers are welcome here

Amish buggies are a common sight on the flat country roads of Elkhart County.

too. You can connect with the **Maple City Greenway** at Abshire Park. There are
other accesses along the way.

The **Elkhart Bike and Walkway** begins just north of downtown **Elkhart,**
off Beardsley Avenue east of Main Street. A network of interconnecting pathways
and bridges over the St. Joseph and Elkhart Rivers allow users to travel from one
park to the others with ease. The **Elkhart Environmental Center** is located in
Elkhart five blocks east of the intersection of South Main and Lusher Avenue.

LUNCH: Before the turnpike trip back, stop for lunch at **Das Dutchman Essenhaus** (240 U.S. 20, Middlebury; 219–825–0455 or 800–455–9471). The moderately priced Amish-style menu features hot sandwiches served with mashed
potatoes and gravy as well as lighter options and full dinners. There are nearly
thirty varieties of pies.

It's about a 50-mile drive across Indiana to the Ohio border, including the 6-
mile ride north to I–90 east.

THERE'S MORE

Bonneyville Mill, 211 West Lincoln Avenue, Goshen; (219) 535–6458. Whether you're in the mood for a walk in the woods or just a nostalgic trip back to the days when the mill along the banks of the Little Elkhart River provided hydroelectric power, livestock feed, and flour to area farmers, you'll enjoy this park. From May through October the gristmill produces buckwheat pancake flour and the park is best for picnicking and hiking. You can pick up the miller's recipe for corn muffins while you watch production.

S. Ray Miller Auto Museum, 2130 Middlebury Street, Elkhart; (888) 260–8566. Shiny vintage automobiles take center stage here. The private collection of the museum's founder preserves these immaculate restorations as well as other symbols of the era: antique toys, music machines, clothing, and even a vast array of sheet music commemorating the arrival of the Model T. Open Monday through Friday 10:00 A.M. to 4:00 P.M. and during the last full weekend of each month from noon to 4:00 P.M. Admission is $4.00 for adults and $3.00 for seniors and students.

College Football Hall of Fame, 111 South St. Joseph Street, South Bend; (800) 440–FAME. There are some interactive areas here, as well as interesting displays of collegiate pigskin notables. If you're a football fan, you'll enjoy a stop here. Open January through June from 10:00 A.M. to 5:00 P.M.; after June, until 7:00 P.M. Admission is $9.00 for adults, $6.00 for seniors and students, and $4.00 for children ages six to fourteen.

Ruthmere, 302 East Beardsley Avenue, Elkhart; (219) 264–0330 or (888) 287–7696. One of the more impressive home museums you'll find anywhere. Built in the Beaux Arts style, it was named after the owners' daughter, Ruth Beardsley, who died during infancy. Because the estate overlooks the St. Joseph River, "mere," meaning water, was added. The tour leads visitors past five Rodin sculptures, a revolutionary war chair, works by Remington, Tiffany lamps and decorative art pieces, and a wealth more. Tours are given Tuesday through Saturday at 10:00 and 11:00 A.M., 1:00, 2:00, and 3:00 P.M. and Sunday at 3:00 P.M. from April through mid-December. Admission is $6.00 for adults, $5.00 for seniors, and $3.00 for students.

Midwest Museum of American Art, 429 South Main Street, Elkhart; (219) 293–6660. Every six weeks or so the temporary exhibit here changes, but the permanent one displays nineteenth- and twentieth-century American works throughout the seven galleries in this neoclassical-style bank building. You'll find treasures like a collection by Norman Rockwell and others from notable periods. Open Tuesday through Friday, 11:00 A.M. to 5:00 P.M.; Saturday and Sunday, 1:00 to 4:00 P.M. Admission is $3.00 for adults, $5.00 for families; free on Sunday from 1:00 to 4:00 P.M. There are often lectures, seminars, and workshops.

SPECIAL EVENTS

September. Autofest, the S. Ray Miller Auto Museum, Elkhart. Displays and competitions of cars, trucks, custom and street rods. Call the Northern Indian Amish Country/Elkhart County Convention and Visitors Bureau at (216) 262–8161 for details.

October. Amish Harvest Festival, 249 U.S. 20, Middlebury, at the covered Bridge Trail of Das Dutchman Essenhaus. (219) 825–5129.

OTHER RECOMMENDED RESTAURANTS AND LODGINGS

Middlebury

Essenhaus Country Inn, 240 U.S. 20; (219) 825–9471 or (800) 455–9471. Rates range from $79 to $130 and include a continental breakfast that becomes more substantial on Sunday when the adjoining restaurant is closed.

Nappanee

The Nappanee Inn, 2004 West Market Street; (800) 773–2011. Located three-fourths of a mile from Amish Acres, Nappanee Inn sits amid cornfields and resembles a barn. Both the inn with its sixty-six rooms and the adjacent buildings are painted barn red with white trim. The interiors reflect the simple style of its neighbors with Amish furnishings and quilts. Standard room rates are $84 based on double occupancy from May through October (less other months).

Inn at Amish Acres, 1234 West Market Street; (219) 773–2011. This inn is located close to the historic farmstead and takes on the historic character of the farm with front porches furnished with rocking chairs. Like the Nappanee Inn, furnishings reflect the Amish surroundings. Rates here are $84 during the high season. Both properties are owned by Amish Acres.

FOR MORE INFORMATION

Elkhart County Convention and Visitors Bureau, 26500 Caravan Drive, Elkhart, Indiana 46514; (800) 262–8161.

Windsor, Ontario

FRIENDLY NEIGHBORS

2 NIGHTS

Parks and manors • Freedom stories
Canada's southernmost point

Windsor, Ontario, is a popular spot for Ohio visitors on several counts. If you're a bird-watcher or nature lover, you may have already discovered the unique and profuse possibilities in southern Canada. Within an hour's drive of Windsor, Point Pelee National Park attracts the monarch butterflies each fall during their migration to Mexico, provides ice skating and cross-country skiing opportunities in the winter, and offers relaxing views and sounds of Lake Erie the rest of the year. You can follow the North Star yourself to discover the important role Windsor and Canada played as the final stop for slaves traveling the Underground Railroad to freedom. Activities abound within Windsor's borders; quaint towns and interesting history dot the map surrounding the city for additional sightseeing opportunities.

Windsor is a convenient stop for those wishing to test Lady Luck. Casino Windsor decorates the skyline with a bright neon rainbow; inside, the Las Vegas–style glitz attracts its share of onlookers and gamblers eager to get more for their wager because of the high exchange rate of the U.S. dollar. The casino offers overnight accommodations, but if you'd like to venture off the beaten track, there are several bed-and-breakfasts offering unique and historical surroundings, whether you're looking for a romantic getaway or just a change of pace and warm hospitality.

Any prices quoted here are in Canadian currency, so the price is even less for U.S. visitors. Also, remember that you are crossing the border. So before entering Canada, prepare to pass customs. You may be asked your citizenship upon cross-

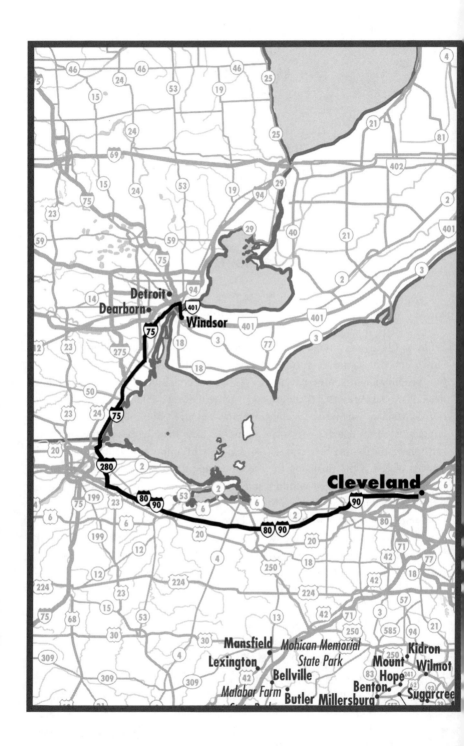

ing so carry a voter registration card, birth certificate, or passport. Your driver's license is not adequate. You will be asked your destination, purpose for visiting, and expected length of stay. Restricted purchases include many foods and plants, animals, fish, and their products.

Police radar detectors are illegal in Ontario and seat belt use is mandatory. Upon re-entering the United States within forty-eight hours, you may bring in $200 worth of goods, ten cigars, fifty cigarettes, and four ounces of alcohol, duty free. Keep receipts. The U.S. agent will ask you to describe any purchases upon your return. For more information, contact the U.S. Customs at (716) 551–4368.

DAY 1

Afternoon

The drive from Cleveland to **Windsor** is an easy one, following interstate and turnpike routes. Get away by early afternoon; the entire trip will take around three hours.

Follow I–80/I–90 west, continuing on the Ohio Turnpike. After logging 100 miles or so, pick up I–280 north around Toledo and then I–75 north into Detroit. As you approach downtown, follow I–375 as well as signs to the Windsor Tunnel. After you drive through the tunnel, stop to clear customs. Then turn left onto Park and right onto Riverside for a drive along the shoreline and picturesque views of downtown Detroit and its Renaissance Center from the opposite shore of the Detroit River.

Stop for a complimentary tour at the **Canadian Club Distillery** (2072 Riverside Drive East, Windsor; 519–561–5499). It is the home of Hiram Walker & Sons Limited, founded in 1858. Along with finding out how whiskey is distilled, you'll learn some of the history of the area and the influence Hiram Walker had on the community known as Walkerville, a historic neighborhood surrounding your bed-and-breakfast. The one-hour tours are offered only on weekdays.

DINNER: During warmer months, make dinner reservations for the **Pride of Windsor Cruise** (Ouellette and Riverside, downtown Windsor; 800–706–7607). From May to October, there are weekend dinner-dance cruises ($59.95) featuring a DJ and dinner buffet, daily one- and two-hour narrated sightseeing cruises ($10–$15), and Sunday brunch ($34.95). They all come with great views of the Detroit River and some Canadian and U.S. points of interest. If you're in town between November and April when cruises are not offered, select **Plunkett's Bistro–Bar** (28 Chatham Street East, just off Ouellette; 519–252–3111). You'll find

For views of Lake Erie and Canada's natural splendor, visit Point Pelee National Park, Canada's southernmost point.

artful and inventive selections and presentations here at moderate prices. There's also seasonal outdoor seating available.

After dinner, stop along the river at **Coventry Gardens** to view the Peace Fountain, lit from mid-May until mid-October.

Continue east on Riverside Drive, turning right onto Walker Road. At Richmond, turn right and then left onto Monmouth. Your B&B is on the corner of Monmouth and Richmond.

LODGING: Ye Olde Walkerville Bed & Breakfast, 1104 Monmouth Road; (519) 254–1507. This conveniently located Victorian B&B was part of the original Hiram Walker Distillery Estates. Walkerville was a town that grew from the distillery industry, but was annexed by Windsor in 1935. Property owners still consider themselves residents of "Olde Walkerville," however, and streets are lined with row houses built for workers and large beautiful homes designed for town executives. Olde Walkerville Bed & Breakfast, in a residential neighborhood, offers a homey, congenial atmosphere. The five guest rooms in this turn-of-the-century manor home are uniquely and comfortably appointed, including queen-size beds (a king bed in one room), and are named after the innkeeper's grandchildren. There's a gazebo and deck in the back and a porch in front. Rates based on double occupancy are $99 to $139, and $199 for "Samantha's Suite."

DAY 2

Morning

BREAKFAST: Your innkeeper, Wayne Strong, boasts of serving the best breakfast in Windsor, and rightly so. He serves a delicious warm coffee cake with streusel topping, fresh fruit, and coffee before he takes your breakfast order. Guests select from a dozen selections, including French toast served with Canadian maple syrup and Canadian bacon. Some repeat guests know to take the coffee cake along for a mid-morning snack. The choice is yours before setting out for Point Pelee National Park, with a few other stops added in for good measure. Strong will prepare picnic lunches for those wishing to dine amid the Lake Erie views at the tip of Point Pelee.

As you leave, take the scenic route along Riverside Drive before turning right onto County Road 19. Take King's Highway 3 south and stop at **Colasanti's Tropical Gardens,** in the little town of **Ruthven** (519–326–3287). You'll find an eighteen-hole miniature golf course indoors here, not to mention a huge greenhouse filled with tropical plants, a petting zoo, a restaurant, and a country store in case you need some homemade fudge for the rest of the drive. You can also pick up a picnic lunch if you didn't bring one from the inn.

From Ruthven continue southeast into **Leamington,** following signs to **Point Pelee National Park** jutting into Lake Erie. Take the train, unless you prefer walking or biking, from the visitor's center to the tip. The free ride to mainland Canada's southernmost point departs every twenty minutes. As they say at the park, "If you don't get to the tip, you've missed the point!" During the fall monarch butterfly migration, the path leading to the water's edge is filled with the prolific species. The best time for viewing is early morning.

Another short but interesting walk is along the Marsh Boardwalk. There is an observation tower with views of the trail as it cuts over one of the Great Lakes' largest freshwater marshes. In summer, you can rent a canoe at the boardwalk and paddle through the marsh. In wintertime, bring your ice skates; weather permitting, the marsh is cleared of snow and open to visitors.

There are many other trails, some of which are handicapped accessible, are interpreted, or have guidebooks to detail the routes. You can cross-country ski the trails during winter.

LUNCH: If you've brought a lunch, picnic in the park. Otherwise, leave the park and journey on County Route 20 into **Kingsville** for lunch at the **Vintage Goose** (24 Main Street West; 519–733–6900). This quaint and uniquely decorated eatery has taken up residence in one of the town's oldest buildings, dating back to the mid-1800s. The menu changes frequently, but you'll find a wide array of creative, moderately priced selections—like a sweet potato torta or a Rueben Merlot—and homemade breads, desserts, and salad dressings plus an extensive wine list. The restaurant, which offers cooking classes, is also open for dinner and Sunday brunch.

Afternoon

Before leaving the fertile farmlands of Essex County, stop for a tour and tasting at **Pelee Island Winery** (455 County Road 20, Kingsville; 800–597–3533). After your first taste of a Riesling dry, a twelve-minute video explains the history of wine making and takes visitors over to Pelee Island, where the winery's grapes are harvested. Guests take a tour of the facility's wine producing plant, followed by more tasting and a lesson in wine appreciation. Cost is $3.00 per person and tours begin at noon, 2:00 and 4:00 P.M. daily year round except for major holidays.

Follow County Road 29 north out of town, picking up Route 3 and continuing back into **Windsor.** Venture to **Erie Street,** the Little Italy of Windsor. It's a microcosm of the country, complete with clothing and tailor shops, markets, and of course, great Italian dining. There are more than a dozen authentic restaurants each offering tastes from the Italian regions of their owners and chefs.

DINNER: You'll find an eclectic menu at **Spago Restaurante** (690 Erie Street East; 519–252–2233). The chef is from Salerno, but entrees highlight other regions as well. Attentive waiters refill the focaccia platter as it nears empty, so don't forget to hold off for the main courses: pastas, carne, pesce, risotto, and many "specialita della casa" (house specials). Dinners range from $9.75 to $18.95, with some market prices for seafood entrees. The house salad and focaccia are included.

For the evening's entertainment stop at **Casino Windsor** (377 Riverside Drive East; 800–991–7777). The parking is free, but once inside you'll find thousands of slot machines and 136 table games where you can part with your dollars. The Las Vegas–style permanent casino on the Detroit River also offers dining and live entertainment options.

LODGING: Ye Olde Walkerville B&B.

DAY 3

Morning

BREAKFAST: Ye Olde Walkerville B&B.

After breakfast walk along Windsor's **Sculpture Garden** on the waterfront. It is just one of several areas managed by the department of Parks and Recreation sprawling on Riverside Drive. This one is like visiting a museum without ever going indoors. Each of the seventeen pieces of outdoor public art conveys a special message, either abstractly or through representational forms. No matter your favorite, the display brought a new moniker to Windsor: "Canada's Sculpture Capital." It's open year-round, dawn to dusk.

For one more tour before leaving Windsor, drive through the charming Walkerville area again to reach **Willistead Manor** (1899 Niagara Street; 519–253–2365). You may already have noticed this unique mansion, sporting several distinct architectural styles. Built in 1906 as the home of Hiram Walker's son Edward and named in memory of another son, Willis, this thirty-six-room mansion reflects the character of an English manor home, built from stone quarried nearby. On the outside, the striking facade is surrounded by acres of parkland, perfect for strolling, and on the inside, tour guides point out the lavish furnishings and beautiful woodwork. Open September through November and January through June, the first and third Sunday of each month; July and August, open every Sunday and Wednesday from 1:00 to 4:00 P.M. Expanded hours during December. Tour prices are $3.75 for adults, $3.25 for seniors, and $2.00 for children under thirteen.

LUNCH: Stop downtown at **Chatham Street Grill** (149 Chatham Street West; 519–256–2555). It has a moderately priced eclectic American menu with interesting selections, perfect for lunch before taking the tunnel across to Detroit and making your return trip home via I–75 and the Ohio Turnpike.

THERE'S MORE

The Great Canadian Trading Post Co., 3025 Huron Church Road, Lambton Plaza, Windsor; (519) 966–4716. Inuit and other Native Canadian art and sculpture. Open every day 9:00 A.M. to 9:00 P.M.

Walker's Candies, 1033 Wyandotte Street East, Windsor; (513) 253–2019. Take a tour of the candy-making operation here, or just stock up on hand-dipped truffles. Open Monday through Saturday, 9:00 A.M. to 5:00 P.M. Group tours of the factory are $1.00 per person.

John Freeman Walls Historic Site and Underground Railroad Museum, East Puce Road, County Road 25, Maidstone; (519) 258–6253. Family members of John Walls, a slave who found his freedom in Canada, retrace his path along the secretive Underground Railroad and retell African slave stories. The interactive presentation is set up for groups, but individuals and families can call ahead and attend one of the group tours costing $4.00 per person. There's an original 1846 log cabin built by John Freeman Walls and a chapel in honor of Rosa Parks, who visits annually. Walls's great-grandchildren have gathered the oral histories, written about the slave experiences in *The Road that Led to Somewhere*, and developed the historical site and program. They created a cross of bricks given to them from the Lorraine Motel, where Martin Luther King Jr. was assassinated. Call ahead for an appointment from May through October. Tours are $4.00 per person, children under five are admitted free.

Pelee Island. Arrive at the largest of the Lake Erie Islands by ferry, either from Leamington or Sandusky. Once on the island, you'll be pleasantly surprised to find another winery tour at the Pelee Winery Vineyards, bird-watching opportunities galore, and great dining at Gooseberry's. There are overnight accommodations at the **Tin Goose Inn** (1060 East West Road; 519–724–2223) and the **Gathering Place** (West Shore Road; 519–724–2656). The island is quaint and quiet.

SPECIAL EVENTS

June. Art in the Park, Willistead Park, Windsor. (519) 253–6382.

June–July. International Freedom Festival. Joint celebration between Canada and the United States in honor of both countries' national holidays. Huge fireworks display on the riverfront. (519) 252–7264.

August. International Gospel Concert and Festival, John Freeman Walls Historic Site and Underground Railroad Museum, Maidstone. (519) 258–6253.

August. Windsor International Busker Festival, Windsor's City Centre and Kieppe's Park on the waterfront. This festival takes its cues from Halifax's unique "Buskers" (street performers). Be entertained as you walk along or stop at the outdoor stages for nightly performances. (800) 265–3633.

August. Willistead Classic and Antique Car Show, Willistead Manor. The beautiful grounds make a lovely backdrop for this car show. (519) 253–2365.

August–October. Harvest festivals, various locations. Nearly every weekend there's some activity related to the locally grown produce. For listings, contact the Windsor, Essex County, and Pelee Island Convention and Visitors Bureau (800–265–3633).

OTHER RECOMMENDED RESTAURANTS AND LODGINGS

Kingsville

Kingswood Inn, 101 Mill Street West; (519) 733–3248. Col. James S. King, founder of Kingsville, built this octagonal home, one of the area's true architectural gems, back in 1859. The current owners added all the accouterments to make it a showplace. There are five guest rooms with private baths, an inground pool, and gardens. Located 40 miles from Windsor, it's a wonderful place for a peaceful and special getaway. The honeymoon suite is $195 midweek, $280 on weekends. Smaller rooms start at $95 during the week.

Windsor

Branteaney's B&B, 1649 Chappus Street; (519) 966–2334; www.bcanada.com/970.html. You can enjoy the outdoors via the orchard, ponds, and award-winning gardens no matter the season and still be close to Windsor attractions. Rates range from $70 to $135 Canadian.

Il Gabbiano Ristorante, 875 Erie Street East; (519) 256–9757. Learn the difference between eating and dining. The posh atmosphere and attention to detail along with strolling minstrels on occasion make it special. Dinners range from $15 to $25.

Tunnel Bar-B-Q, 58 Park Street East (across from the Windsor-Detroit tunnel exit); (877) 285–3663. Famous for award-winning ribs ($15.95) and chicken. Homemade desserts.

Leamington

Marlborough House Bed & Breakfast, 49 Marlborough Street West; (519) 322–1395. Located 30 miles from Windsor, this B&B is a good choice for naturalists looking for a stay convenient to Point Pelee National Park. It is also one of the least expensive B&Bs, with rates under $100.

FOR MORE INFORMATION

Windsor, Essex County, and Pelee Island Convention and Visitors Bureau, City Centre Mall, Suite 103, 333 Riverside Drive, Windsor, ON N9A 5K4; (800) 265–3633.

Detroit, Michigan

MORE THAN THE MOTOR CITY

2 NIGHTS

Greektown • Historic sites • Hitsville

There are historic remnants of early Detroit, dating back to the 1700s when the French explorer Antoine de La Mothe Cadillac first paddled along the Detroit River, but these days some of those not-too-positive stereotypes that came about as Detroit grew into the Motor City capital are becoming history too. If you haven't visited Detroit lately, now is a good time.

Downtown is undergoing revitalization, not unlike what Cleveland experienced a few years back. The skyline is changing, but the process will continue over the next several years, with new sports complexes, gambling casinos, and lively restaurant and shopping areas adding big doses of vitality. You'll be pleasantly surprised at the friendly service, selection in shopping and sightseeing opportunities, and upscale atmosphere in Detroit.

Many outdoor ethnic festivals take place at Hart Plaza during the summer months, and there are often major exhibits showing at the Detroit Institute of Arts.

Whatever your interests, you can't visit the Motor City without getting caught up in automotive history. A trip to Dearborn familiarizes visitors not only with Henry Ford's accomplishments, but with other inventors of his time in the living history setting of the Greenfield Village and with inventions and memorabilia of times past in the Henry Ford Museum. Repeat visitors and architectural and art buffs should opt to tour the mansions of the auto barons.

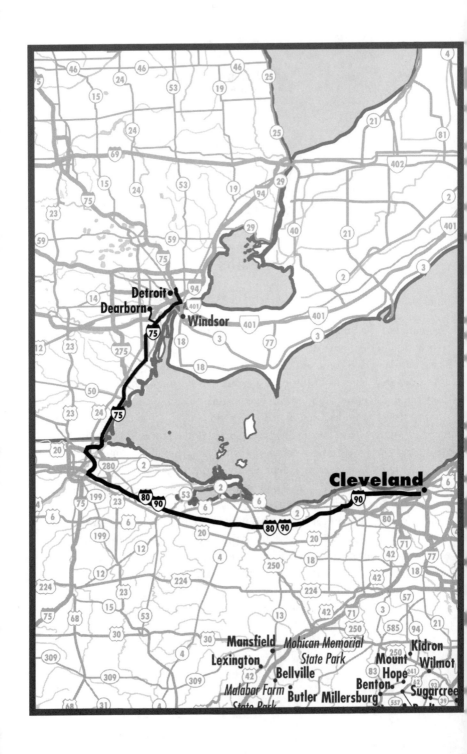

DAY 1

Afternoon

If you can get away early on Friday, by all means do so. The drive to **Detroit,** just shy of 180 miles, is an easy one, but there's so much to see and do, you'll be able to fit more options in if you leave by noon. You'll pick up I–90 west, ultimately traveling the Ohio Turnpike heading toward Toledo. Take I–280 north and then I–75 north from Toledo.

Follow I–75 north to M–10 (the Lodge Freeway) north. Exit at Warren Avenue and turn right (east), passing Wayne State University's main campus. Continue on Warren to your first stop, the **Charles H. Wright Museum of African American History** (315 Warren Street; 313–494–5800). There's a public parking lot behind to the museum.

You'll be impressed with the building's highly recognizable architecturally unique circular facade. Inside, the glass rotunda surrounded by flags of African countries introduces visitors to *Of the People: The African American Experience,* the museum's permanent exhibition tracing more than 600 years of African-American history.

There are eight themes presented here, such as "The African Memory" detailing the importance of remembering one's origins and history. In the next display, "The Crime," students from modern-day Detroit's schools posed for the human-like clay renderings in the bow of a slave ship. Each of the eight stations portrays another aspect of African-American life, and two interactive "studios" allow guests to listen to influential musical styles and readings. The museum makes a poignant statement, no matter the viewer's cultural background.

The gift shop stocks an excellent selection of books and gift items. Open Tuesday through Sunday 9:30 A.M. to 5:00 P.M. Admission is $3.00 for adults, $2.00 for children twelve and younger.

If you're traveling on the first Friday of the month, you'll get in a visit at the noted **Detroit Institute of the Arts** (5200 Woodward Avenue; 313–833–7900), which is open until 9:00 P.M. on those evenings. It is within walking distance of the African American museum.

When you are ready to leave, take Warren to I–75 south to I–375 south. Take the Lafayette exit and turn right on Lafayette.

DINNER: Great Cajun cuisine awaits at **Fishbone's Rhythm Kitchen Cafe** (400 Monroe Street, Detroit; 313–965–1449). Pick out your plastic beads as a souvenir of your Mardi Gras experience, one that might include such specialties as catfish

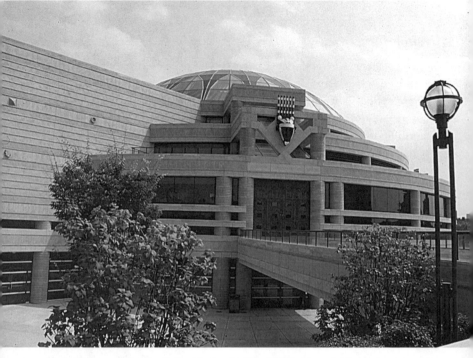

The architectural design of the Charles H. Wright Museum of African American History blends linear and circular elements for a striking facade.

or crawfish étouffée and luscious desserts like Bourbon Street bread pudding and bananas Foster. Prices are moderate.

Greektown delicacies abound within a block's walk for additional alternatives, or at least a serving of baklava and a cup of Greek coffee. By press time, the new **Greektown Casino** will likely be open to test Lady Luck. It's located right behind your hotel.

LODGING: The **Atheneum Suite Hotel and Conference Center,** 1000 Brush Avenue; (313) 962–2323 or (800) 772–2323. Located at the edge of Greektown, this hotel started out as an office building. It has been refitted with contemporary furnishing and designs, offering queen or king beds, marble bathrooms, and whirlpool bathtubs. Rates normally start at $155 and go as high as $700 for the presidential suite, but there are weekend special packages. The Greektown "OPA" package includes accommodations, continental breakfast, dinner for two at Fishbone's or Pegasus, and valet parking for $195, $115 for the second night.

DAY 2

Morning

BREAKFAST: The Atheneum Suites Hotel.

Today will be spent in **Dearborn,** visiting the Henry Ford Museum and Greenfield Village, with a stop at the Spirit of Ford across the street, so wear your walking shoes.

As you exit the hotel, turn right onto Monroe Street at the next block and then watch for I–75 north. Take this interstate to I–94 west and take the first exit (Oakwood Boulevard). Follow signs to **Henry Ford Museum and Greenfield Village** (20900 Oakwood Boulevard, Dearborn; 313–271–1620). The easy drive will take about twenty minutes.

Begin your visit to Greenfield Village with a half-hour horse-drawn omnibus tour. It's an extra $5.00, but the narration will provide an overview of the village, which was created by Henry Ford in celebration of the spirit of innovation and dedicated to his friend, Thomas Edison. There are also train rides, surrey rides, and Model A shuttles.

There are numerous links to Ohio and its famous citizens throughout the village. The Wright Brothers' family home and cycle shop are here, as well as Thomas Edison's Menlo Park laboratory, a laboratory from his Ft. Myers residence, and the Sarah Jordan Boardinghouse—the first home he wired for electricity. An 1880s-style seven-acre farm operates year-round just as it would have when Harvey Firestone was growing up.

As you peek into various homes and businesses, you'll meet characters from the 1800s who are eager to share anecdotes from the time or explain how their crafts were created. Especially interesting are some of the earlier buildings: a 1600s windmill from Cape Cod and cottages from the Cotswolds in England.

The Henry Ford Museum and Greenfield Village are open 9:00 A.M. to 5:00 P.M. daily; closed Thanksgiving and Christmas. Interiors of Greenfield Village are closed January through March. Admission to the museum or village is $12.50 for adults, $7.50 for children age five to twelve, and $11.50 for seniors.

LUNCH: For a quick, delicious lunch before leaving Greenfield Village, stop at **Taste of History,** which serves historical favorites. The most popular lunch item is a hot beef and mashed potato sandwich served in a scooped out bread bowl, but the railroader's lunch, a turkey and cheese combo on "hobo" bread baked in a can, is equally delicious. Prices are moderate, some items are available in five-ounce tasting portions, and all the breads and pastries are baked on-site.

Afternoon

Begin the afternoon at the Henry Ford Museum. Make sure to stop at the rocker President Lincoln was sitting in when shot at Ford's Theatre, and pause for a moment at the 1961 Lincoln in which President Kennedy was assassinated. The car was a convertible at the time but was later modified for use by Presidents Johnson, Nixon, Ford, and Carter. These days, presidential limousines are destroyed in Secret Service safety experiments after their tenures. More modern exhibits show off the robotics of the '90s. And in between, *100 Years of the Automobile in American Life* not only includes the popular and not-so-popular models, but reflects the influence they had on America. The diners, motels, and fast-food chains that cropped up as a result of America's mobility take center stage here. The most recent addition is a new 3-D IMAX Theatre.

Open 9:00 A.M. to 5:00 P.M. daily, except major holidays. Closed on Monday during January and February. Admission is $6.00 for adults, $4.00 for children ages five to twelve, and $5.00 for seniors. Certified teachers and Ford employees or retirees and their immediate families admitted free.

Before leaving the area, walk across the street to the **Spirit of Ford** (313–31–SPIRIT). Ford factory tours used to be a popular visitor destination. They are no longer offered, but you can now take the Turbo Tour in the theater of this new museum. The short video is worth the price of admission and better than an amusement park ride.

As you leave the Henry Ford Museum, turn right onto Michigan Avenue and then left onto Evergreen, following the signs to Fairlane Drive, where you will find the Henry Ford Estate, **Fair Lane** (4901 Evergreen Road, Dearborn; 313–593–5590). This fifty-six-room, fifteen-bath, eight-fireplace mansion has seen the likes of presidents and dukes and is open for guided tours. The last tour begins at 3:00 P.M. and costs $7.00 for adults, $6.00 for seniors and students. Afterward, explore the Ford Discovery Trail, a self-guided walking tour to the tree house, boathouse, gardens, and unique landscape treasures.

Retrace your previous route to I–94, I–75, and I–375. Take Gratoit Avenue to Harmonie Park, a few blocks from the hotel.

DINNER: Intermezzo Italian Ristorante, 1435 Randolph Street; (313) 961–0707. This upscale restaurant has interesting decor and cuisine. During warm months, opt for alfresco dining. Moderate to expensive.

Nearby you'll find theaters, opera, and Second City for live entertainment after dinner. The hotel guest services can provide information about current performances at theaters including Fox Theatre (2211 Woodward Avenue; 313–202–1252), the Gem Theatre (333 Madison Avenue; 313–963–9800), the Masonic Temple Theatre (500 Temple Drive; 313–202–1952), or the Michigan Opera Theatre (1526 Broadway; 313–961–3500).

LODGING: The Atheneum Suite Hotel.

DAY 3

Morning

BREAKFAST: Enjoy Sunday brunch in Greektown at **Pegasus Taverna Restaurant** (558 Monroe Street; 313–964–6800). You'll find Greek and American fare at moderate prices.

Check out of the hotel and head to north to **Bloomfield Hills** for a visit to **Cranbrook** (1221 North Woodward Avenue, Bloomfield Hills; 877–GO–CRANBROOK). Take I–75 north to the Big Beaver exit, turning right onto Woodward Avenue. Cranbrook will be on the left. The center consists of a world-renowned art museum, a science institute, the house, gardens, and schools. You'll enjoy touring the Saarinen House, the restored home of the community's architect, as well as the outdoor sculpture gardens and the natural history museum, complete with a 15-foot-tall Tyrannosaurus rex. Admission to Cranbrook Art Museum is $4.00 for adults, $2.00 for students and seniors. Admission to the Cranbrook Institute of Science is $7.00 for adults, $4.00 for seniors and children.

When you are finished at the Cranbrook museums, head over to the Somerset Collection in **Troy** at Coolidge and Big Beaver Roads for a little upscale shopping.

LUNCH: Stop for lunch at **Portabella** (2745 West Big Beaver Road, Troy; 248–649–6625). It's located in the Somerset Collection. There's a casual atmosphere and interesting lunch entrees between $5.95 and $12.95. It's one of local restauranteur Matt Prentice's dozen Detroit eateries.

Afternoon

Head back to Cleveland by traveling east on West Big Beaver Road from the mall to I–75 south, taking I–280 south near Toledo. Follow signs for the Ohio Turnpike east into Cleveland.

THERE'S MORE

The Detroit People Mover, accessible from any of its thirteen stops, can act as your trolley for a quick fifteen-minute sightseeing overview of the downtown business district or a means of fast transportation. Stops include the Cobo Conference/Exhibition Center, Joe Lewis Arena, the Renaissance Center and Greektown. The exact change of fifty cents or a token is required.

The Detroit Science Center, University Cultural Center, 5200 John R. Street, Detroit; (313) SCIENCE. Home of the IMAX Dome Theatre and Discovery Theater, where live science demonstrations and interactive presentations take place. There are more than fifty hands-on exhibits as well as Internet experiences. Hours are Monday through Friday from 9:30 A.M. to 2:00 P.M., Saturday from 10:30 A.M. to 5:00 P.M., and Sunday from 11:30 A.M. to 5:00 P.M. Admission is $3.00 for adults and $2.00 for seniors and youths ages three to seventeen.

Detroit Historical Museum, 5401 Woodward, in Detroit's Cultural Center; (313) 833–1805. Come here to learn about Detroit's past. Street scenes dating from the 1840s through the 1900s are re-created in the *Streets of Old Detroit* exhibit. The *Motor City* exhibit shows off 100 years of automotive history. Open Tuesday through Friday from 9:30 A.M. to 5:00 P.M., Saturday and Sunday from 10:00 A.M. to 5:00 P.M. Admission is $4.50 for adults, $2.25 for seniors and children ages twelve to eighteen.

Holocaust Memorial Center, 6602 West Maple Road, West Bloomfield; (248) 661–0840. This was the first memorial museum in the United States dedicated to the Holocaust. Open from September through June, Sunday to Thursday 10:00 A.M. to 3:30 P.M., Friday 9:00 A.M. to 12:30 P.M. Admission is free.

Automotive Hall of Fame, 21400 Oakwood Boulevard, Dearborn; (888) 29–VISIT). Located next door to the Henry Ford Museum and Greenfield Village. Open Memorial Day through October 31, daily from 10:00 A.M. to 7:00 P.M.; November through Memorial Day, Tuesday through Sunday from 10:00 A.M. to 5:00 P.M. Admission is $6.00 for adults, $5.50 for seniors, and $3.00 for youths five to twelve.

Belle Isle Park; (313) 852–4074. An urban park 3 miles from downtown via the MacArthur Bridge. Perfect for picnicking, fishing, and just relaxing. It is also home of the Dossin Great Lakes Museum, the Belle Isle Zoo, the Belle Isle Aquarium, and a nature center and conservatory. There is an admission charge for the aquarium and conservatory.

Professional Sports. You can watch the NHL Detroit Red Wings at the Joe Louis Arena or the NBA Detroit Pistons and the WNBA Detroit Shock at The Palace of Auburn Hills. Detroit is also home to the American Baseball League's Detroit Tigers, playing in a new park, and the NFL's Detroit Lions, scheduled for a new stadium. For tickets call the Pistons at (248) 377–0100; Red Wings, (313) 396–7444; Rockers Soccer, (248) 366–6254; Vipers IHL Hockey, (248) 377–0100; Tigers, (313) 962–4000; Lions, (248) 335–4131.

Hitsville, U.S.A. and the **Motown Historical Museum,** 2648 West Grand Boulevard; (313) 875–2264. Stroll down memory lane and tour the original "Studio A" where Diana Ross and the Supremes, the Jackson Five, Stevie Wonder, and others recorded long before the site became a museum. Admission is $6.00 for adults, $3.00 for children. Open Tuesday through Saturday 10:00 A.M. to 5:00 P.M., Sunday and Monday noon to 5:00 P.M., other times by appointment.

Windsor, Ontario. Just a few minutes away via the Windsor Tunnel or the Ambassador Bridge. Americans like to gamble at the Casino.Windsor because of the exchange rate, but you'll also discover sightseeing and dining possibilities (see Western Escape Two).

SPECIAL EVENTS

May. Budweiser Downtown Hoedown, Hart Plaza, downtown. Considered the world's largest free country music festival, it attracts more than 800,000 fans. (734) 459–6969.

August. Tenneco Automotive Grand Prix of Detroit, Belle Isle. Belle Isle Park becomes a state-of-the-art contemporary street course when race fans and cars gather here. Tickets vary in price; free admission during time trials. (313) 393–7749.

August. African World Fest, Hart Plaza, downtown. More than 150 artisans sell handcrafted African fine art, apparel, dolls, and more. The plaza resembles an open-air marketplace in Africa or the West Indies. (313) 494–5853.

September. Detroit Festival of the Arts, University Cultural Center area, off Woodward Avenue. This lively festival includes something for everyone: a marketplace of artists selling their crafts, stage performances, ethnic foods and music, and some fifty hands-on activities for children. Free. (313) 577–5088.

November. Annual "America's Thanksgiving Parade" through the heart of downtown along Woodward Avenue from Mack Avenue to Jefferson Avenue.

OTHER RECOMMENDED LODGINGS AND RESTAURANTS

Detroit

Omni Detroit Hotel River Place, 1000 River Place; (313) 259–9500. Recently refurbished and reopened; one of the few riverfront hotels with views of Windsor, Canada, and Belle Isle Park.

New Parthenon Restaurant, 547 Monroe Street; (313) 961–5111. This restaurant serves authentic Greek fare. You'll find all the well-known favorites, including the district's famous flaming *Saganaki "Opa!"* cheese appetizer.

Duet's, 3663 Woodward Street; (313) 831–3838. It's an upscale and innovative restaurant. Expensive.

Ja-Da, A Barbecue Grille, 546 East Larned Street; (313) 965–1700. The place for upscale (and expensive) soul food and live jazz entertainment.

Dearborn

The Dearborn Inn, 20301 Oakwood Boulevard; (313) 271–2700. This Marriott was originally built as a hotel for those arriving at Henry Ford's airport. Ford planned to re-create a community of famous homes for his guests, but got only as far as erecting five. Prices for standard rooms begin at $79, depending on the season. Suites, including the colonial homes, range from $200 to $275, but there are often weekend rates and honeymoon and special occasion packages. There are also two restaurants, one for fine dining and another with a pub atmosphere.

The Ritz Carlton, 300 Town Center Drive, Fairlane Plaza; (313) 441–2000 or (800) 241–3333. This pink luxury hotel lives up to its reputation. Weekend rates and a variety of special packages bring rates down as low as $135.

The Dearborn Bed & Breakfast, 22331 Morley Street; (313) 563–2200. Offers four guest rooms with private baths and continental breakfast.

Birmingham

Big Rock Chop & Brew House, 245 South Eton; (248) 647–7774. Located in the historic Birmingham train station. Like the area, it's upscale and eclectic, featuring handcrafted beers and dining on the terrace. There's also a martini and cigar bar upstairs. Moderate to expensive.

FOR MORE INFORMATION

Detroit Metro Convention and Visitors Bureau, 211 West Fort Street, Detroit, Michigan 48226; (800) DETROIT.

Lake Michigan's Shore

STOPS ALONG THE CIRCLE TOUR

2 NIGHTS

Dunes • Tulips • Maritime mystique

Even if you could spend your entire vacation strolling beaches, you'd leave miles of sand untouched. And you don't have to travel to the Caribbean to try—it's only a five-hour drive to the start of Lake Michigan's beautiful beaches and quaint villages, a great destination to get away from it all. A weekend visit will only whet your appetite for a full-fledged vacation.

The only trouble with planning a getaway along western Michigan's "Circle Tour" following the Great Lake's coastline is there are just too many choices. The state boasts outrageous statistics to prove it. It has 3,200 miles of shore—more than any other state except Alaska—and it ranks at the top of the lighthouse category too, with 115. Some 950,000 registered recreational boats ply the waters encircling the mitten of Michigan, further attesting to its popularity as a waterfront haven.

DAY 1

Morning

Plan a long weekend, leaving first thing Friday morning to allow time to explore some of the region and take a few leisurely detours off the beaten path.

The 280-mile trip begins on I–90 to I–80/I–90 (the Ohio Turnpike). After about three hours, take a break from turnpike travel. Midway across Indiana, take the Howe exit and travel south on State Route 9 to U.S. 20.

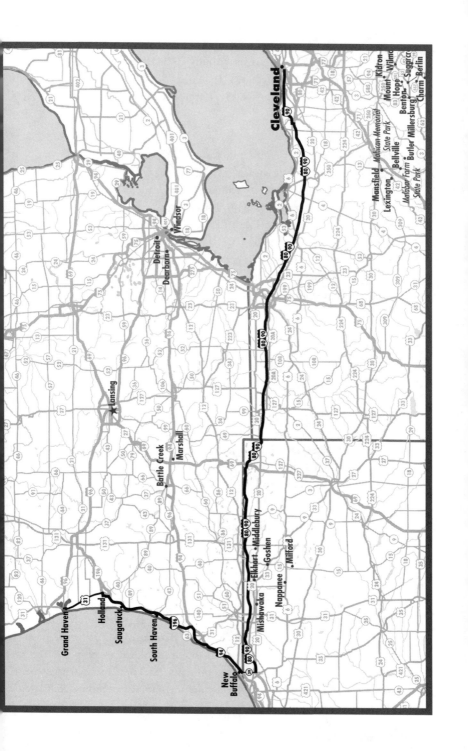

LUNCH: Stop at **Das Dutchman Essenhaus** (240 U.S. 20; 800–455–9471) in the heart of Indiana's Amish settlements. Touted as the largest Amish restaurant in northern Indiana, it features inexpensive yet hearty home-cooked meals.

Afternoon

Return to the highway and continue across Indiana, entering Michigan near New Buffalo, one of eight little towns in "Harbor Country" that all share a common thread of the Red Arrow Highway running through them. Any is a good stop for antiques, boutique and gallery hopping, or dining.

Exit the toll road onto I–94 east (but you will be heading north) to exit 1. At the end of the ramp, turn left onto La Porte Road. Drive 1½ miles into **New Buffalo** to the beach. Here you'll get your first glimpse of sand dunes. They are an integral part of the landscape along this scenic shoreline stretching to the Straits of Mackinac. Even on less than perfect beach days, locals and visitors alike take time to climb the narrow, hilly sand trails through the brush and grass for spectacular views. Remember to leave the tall grasses amid the dunes undisturbed; they help protect the sand from wind erosion.

After discovering small dunes in New Buffalo you'll be eager to explore the nearby **Warren Dunes State Park** (12032 Red Arrow Highway, Sawyer; 616–426–4013), with dunes 240 feet high.

Consider stretching your legs by visiting the **Bicycle Museum** (One Oak Street, Three Oaks; 616–756–3361). You can rent a bike and traverse one of eighteen "Backroads Bikeways" trails or just enjoy the exhibition, beginning with an 1860s wooden "boneshaker."

Go south on Elm Street to U.S. 12. Turn right and drive the 7 miles back to New Buffalo.

DINNER: Restaurants in this area combine the quality you'd expect in the city with the ambience of friendly small towns. One such place is **Brewster's Deli & Cafe** (11 West Merchant Street; 616–469–3005), a tiny Italian bistro brimming with authenticity. During warm seasons, you can dine alfresco on the patio. Wood-fired pizzas and pastas are specialties, moderately priced.

LODGING: Head west on Merchant Street one block. Turn left on North Barton for a step back in time, but not too far, at the **Bauhaus on Barton** (33 North Barton Street; 616–469–6419). This B&B is a cruise down memory lane to the 1950s, with its retro furnishings from the post-war era. There's an extensive memorabilia collection neatly arranged throughout the pink stucco structure, located a short walk from downtown shops, eateries, and lake views.

Each of the four guest rooms is named for a TV program of the day and has its own selection of '50s magazines, blond American Modern furniture, and a chenille bedspread, of course. Prices range from $95 for the "I Love Lucy" to "The Millionaire Suite" for $135. A two-bedroom suite is $200. Innkeeper Roger Harvey gave up the Chicago-style rat race to paint and to run his B&B. Many of his paintings decorate the walls.

DAY 2

Morning

BREAKFAST: Although breakfast is served at the B&B, you'll want to stroll the shops, stopping around the corner for a morning cappuccino or something more substantial at **Cafe at Michigan Thyme** (107 North Whittaker Street; 616–469–6604). It's an especially good choice for the health conscious and vegetarians and offers breakfast specialties like stuffed French Toast. Breakfasts average $4.00.

After checking out of the Bauhaus, stop at **Warren Woods Natural Area** (12032 Red Arrow Highway, Sawyer; 616–426–4013) for a quiet hike. To reach the area from the Red Arrow Highway going north, turn right onto Sawyer Road, then right on Three Oaks Road. Continue 3 miles to Elm Valley Road, turning right. The park entrance is 1 mile ahead on the right.

Continue 40 miles north along scenic highway U.S. 31 toward **South Haven,** a favorite coastal town and a great spot for learning more about Michigan's maritime tradition. South Haven's convenient location makes it perfect for dropping anchor, whether or not you're traveling by boat. Many B&Bs and a waterfront hotel dot the area and it's well situated for day-tripping to nearby parks and ports, but its main appeal is in its "walkability." Once you park your car, public beaches and lighthouses, parks, restaurants, and quaint shops are all within walking distance. Restaurants offer casual dining throughout South Haven and as in most of these waterfront towns, cater to tourists by providing many options.

A stop at the **Michigan Maritime Museum** (260 Dyckman Avenue; 800–747–3810), located along South Haven's Black River, will teach you more about the towns, history, and activities centered here. The historical picture begins with prehistory, predating European contact, before visitors look at the birch bark Ojibwa canoe replica used for rice harvesting. The timeline continues through commercial fishing and transportation to the extensive shipbuilding industry along the Great Lakes. Interesting historic ship models and memorabilia provide details.

One-day workshops and classes of longer duration are offered at the Padnos Boat Shed, another of the museum buildings, if you'd like to learn maritime skills

Dutch artifacts, like those found in this Dutch fishing cottage, are numerous and delightful at the Holland Museum in Holland, Michigan.

like wooden boat building, sailmaking, canoeing, rowing, and kayaking. Even if you don't sign up for a class, you can practice your knot hitches at the kiosk in the center of the exhibit space, visit the gift shop, and stroll the boardwalk. Open Tuesday through Saturday, 10:00 A.M. to 5:00 P.M., Sunday noon to 5:00 P.M. Admission is $2.50 for adults, $1.50 for seniors and children ages five to twelve.

LUNCH: After the museum, park downtown and have lunch at **Clementine's Saloon** (500 Phoenix Street; 616–637–4755). This local favorite has moderate prices and a varied selection—entrees as well as many sandwiches, salads, and appetizers.

Afternoon

The trailhead for **Kal-Haven Trail State Park** (23960 Ruggles Road, South Haven; 616–637–4984), one of Michigan's linear state parks, is also located downtown. The multiuse park follows an old railroad bed through covered bridges, past lakes and great scenery for 33 miles into Kalamazoo. Those with less enthusiastic goals can take the **Harbor Walk,** decorated with historic markers, stretching between the North and South Piers and the lighthouse.

After time outdoors, check into your lodging, **The Carriage House Inn** (233 Dyckman Avenue and 118 Woodman; 616–639–1776). One location overlooks Stanley Johnson Park; the other is above the marina on the Black River. Choose among accommodations at either location (twenty rooms) for a luxurious stay. Only one wall remains of the former's century-old structure; the rest is only a few years old, so the decor and style could be considered new-Victorian. Fireplaces are scattered among the common areas and guest rooms; complimentary home-baked goodies, afternoon hors d'oeuvres, and fresh popcorn are part of the hospitality, so plan to arrive by late afternoon. Rates, including breakfast, range from $95 to $180.

DINNER: For great views try the **White Rose Dinner Cruise** (815 East Wells Street, South Haven; 888–828–7673). Two-hour dinner cruises are $35 and depart at 5:00 P.M. Sunset cruises are $15.

Entertainment is generally of an outdoors variety, but first-run flicks at the local theater are a bargain at $3.50 per ticket.

LODGING: Carriage House Inn.

DAY 3

Morning

BREAKFAST: Breakfast is scrumptious at the inn. Lavish main courses follow freshly baked fruit scones and muffins. It is served in the screened sunroom, with a cozy wood-burning fireplace stoked during cool months, or in the airy dining room, overlooking the river.

It's a short drive up U.S. 31 to downtown **Saugatuck,** located on the Kalamazoo River, where more shops, restaurants, and about thirty galleries await. Another fifteen minutes north on U.S. 31 and you'll be in **Holland,** where tulips by the thousands celebrate the city's Dutch heritage during the annual Tulip Time Festival (800–822–2770) each May. Even if you don't visit when the tulips are in full bloom, do stop at **Holland Museum** (31 West Tenth Street; 888–200–9123) to experience the town's fascinating link to the Netherlands. An extensive collection—artifacts from the World's Fair of 1939, dolls, Delft pieces, and even a room depicting a Dutch fisherman's dwelling—blends with the local story.

Begin your five-hour return trip by going south on U.S. 31 from Holland and then east on M–89 past Saugatuck.

LUNCH: Stop for lunch at **Crane's Pie Pantry Restaurant, Bakeries and Cider Mill** (6054 124th Avenue; 616–561–5545). It will be on your right before you reach Fennville. Don't leave without cider and pie for dessert or one for the road.

Continue back to Ohio via M–89 east to U.S. 131 south. In Kalamazoo, take I–94 east 36 miles to I–69. Follow I–69 south to the Indiana turnpike and continue east to Ohio.

THERE'S MORE

Saugatuck Dunes State Park, 2215 Ottawa Beach Road, Holland; (616) 399–9390. More outdoor options; check into dune buggy rides.

Saugatuck Dune Rides, 6495 Washington Road, Saugatuck; (616) 857–2253. Jeep-like vehicles holding about twenty people travel through the woods, through the sand dunes and onto Lake Michigan's shore, stopping for photo opportunities of wildlife. This isn't a carnival ride, but a fun and scenic attraction. Rates are $10.00 for adults, $6.50 for children ten and under. Hours are Monday through Saturday from 10:00 A.M. to 7:30 P.M., Sunday noon to 7:30 P.M.

OTHER RECOMMENDED RESTAURANTS AND LODGINGS

New Buffalo

The New Buffalo All Suites Inn, 231 East Buffalo Street; (800) 469–7668. Recently constructed by gutting an apartment building six blocks from the beach. Includes suites with kitchen facilities, entertainment centers, whirlpool tubs, and/or fireplaces. Grills, decks, and a hot tub are among the outdoor amenities. One handicapped-accessible suite has a washer/dryer. Rates for the six units range from $95 to $185. They are also available by the week, from $570 to $1120.

Saugatuck

The Wickwood Inn, 510 Butler Street; (616) 857–1465. Owned by Julee Rosso, co-author of *The Silver Palate Cookbook.* If you know of her cooking expertise, then your expectations will be met by the delectable array of cocktail hour appetizers and breakfast buffets. The inn is chock-full of antiques with both English pub and Laura Ashley/Ralph Lauren–style furnishings. It's a leisurely walk to shops and waterfront dining. Rates: $135–$275, depending on season and room choice. Two-night minimum on weekends.

Sherman's Dairy Bar, 72338 County Road 388; (616) 637–8251. Located a mile from downtown, stop here for world-famous premium ice cream. If you have a huge appetite, order the "Pig's Dinner," a sundae concoction for $7.75. This landmark establishment has been around for more than a century. Open March through October.

Union Pier

The Sandpiper, 16136 Lakeview Avenue; (616) 469–1146. Combines luxurious accommodations and picture postcard views. Breakfast and afternoon snacks overlooking Lake Michigan. Tranquil beach walks, private screened-in balconies, and whirlpools for two make it a perfect romantic getaway or honeymoon stay. Adults-only Georgian-style lake inn; airy and comfortably upscale. Rates: $195–$235.

Miller's Country House, Red Arrow Highway; (616) 469–5950. Locals say you can catch up with Chicago television celebrities who have seasonal homes in the area when you dine here. Dining is moderately expensive and casual, ranging from burgers to the house specialty, New Zealand rack of lamb.

Grand Haven

The 1873 Khardomah Lodge, 1365 Lake Avenue; (616) 842–2990. Guests bring their own food, cook in the community kitchen, and do their own dishes, sans a dishwasher. This historical landmark, located within the wooded dunes overlooking Lake Michigan, offers sixteen guest rooms that share five baths in a cottage atmosphere typical of early days. It's popular for retreats and reunions. Rates are $49.50 to $55.00 based on double occupancy, depending on season. A new two-bedroom unit with outdoor hot tub and private bath runs $125 to $145.

FOR MORE INFORMATION

West Michigan Tourist Association, 1253 Front Avenue Northwest, Grand Rapids, Michigan 49504; (800) 442–2084.

South Haven–Van Buren County Lakeshore Convention and Visitors Bureau, 415 Phoenix Street, South Haven, Michigan 49090; (800) 764–2836.

Saugatuck/Douglas Convention and Visitors Bureau, P.O. Box 28, Saugatuck, Michigan 49453; (616) 857–1701.

Holland Area Convention and Visitors Bureau, 76 East Eighth Street, Holland, Michigan 49423; (800) 506–1299.

Battle Creek and Marshall, Michigan

A TOWN THAT CEREAL BUILT AND MORE HISTORIC GEMS

2 NIGHTS

Landmark districts • Fancy architecture
The cereal capital

Crunch a few numbers and you'll understand how Marshall, Michigan, with a population of only 8,000, can fill your weekend if you're a history buff. It's not high on designer boutiques, but you'll be in heaven if you like to browse museums, hunt down antiques, and enjoy some local fare. The charming little community centers around its National Historic Landmark District, the largest in the United States in the small urban category. It's won other accolades as well for the distinction of having more than 850 nineteenth-century structures along its streets. Trees are plentiful here too; armed with a self-guided tree tour pamphlet, you can count off thirty distinctive varieties in Marshall.

Add a stay in a cozy 1836 stagecoach stop and some delightful meals and you have the makings of a pleasant adult getaway, but Marshall is family friendly. If you've brought the troops, simply add a few varied attractions in Battle Creek (only 15 miles away) and everyone in the group will have something to rave about. The Marshall Chamber of Commerce markets its highlights with the ones in Battle Creek, so they are very accommodating to families looking for a little of both worlds.

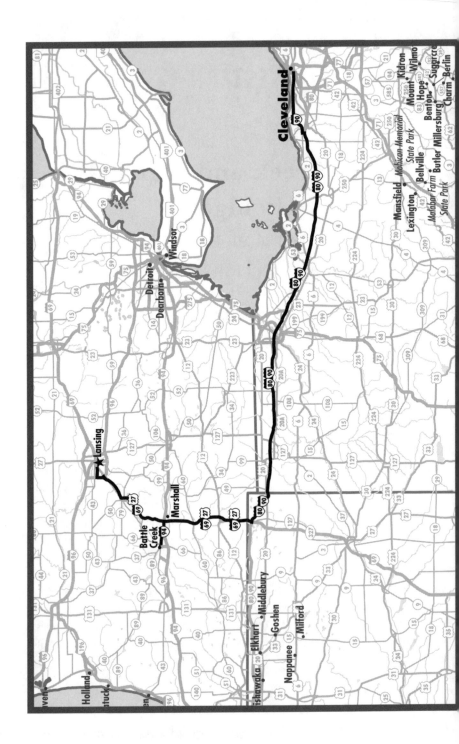

DAY 1

Afternoon

It's about 220 miles to **Marshall** from Cleveland, but an easy three-and-a-half-hour drive. Just follow the Ohio Turnpike west into Indiana and then I–69 north into Michigan and you're there.

Leave by noon to arrive in time for afternoon tea and refreshments. Take exit 36 off I–69 and drive east on West Michigan Avenue 1.3 miles to the **National House Inn** (102 South Parkview Street; 616–781–7374). The staff serves homemade goodies about 3:00 P.M.

After a snack, you'll have some time to explore the **Honolulu House Museum,** practically across the street from the inn at 107 North Kalamazoo Avenue; (616–781–5163). Built in 1860 as a private residence for Judge Abner Pratt after returning from his term as U.S. Consulate to the Sandwich (Hawaiian) Islands, it is patterned after the island architecture he left behind. Bright colors, Polynesian murals, and period furnishings fill the house. It serves as the home of the Marshall Historical Society with continuing renovations. Hours are daily noon to 5:00 P.M. from May to September, noon to 5:00 P.M. Thursday through Sunday in October. Special seasonal exhibits are displayed. Admission is $3.00.

DINNER: Dinner is at another landmark, **Schuler's Restaurant** (115 South Eagle Street, Marshall; 616–781–0600). There are too many signature items to mention, from the Schuler salad to the prime rib, but perhaps the most unique are the Austrian specialties, like Wiener schnitzel ($17.95) and homemade apple strudel ($4.50).

After dining, walk around downtown for a flavor of the historical district, stopping at the **Brooks Memorial Fountain,** where a light show beams nearly a hundred colors spring through fall. Patterned after Marie Antoinette's *The Temple of Love* fountain in Versailles, the white pillars spew water 30 feet high.

LODGING: The National House Inn is just across the street. Part of the sixteen-room inn's charm is its well-worn and comfortable feeling. There's popcorn for popping over the open hearth in the entryway and rooms are decorated with nineteenth-century antiques commemorating earlier times. Rates at the National House range from $105 for a standard queen to $145 for the Ketchum Suite.

DAY 2

Morning

BREAKFAST: Served buffet style, breakfast is a friendly, cheerful time at the inn. Guests help themselves to a full breakfast—including delicious morning cream tea cake still warm from the oven—and join others at small tables.

Begin your day by visiting a few more of Marshall's many small museums. Several are open by appointment only, so call ahead to arrange for guided tours. One of the town's popular house museums is the **Governor's Mansion** (612 South Marshall Avenue; 616–781–5163). It was built in 1839 in hopes of Marshall becoming the state capital, but it lost by one vote. Open by appointment only; donations are appreciated.

The Postal Museum (202 East Michigan Avenue; 616–781–2859) is, aptly enough, in the post office. Located in the basement, this small museum displays old-time artifacts. A horse-drawn mail buggy and an 1890s storefront post office are exhibited, along with old uniforms and mailboxes. By appointment only; free.

Battle Creek is but a fifteen-minute drive west on I–94. Drive over for the afternoon, but as you leave Marshall, notice the many architectural styles. Once in Battle Creek, it doesn't take long to realize the truth in its moniker, "Cereal Capital of the World." Where Kellogg's name isn't, Post's is.

The Kellogg brothers accidentally invented corn flakes in the mid-1800s at their Seventh Day Adventist hospital and health spa. Later, W. K. Kellogg would continue growing the cereal business while Dr. John Harvey Kellogg stayed with the clinic, inventing products for use in the hospital. The cereal magnate left behind one of the world's largest philanthropic organizations and endowed much of the community. C. W. Post came to town as a patient at the Battle Creek Sanitarium.

LUNCH: Stop for lunch at **Clara's on the River** (44 McCamly Street North; 616–963–0966). The sixteen-page menu is chock-full of American favorites— sandwiches and pizza—with a bit of Mexican and Asian, moderately priced.

Afternoon

Clara's is located right on the city's Linear Park, which has more than 17 miles of paved multiuse trails linking other parks, woodland, and historical and cultural sites along the rivers. Walk east from the restaurant to the Underground Railroad Sculpture. Look for it next to the Kellogg House between Capital Avenue and

Cereal City, USA offers a factory style tour filled with brightly colored interactive exhibits.

Division Street. It pays tribute to the efforts of Harriet Tubman and other abolitionists. Farther down Michigan Avenue you'll find a monument to Sojourner Truth. She lived part of her life in Battle Creek and died here in 1852. She is buried in historic Oak Hill Cemetery on South Street.

A few blocks away is **Full Blast** (35 Hamblin Avenue; 616–966–3667). It's a 185,000-square-foot family entertainment and recreational center featuring an indoor and outdoor waterpark with water playground, a three-story indoor playground, climbing wall, full-service health club, laser tag, video arcade, teen night club, sports forum (indoor running track, three full-size basketball courts), and indoor and outdoor food courts. Hours vary depending on season and are extended during school breaks. Admission to the facility is $3.00, another $2.00 for wintertime swimming and $3.00 when all water activities are open from Memorial Day to Labor Day. There are extra charges for specific events ($1.00 per climb on the climbing wall, $7.00 for two laser tag plays).

Next stop is **Cereal City, USA** (171 West Michigan Avenue; 616–962–6230). Corn flakes never tasted as good as they do at the end of the production line simulation—they're warm. Brightly colored climbing and playing activities, bigger-than-life characters, and memorabilia are fun, especially for preschoolers. Admission is $6.50 for adults, $4.50 for children, and $5.50 for seniors. Hours vary.

More exciting for older children and adults is the new **Dr. J. H. Kellogg Discovery Center** (300 Michigan Avenue; 616–963–4000). John Harvey Kellogg ran the wellness center, called the Battle Creek Sanitarium in those days. He invented numerous remedies and healthful treatments for his patients. Many are among the ones you can try at the interactive center. You may even pick up a tip or two for improving your current-day lifestyle. Visitors can ride the mechanical horse, take a heat and sunbath, or try Dr. Kellogg's posture chair. Open Memorial Day through Labor Day, Sunday through Friday 10:00 A.M. to 5:00 P.M., and Saturday 1:30 to 6:30 P.M., with slightly shorter hours other seasons. Donation is $2.00 per person, $5.00 per family.

Head back to Marshall, and visit a few of the downtown shops before dinner. Local artists run a cooperative guild, **Gallery 127** (127 West Michigan Avenue; 616–781–1902). They sell fine art and high-quality craft items. Antique and collectible shops dot the district.

DINNER: Malia's Italian Bistro, 130 West Michigan Avenue; (616) 781–2171. Choose an Italian specialty from the menu or create your own by selecting a sauce, meat or seafood, and your favorite pasta. It's cooked to order so don't be afraid to customize, but save room for dessert. Dinners start around $10; rock shrimp with bay scallops in a lemon dill sauce over linguine is $19.95. Weather permitting, walk from the inn to burn off a few calories.

LODGING: National House Inn. Check at the inn or at Malia's for cooking classes and other planned events.

DAY 3

Morning

BREAKFAST: For a little local flavor, try the **Dug Out Restaurant** (107 West Michigan Avenue, Marshall; 616–781–8373). It's a family spot with inexpensive prices. The country omelette topped with sausage gravy ($5.59) will keep you full until you get back home.

Pick up a "Walking Tour of Marshall" brochure at the inn or the Chamber of Commerce (424 East Michigan Avenue) and set out to explore the historic architecture in this quaint town. Many of the downtown merchants will provide maps also. Arrange to visit another museum before leaving town. The **American Museum of Magic** (107 East Michigan Avenue; 616–781–7674) is a unique choice. Set within a Victorian renovation, the collection of magic-related memorabilia and apparatus is said to be the largest publicly displayed and privately owned collection in the world. Guided tours are given May 25 to September 2, Saturday at noon, 2:00, and 4:00 P.M. and Sunday at 1:00 and 3:00 P.M. Admission is $4.00 for adults, $2.00 for children through age twelve. Not suitable for children under eight.

Drive west on Michigan Avenue to I–69. Take I–69 south to the Ohio Turnpike and continue east to Cleveland. The return trip will take three and a half hours.

THERE'S MORE

Binder Park Zoo, 7400 Division Street, Battle Creek; (616) 979–1351. The newest addition, Wild Africa, takes visitors to an eighteen-acre African savannah where eighty animals roam free. Passengers board a tram that takes them to an authentic-feeling African Village. Feed a giraffe or ride a camel if you wish. Open Monday through Friday 9:00 A.M. to 5:00 P.M., Saturday 9:00 A.M. to 6:00 P.M., and Sunday 10:00 A.M. to 6:00 P.M. Admission is $7.95 for adults, $6.95 for seniors, and $5.95 for children three to twelve.

Gilmore Classic Car Club of America Museums, M–34 at Hickory Road, Hickory Corners; (616) 671–5089. Learn the history of American autos by touring the eight red exhibit barns containing about 140 cars dating from an 1899 steam-driven locomobile to a 1992 Cadillac Seville. Admission is $6.00 for adults, $5.00 for seniors and AAA members, $3.00 for children seven to fifteen. Open from May to October, 10:00 A.M. to 5:00 P.M. daily.

Wolverine Fire Company Museum, 13280 Verona Road, Battle Creek; (616) 968–2998. Privately owned memorabilia displayed in a re-created Romanesque Revival–style firehouse. Open 1:00 to 5:00 P.M. the first Sunday of each month from May through October, other times by appointment.

Capitol Hill School Museum, East Washington Street, Marshall; (616) 781–8544. This two-room schoolhouse, built in 1860, served the community for one hundred years. One room replicates a nineteenth-century school, the other is filled with antique toys. Open by appointment.

G.A.R. Hall, East Michigan and Exchange Street, Marshall; (616) 781–5162. This museum shouldn't be missed by history buffs interested in artifacts from the Civil War, Spanish-American War, and World Wars I and II. There is also a substantial collection reflecting local history. Open noon to 4:00 P.M. Saturday from May through September, by appointment other days.

SPECIAL EVENTS

July. Battle Creek Hot Air Balloon Championship, W. K. Kellogg Airport, Battle Creek. (616) 962–0592.

July. Welcome to My Garden Tour, Marshall. Self-paced tour of private and public gardens. (800) 877–5163.

September. Annual Home Tour, Marshall. Museums and private homes are open for touring, encampments, musical entertainment and antique shows. Tickets are $15. (800) 877–5163.

November–January. Zoolights Festival, Binder Park Zoo, Battle Creek. (616) 979–1351.

November. Annual Christmas Parade, downtown Marshall. (800) 877–5163.

OTHER RECOMMENDED RESTAURANTS AND LODGINGS

Marshall

Kate's Diner, 129 West Michigan Avenue; (616) 781–9577. Open for breakfast and lunch. Decorated with 45-rpm records and Elvis pictures for a '50s diner appeal. Moderate.

Denny's Diner, 15250 Old U.S. 27 North, off exit 110 on I–94. Old-fashioned diner featuring shakes and burgers of Denny's chain.

Cornwell's Turkeyville U.S.A. and Dinner Theatre, 18935 15½ Mile Road; (800) 228–4315. If you like turkey, you'll like Turkeyville. They serve turkey sandwiches, hot plates, dinners, and stir-fry. Homemade pies and ice cream concoctions from the Ice Cream Parlour. County fair atmosphere with reasonable prices. Call for theatrical schedule and pricing.

Rose Hill Inn, 1110 Verona Road; (616) 789–1992. This charming 1860 Italianate mansion was once the home of William Boyce, the founder of the Boy Scouts of America. It offers six guest rooms with private baths for $125 per night. Sunday night stays are $99. Antiques, floral carpeting, screened porches, a swimming pool along with great views overlooking Marshall and gourmet breakfasts. The grounds surrounding the home were previously owned by author James Fenimore Cooper.

Amerihost, 204 Winston; (616) 789–7890. Rates at this chain range from $76 for a standard room to $81 for a whirlpool suite. Swimming pool and continental breakfast.

Battle Creek

Pierre Lamorghinistein's Deli and Bakery, 80 West Michigan Avenue, Suite D; (616) 692–8599. Overstuffed deli sandwiches (110 to choose from), homemade breads and desserts. Sandwich fare ranges from $3.50 to $7.50.

McCamly Plaza Hotel, 50 Capital Avenue Southwest; (800) 777–5292. Full-service high-end hotel. Regular weekend rates begin at $129 for two, but there are often specials beginning at $99, including a full breakfast buffet served in the hotel's dining room.

FOR MORE INFORMATION

Battle Creek and Calhoun County Convention and Visitors Bureau, 34 West Jackson Street, Battle Creek, Michigan, 49017; (800) 397–2240.

Marshall Area Chamber of Commerce, 109 East Michigan Avenue, Marshall, Michigan, 49068; (800) 877–5163; www.marshall.org.

AIRBORNE
ESCAPES

AIRBORNE

Nashville

MUSIC CITY, U.S.A.

2 NIGHTS

Country two-stepping • Antebellum Trail
Southern hospitality

Nashville, Tennessee, may seem too far away for a weekend getaway, but it isn't if you hop one of the frequent, inexpensive, and quick nonstop flights. At around $100 round-trip, Southwest Airlines, for example, offers the Cleveland/Nashville connection several times each day. The flight takes a little over an hour to bring you face to face with the lively sounds of country music, southern hospitality, and a true change of scenery.

It's easy enough to get around via public transportation, a touring trolley, on foot, and flagging a few taxis, but travelers who opt for a weekend car rental will enjoy greater flexibility. Including a Gray Line tour with some of the suggested stops lets you explore the outlying region without any driving hassles, if you prefer. Either way, embellish your Nashville experience with visits to plantations, mansions, and local events.

Whether you have a car or not, follow the downtown-based itinerary to make the most of your time, choosing appropriate activities that fit your mobility. If this is your first time visiting Music City, U.S.A., you'll soon discover Nashville's musical energy. Repeat visitors can easily add a few of the cultural and sporting events to add to the excitement.

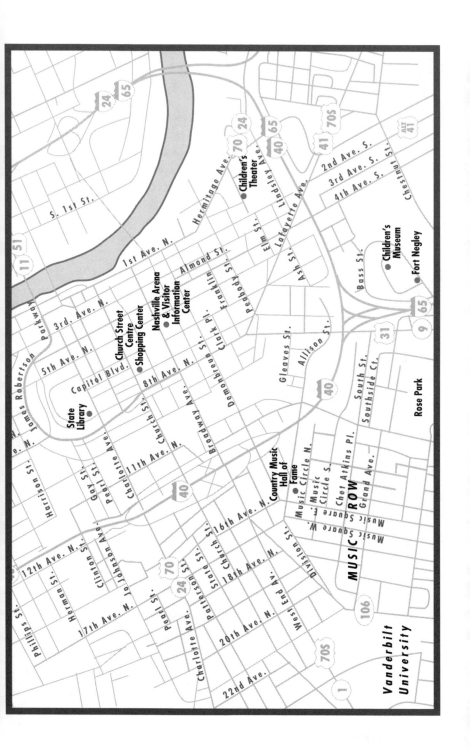

AIRBORNE

DAY 1

Morning

Take a midmorning flight so you'll arrive in **Nashville** before lunch. Either pick up your rental vehicle at the airport or travel downtown to your hotel by airport shuttle, costing $15 round-trip. Check into the **Renaissance Nashville Hotel** (611 Commerce Street; 615–255–8400 or 800–HOTELS–1). It's conveniently located in the midst of downtown activities and brimming with a full range of amenities. Reduced weekend rate specials begin at $99.

Drop off your luggage, don comfortable walking shoes, and head to the Visitors' Center around the corner in the Gaylord Entertainment Center at Fifth and Broadway. Pick up discount coupons and a CityWalk guide. If you prefer, have materials sent to you before you depart by calling (800) 657–6910. Refer to *Nashville Scene,* a free weekly publication, to find out who's performing on the various stages around town. The concierge and ticketing service at the Convention and Visitors Bureau provide discounted prices on most tickets.

As soon as you venture out of the hotel, you'll notice a wide teal blue City-Walk strip painted on the sidewalk. If you merely toe the line, so to speak, you'll stroll past fifteen of the historical sights throughout the downtown "District" and get in a 2-mile walk, as you discover many of the shops for which Nashville is famous. At least keep the map handy to identify points of interest while discovering this popular area along Broadway from Fifth Avenue to the Cumberland River and encompassing such streets as Printers Alley, Commerce, Church, and Union Streets.

LUNCH: Stop at a local favorite, **Jack's Bar-B-Que** (416 Broadway; 615–254–1020). It's inexpensive and very casual—paper plates and self-serve. Standard and jumbo sandwiches are piled high with Tennessee pork, Texas brisket, smoked turkey, sausage, or chicken. Of course, there are ribs. Customers add their own hot or mild sauce to each order. It's in the midst of the District.

Afternoon

Continue to explore the District. Make sure you stop at the **Ryman Auditorium** (116 Fifth Avenue North; 615–889–3060), the original home of the Grand Ole Opry and the Union Gospel Tabernacle before that. With its exceptional acoustics, it is still a showplace attracting live performances and is a good choice for an evening's entertainment. Several concerts and theatrical productions occur throughout the year; guided tours are offered.

Another must-see is **Hatch Show Print** (316 Broadway; 615–256–2805). You may have noticed this deco art form decorating the airport corridors when you arrived. You can see how these prints, which have advertised Grand Ole Opry stars, circuses, and vaudeville acts since 1879, are created, and purchase them as well.

Country music wafting along Broadway may sound alluring, but try to resist until later by hopping aboard a green and red Nashville Trolley. The one-hour tours are run by Gray Line, corner of Second and Broadway (615–248–4437). The trolley stops at the Country Music Hall of Fame and drives past the numerous studios along Music Row to put you in the mood. Fares are $10.00 for adults and $5.00 for children. Passengers can get off the trolley and then catch the next one, if desired.

After the tour, it's time for some free line-dance lessons at the **Wildhorse Saloon** (120 Second Avenue North; 615–902–8200). There's no cover charge before 5:00 P.M., but the lessons continue at 6:00, 7:00, and 9:00 P.M. on Friday and on the hour from 2:00 to 6:00 P.M. on Saturday.

DINNER: After your lesson, walk to **Merchants Restaurant** (Fourth and Broadway; 615–254–1892). It's a casual and relaxed atmosphere and the food is upscale and inventive. Reservations are needed for the upper level, where the only dress code is no T-shirts or jeans, but at street level there are no restrictions.

For the evening's entertainment, take a club crawl along Honky Tonk Highway, the local term for Broadway. Make sure you stop at **Tootsie's Orchid Lounge** (422 Broadway; 615–726–0463). It's where many of the famous Grand Ole Opry stars stopped for some reinforcements before they went out the back door and onto the stage at the Ryman. Talented musicians performing just inside the door crowd the tiny bar.

LODGING: The Renaissance Hotel

DAY 2

Morning

BREAKFAST: Perhaps the whole mood of Nashville's country ambience can be summed up at breakfast at the **Loveless Cafe** (8400 Highway 100; 615–646–1056; www.lovelesscafe.com). It's at least a twenty-minute drive from downtown, available on several tour itineraries if you don't have a car. From the outside, this vintage motel/restaurant looks like a movie set, and reminds visitors of what it was like driving through the south before freeways were built. Once inside, the only addition to the country look is the gallery of photos autographed by the rich and famous who have dined on the country ham and biscuits here.

It's impressive to have the waitress ask if you'd like to start over with a fresh cup of coffee after she's topped off your warm cup several times. Don't look for any lowfat substitutes here: The salty red-eye gravy accompanying breakfast has coffee and lard in it. The scratch biscuits for which this place is so popular are served with homemade preserves, honey, and sorghum. Purchase the cookbook if you'd like recipes for some of the other down-home fare. Food prices range from $10 to $20.

From the everyday, local flavor of the Loveless, head back along State Route 100 to **Cheekwood** (1200 Forrest Park Drive; 615–356–8000) for a look at the opposite lifestyle in Nashville. Here, the Georgian mansion and fifty-five-acre estate of Maxwell House Coffee founders Leslie and Mabel Cheek become one of the focal points of the city's arts and gardens stops. The home recently received revitalization, restoring it to its original grandeur, and it serves as a backdrop for permanent collections of decorative arts and nineteenth- and twentieth-century paintings and sculpture. Galleries are organized by themes like "Body, Mind & Spirit" and "History, Legend & Myth" which are interestingly defined with both art and text.

Looking through the windows will frame a bit of the pastoral surroundings, but strolling the lush grounds is a must. You'll find little brooks, carefully manicured formal gardens, and a great mile-long wooded sculpture path.

Just 2 miles north of Cheekwood is another southern mansion at **Belle Mead Plantation** (5025 Harding Road; 615–356–0501). Take the one-hour tour guided tour of the mansion, which dates back to the 1800s. The 5,400-acre plantation, famous for its Tennessee walking horses and racetrack thoroughbreds, still displays remnants of equine wealth. With fireplaces in each room, pocket windows and doors, and high ceilings, Belle Mead showcases the opulence of the Victorian era; a log cabin, one of the first in Tennessee, and about a dozen other outbuildings reflect on earlier times. Admission is $8.00 for adults, $7.50 for seniors, and $3.00 for children. Open 9:00 A.M. to 5:00 P.M. daily, until 8:30 P.M. on Thursday, Friday, and Saturday.

LUNCH: While you're at the plantation, visit the **Belle Mead Cafe** (615–356–6229). It's run by the Loveless Cafe folks, so you can enjoy more of the same scratch biscuits and homemade preserves, along with more creative luncheon efforts. Prices range from $8.00 to $16.00.

Afternoon

After the plantation outing, tour the **Country Music Hall of Fame and Museum** (4 Music Square East; 615–256–1639 or 800–816–7652) and walk **Music Row.** The Hall of Fame will be moving to its new District location in 2001, but for now the stars are still along Music Row, lined with recording studios. It's necessary to take some time and read about the old-time performers, like Hank Williams, who died in an auto crash on his way to perform one New Year's Eve in Canton, Ohio. There is also memorabilia from Nashville's current stars and an opportunity to tour Studio B next door.

Many of Nashville's most prominent artists have unmarked studios, but locals will often be able to point them out between the mega-size studios owned by all the major recording labels.

After an afternoon of sightseeing, head back to the hotel. A taxi between the hotel and Music Row costs about $4.00. Freshen up before departing for dinner and an evening at the Grand Ole Opry, "the radio show worth watching."

DINNER: Stop for a casual dinner at **Market Street Brewery** (134 Second Avenue North; 615–259–9611). You'll find local microbrews and typical pub food at moderate prices while you await a river taxi that will take you to **Music Valley** and the **Grand Ole Opry House,** 2804 Opryland Drive.

The Grand Ole Opry is the world's longest-running radio show and the most watched, with seating for 4,400 enthusiasts. Even if the Nashville Sound isn't your first choice in music, the performance is a must-see. Because the show runs in thirty-minute broadcast segments, it's easy enough to leave early for a later dinner reservation or another performance. Shows begin at 6:30 and 9:30 P.M. on Saturday, with reserved tickets ranging from $16 to $18. Call (615) 889–3060 for advance reservations, but don't hesitate to check at the last minute for cancellations. The lineup of the concert's performers is listed in the *Tennessean* each Thursday.

If you want to follow up the evening with yet another bout of country music, head over to the Ernest Tubb Midnight Jamboree at the **Texas Troubadour Theatre** (2414 Music Valley Drive; 615–885–0028). It's a free radio broadcast made up of some of the acts that were just on stage at the Grand Ole Opry nearby.

LODGING: The Renaissance Nashville Hotel.

After touring Hermitage, the home of Andrew Jackson, walk the grounds stopping at the memorial garden and monument he built for his wife, Rachel.

DAY 3

Morning

BREAKFAST: Check out of the hotel before leaving for breakfast at **Pancake Pantry** (1796 Twenty-first Avenue South; 615–383–9333). It's a couple miles southwest of the district, adjacent to Vanderbilt University in Hillsboro Village. The neighborhood is a lively mix of shops and some of the best dining options in Nashville. Expect to wait in a long but fast-moving line encircling the pancake house—their extensive list of varieties is that popular. Prices are reasonable ($5.25 for fifteen silver dollar pancakes).

Spend time enjoying the area before leaving for the **Hermitage,** the plantation home of Andrew Jackson. It's north of Nashville at exit 221 of I–40 east, minutes from the airport at 4580 Rachel Lane, Hermitage; (615) 889–2941. During the introductory video at the visitors' center, you'll find out how Jackson got the name "Old Hickory" before glancing over memorabilia displays there and following the path to the mansion and outbuildings.

During the mansion tour, visitors are provided audio wands that explain artifacts in each of the rooms. Unfortunately, views are restricted from the glass-covered doorways of each room. A separate kitchen is connected to the main house by a walkway; the family's springhouse, smokehouse, and the log cabin in which the Jacksons first lived after coming to Tennessee are also on the grounds. Perhaps the most poignant area is the garden where Jackson built a monument for his wife, Rachel, when she died right before his inauguration. His tomb is also here. Admission is $9.50 for adults, $8.00 for seniors, and $4.50 for children. On January 8, in commemoration of the Battle of New Orleans, admission is free, and prices are reduced on March 15, Andrew Jackson's birthday.

LUNCH: Drive west on I–40 to the Nashville International Airport exit, turn right to find **Darfon's** (2810 Elm Hill Pike; 615–889–3032). It's a local eatery and a good stop for lunch before heading home. If you haven't tried a "Hot Brown Sandwich," a southern favorite of ham and turkey covered with a melted cheese sauce and served slightly browned with tomato, bacon, and hollandaise, it's available here along with lighter fare at reasonable prices.

Turn left and head in the opposite direction to the airport and your departure.

THERE'S MORE

Belmont Mansion, 1900 Belmont Boulevard; (615) 460–5459. This 1850s mansion was the summer home of Adelicia Acklen, one of the wealthiest women in America. Tours are guided, detailed, and show off fifteen rooms of original furnishings. Admission is $6.00 for adults, $2.00 for children ages six to twelve. Open June through August, Monday through Saturday, 10:00 A.M. to 4:00 P.M., Sunday 2:00 to 5:00 P.M.; September through May, Tuesday through Saturday, 10:00 A.M. to 4:00 P.M.

Carl Van Vechten Art Gallery at Fisk University, Jackson Street and D. B. Todd Boulevard; (615) 329–8720. This museum houses the Alfred Stieglitz Collection of Modern Art—a gift from Georgia O'Keeffe—and an extensive collection of African-American works. Admission is free but donations are appreciated. Open Tuesday to Friday 10:00 A.M. to 5:00 P.M., Saturday and Sunday 1:00 to 5:00 P.M.

Texas Troubadour Theatre, 2414 Music Valley Drive; (615) 885–0028. Located in the midst of Grand Ole Opry sights. *A Closer Walk with Patsy Cline* runs continuously from April through December. Tickets are $18.00 for adults, $15.00 for seniors, and $5.00 for children. The Nashville Cowboy Church begins at 10:00 A.M. each Sunday. It's free.

The Tennessee Antebellum Trail begins at the Belle Meade Plantation and includes tours of eight other sites, but there are more than fifty-five historic stops along the 90-mile self-guided loop drive. Maps are available at each of the stops and at the Visitors' Center at the Gaylord Entertainment Center. Discount trail tickets are available by calling (800) 381–1865.

The Tennessee State Museum, Fifth Avenue between Deaderick and Union Streets, (615) 741–2692. This museum puts the Nashville you're enjoying in a historical perspective, beginning with prehistory and adding segments of Native American history, the settling of Nashville by French fur traders, the Civil War, and life in the 1900s. Traveling exhibits are also displayed. Open Tuesday through Saturday from 10:00 A.M. to 5:00 P.M., and on Sunday from 1:00 to 5:00 P.M. Admission is free for permanent exhibits but there is a charge for traveling exhibits.

The Tennessee Performing Arts Center, commonly referred to as TPAC, 505 Deaderick Street; (615) 782–4000. Special performances and concerts, including the Broadway series, take place here. Contact TicketMaster at (615) 255–ARTS or obtain information and purchase tickets at the Visitors' Center.

NashTrash Tours, P.O. Box 60324; (615) 226–7300 or (800) 342–2132. When you board this hot pink school bus, be ready for an irreverent tour of Nashville with the Jugg Sisters. Prices are $20 for adults, $18 for seniors, and $15 for children. Tours begin at 11:00 A.M. and 2:00 P.M. on Saturday and Sunday. Reservations are required.

The Parthenon, West End and Twenty-fifth Avenue behind Centennial Park; (615) 862–8431. You'll be surprised to see this exact replica of the Greek Parthenon housing a 42-foot-tall Athena statue. There are rare artworks and traveling exhibits. Admission is $2.50 for adults, $1.25 for children and seniors. Open year-round, Tuesday to Saturday 9:00 A.M. to 4:30 P.M., and on Sunday afternoon from April through September.

Tennessee Fox Trot Carousel, Broadway at Riverfront Park, (615) 259–4747. This carousel is interactive art and history at its best. Artist and Nashville native

Red Grooms's whimsical and colorful characters (thirty-six in all) have roots in Tennessee. Rides are $1.50 per person. Open Monday through Saturday 10:00 A.M. to 9:00 P.M., Sunday noon to 6:00 P.M.

SPECIAL EVENTS

February. Nashville Entertainment Association Extravaganza. Every kind of music is showcased all over town during this three-day event when talented musicians hope to catch the ear of the listening public and recording executives. There may be charges, depending on venue. (615) 327–4308.

April. Nashville River Stages, Riverfront Park. This relatively new event draws some sixty bands performing on five different stages. Call TicketMaster at (615) 255–9600 for advance tickets or purchase at the door.

May–August. Dancin' in the District. Every Thursday from 5:00 to 10:00 P.M., crowds gather downtown to hear the free concerts at Riverfront Park. (615) 256–2073.

October. Southern Festival of Books, War Memorial Plaza. Activities, book signings, readings and discussions by authors from all over the country. Free admission. For details, call the Tennessee Humanities Council, (615) 320–7001.

November–December. Nashville's Country Holidays. Nashville sparkles during the holidays with special packages from various hotels, candlelight tours, and seasonal displays. For information contact the Nashville Convention and Visitors Bureau, (615) 259–4700 or (800) 567–6910.

OTHER RECOMMENDED RESTAURANTS AND LODGINGS

Nashville

Sunset Grill, 2001 Belcourt, Hillsboro Village; (615) 386–FOOD. One of the few restaurants with many heart-healthy suggestions, but you'll be tempted to try the other creative and delectable suggestions. Bistro atmosphere; moderate.

Swett's Restaurant, 900 Eighth Avenue North; (615) 742–0699. Southerners enjoy their "meat 'n' threes," which translates into a meat entree and three side dishes, usually comfort foods. This family-owned establishment is one of the locals' favorites. Open for lunch and dinner from 11:00 A.M. to 8:00 P.M. Inexpensive.

Bound'ry, 911 Twentieth Avenue South; (615) 321–3043. Unique flavors: new southern and continental and an eclectic mix. You can order tapas-style as well as entree-size portions. Pizzas are baked in wood-fired ovens. Moderate to expensive.

The Pineapple Room Restaurant at Cheekwood; (615) 352–4859. Stop here on your way from the Cheekwood mansion for homemade soup and a salad or sandwich amid the botanical atmosphere. There's outdoor seating, weather permitting. Varied menu, moderate prices.

Jimmy Kelly's, 217 Louise Avenue at State Street; (615) 329–4349. This landmark establishment, in a Victorian home, has been a popular steak and seafood restaurant for more than sixty years. Entrees are served with signature corn cakes and other side dishes, making them more reasonable than other steakhouses.

Westin Hermitage, 231 Sixth Avenue North; (615) 244–3121 or (800) WESTIN–1. This historic landmark has all the grandeur of its earlier days. Weekend specials are available, such as a romance package that includes truffles, champagne, breakfast, and late checkout. This is an all suites hotel. Rates: $129 weekends.

Hilton Suites Nashville, 121 Fourth Avenue South; (615) 620–1000 or (800) HILTONS. Nashville's newest hotel in downtown across from Gaylord Entertainment Center. There's a fitness center. Weekend rates include breakfast. Rates: $119 to $169.

Courtyard by Marriott, 170 Fourth Avenue North; (615) 256–0900 or (888) 391–8738. Convenient location in a historic building full of character. Rates: $99 weekends; $119 weekdays.

Downtown hotels are emphasized because of their accessibility for a weekend getaway, but interesting B&B accommodations along the Tennessee Antebellum Trail are listed in the *Antebellum Trail Guide*. Phone (800) 381–1865.

FOR MORE INFORMATION

Nashville Convention and Visitors Bureau, 161 Fourth Avenue North, Nashville, Tennessee 37219; (800) 657–6910.

Nashville Information Center, Gaylord Entertainment Center, Fifth Avenue and Broadway; (615) 259–4747. Walk-in ticket and information center. Open daily.

AIRBORNE

Baltimore

DISCOVERING "CHARM CITY"

2 NIGHTS

Lively nieghborhoods • Crabcakes • Visionaries
Star-spangled pride

Cheap fares—well below $100 round-trip through Southwest Airlines, Continental, and U.S. Airways—and frequent flights make Baltimore a great weekend escape. After an airport shuttle (fifteen minutes, less than $15) to an Inner Harbor lodging, the inexpensive and scenic water taxi service will help you discover the rest of Baltimore.

Baltimore's Inner Harbor rejuvenated the city twenty years ago and continues attracting tourists eager to enjoy the latest entertainment venues, the Ravens PSINet Stadium, Oriole Park at Camden Yards, and delicious Maryland crab. The fun of Baltimore extends beyond the Inner Harbor, but most tourists don't get past the shopping and dining there. If you're one of these types, add a few "charms" to your next getaway and learn why Baltimore is "Charm City."

Must-see spots describe Baltimore's history, while bustling old-fashioned neighborhoods reflect quirks that set Baltimore apart from the rest of the East Coast. Take an architectural walk through Mt. Vernon and Fell's Point, and don't leave without discovering Fort McHenry, even if you're not a history buff. Visit Hampden's "Honville," where girls with high hair and way-out art flourished, and you'll feel like you've stepped back to the '50s.

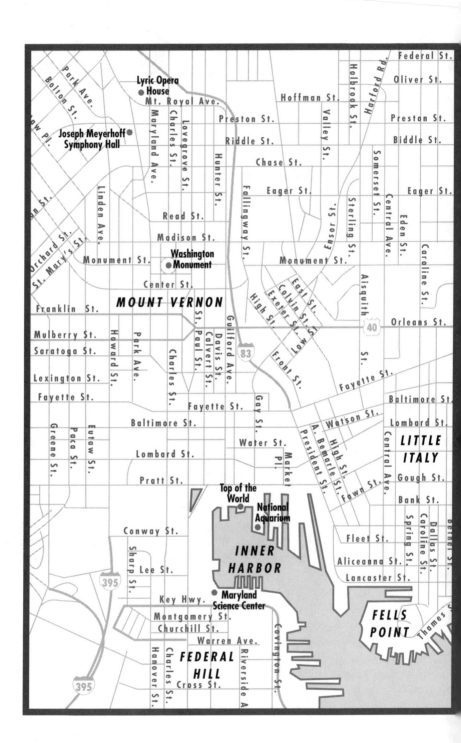

DAY 1

Morning

If your schedule permits, catch a morning flight to arrive by noon for an extra half day of R&R. Even if you can't leave before 5:00 P.M., you'll arrive in time for a wonderful dinner.

Once in **Baltimore,** board the BWI Airport Shuttle ($11 each way) for the **Hyatt Regency Baltimore** on the Inner Harbor (300 Light Street; 410–528–1234), one of several full-service luxury hotels connected to the Inner Harbor by aboveground walkways. It's convenient to the rest of the itinerary, as you will soon discover. Check your luggage and make dinner reservations at Pisces, the rooftop seafood restaurant. In addition to acclaimed food (for landlubbers too), it offers the prized harbor view.

Don comfortable walking shoes for a fifteen-minute hike up Charles Street for lunch and some noteworthy stops in the Victorian Mt. Vernon neighborhood later in the day. On your way to lunch, pick up a free self-guided walking tour at the **Downtown Partnership** (217 North Charles Street; 410–244–1030). Walking itineraries may lead you past the former home of the original "Miss Manners," Emily Post, at 14 East Chase Street or to 215 East Biddle Street, where Wallis Warfield Simpson, the Duchess of Windsor, resided. You'll find background information and directions to the area's well-known homes and attractions.

LUNCH: Stop for lunch at **Louie's Cafe** (518 North Charles Street; 410–230–2998). Students from the Peabody Conservatory of Music a block away perform and wait tables. You can count on some jazz or perhaps classical guitar accompaniment with your lunch, dinner, or Sunday brunch. With a "living room" area, a bookstore downstairs, and chandeliers from the Waldorf Astoria, it's a terrific reuse of vintage space. There's falafel ($5.50) or more sophisticated wraps and sandwiches ($5.25 to $8.95) for lunch.

Afternoon

Mt. Vernon gets its name from the marble Washington Monument in the square. After lunch you should have the energy to climb the 228 steps to the top for a close look at the Washington statue and monument.

You won't find a sign on the door, but the **Mount Vernon Museum of Incandescent Lighting,** next to the Washington Monument at 717 Washington Place, is the neighborhood "highlight." Prearrange your visit by calling Hugh Francis Hicks at (410) 752–8586. At 77, he still practices dentistry at this address.

Shop, dine, and stroll the streets encircling quaint Fells Point in Baltimore.

He will gladly show his display of 8,000 bulbs dating from the 1880s. This free stop isn't handicapped accessible, but well worth a chat with the congenial and knowledgeable curator.

Nearby you'll find the magnificent **Peabody Library** (600 North Charles Street; 410–756–9000). Stop to peruse the interior architecture of the stack room, with elaborate balconies, skylights, and marble. Another must-see is the **Walters Art Gallery** (1 West Centre Street; 410–547–9000 or 410–547–ARTS). The gallery, in Italian Renaissance–style, exhibits one of the finest private collections in the United States, spanning 5,000 years of antiquities and works of art. Admission is $4.00 for adults, $3.00 for seniors, and free to students. Special exhibits may require a fee. Open Tuesday through Sunday from 11:00 A.M. to 5:00 P.M. An $18.5 million revitalization will close a portion of the museum temporarily, but the original Walters building will remain open.

Also nearby, the **Contemporary Museum** (100 West Centre Street; 410–783– 5720) hosts exhibits featuring works of artists with a mission of bringing art to the community.

The Mt. Vernon shops will lure you inside for a closer peek. Favorites include the Nouveau (519 North Charles Street; 410–962–8248) for contemporary furnishings, Steven Scott Gallery (515 North Charles Street; 410–752–6218), Meredith Gallery (805 North Charles Street; 410–837–3575) for contemporary handmade furniture, and Craig Finner Gallery (505 North Charles Street; 410–727–1863) for interesting vintage poster and antique prints.

DINNER: It's all downhill back to the Hyatt for dinner. Take the specially marked elevator to the fifteenth floor to **Pisces** for dinner (410–605–2835). Start out with a cocktail and selection from the raw bar. The Pisces appetizer sampler for two has a little of everything—tempura shrimp, baked oysters, clams casino, and lemon pepper calamari served with roasted pepper marinara for $16. You probably won't be able to resist the jumbo (and they aren't exaggerating) lump crab cakes at market price. Try to save room for one of the delectable desserts. If that's impossible, stay for live jazz beginning at 10:00 P.M. on weekends and enjoy dessert later.

LODGING: Accommodations at the Hyatt. Amenities such as rooftop tennis, a running track, and a swimming pool set this hotel apart from others in the harbor area. There's also a coffee and espresso bar overlooking harbor views, but the best views are from the restaurant. Very convenient location. Weekend rates begin at $150, but climb higher depending on season and events.

DAY 2

Morning

Brew coffee or tea in your room while getting ready for the day—comfortable walking shoes are a must. Cross over to the Light Street Pavilion of Harborplace via the skywalk from the Hyatt.

BREAKFAST: You'll find quick and inexpensive breakfast at an assortment of eateries in the food courts, but **Wayne's Bar-B-Que** (301 Light Street; 410–539–3810) is a full-service restaurant that serves breakfast. Moderate.

Discover some of Baltimore's unique attractions and history the easy way: Board the **Harbor City Tour** bus at Light and Conway Streets (410–254–TOUR). Energetic guides narrate the ninety-minute informative tour. It costs $10.00 for adults and $5.00 for children six to twelve and departs at 10:00 A.M., noon, and 2:00 P.M. daily, rain or shine. You'll pass Edgar Allen Poe's grave, historic neighborhood markets, area universities, and attractions like the National Aquarium.

LUNCH: After your return, try the seafood at **Phillip's Harborplace** (301 Light Street; 410–685–6600). The bus tour furnishes discount coupons and stops in front of the eatery. There's a sit-down restaurant, as well as fast food and to-go options. Buffet lunch at Phillip's is $12.99 for adults and $6.99 for children ages six to twelve. The main restaurant menu ranges in price from $10 to $25, offering the same selections as dinner with a few smaller portions available.

Afternoon

For $15, a combination "land and sea" tour package includes an all-day pass for **Ed Kane's Water Taxi** (800–658–8947), stopping seventeen times along the harbor. Hop on the water taxi at stop #1 (Aquarium) and take it to stop #10, where two uniquely Baltimore museums vie for your time.

At the **Museum of Industry** (1415 Key Highway; 410–727–4808), you may think you're in the midst of remnants of Baltimore's gritty past. After closer scrutiny you'll discover stories of shipbuilders, canneries, print shops, sweatshops, oyster shucking, and truck manufacturing through the museum's interactive exhibits. From Memorial Day through Labor Day it's open Monday through Friday noon to 5:00 P.M. (opening again from 6:00 to 9:00 P.M. on Wednesday) and Saturday 10:00 A.M. to 5:00 P.M. The rest of the year, hours are Wednesday 7:00 to 9:00 P.M.; Thursday, Friday, and Sunday noon to 5:00 P.M.; and Saturday 10:00 A.M. to 5:00 P.M. Admission is $5.00 for adults, $3.50 for seniors and students, $17.00 for a family.

Nearby, the **American Visionary Art Museum** (800 Key Highway; 410–244–1900) exhibits work of self-taught artists and their "creations born of tuition and self-styled imagination." Undoubtedly this museum is unique in structure, philosophy, and offbeat content. Blinking robots created of found objects, detailed toothpick constructions, and bottle cap aliens showcase just a few of the media utilized by a cross section of untrained artists, including mentally and physically disabled individuals, homeless people, housewives, mechanics, neurosurgeons, and children. The museum's mission includes such uplifting ideals as "engendering respect for and delight in the gift of others and promoting creative self-reliance." Admission is $6.00 for adults, $4.00 for seniors and children. Hours are Tuesday through Sunday 10:00 A.M. to 6:00 P.M.; closed Monday.

Reboard the water taxi for **Fort McHenry National Monument and Historic Shrine** (East Fort Avenue; 410–962–4290). Don't miss the fifteen-minute video in the visitor center. Shown every half hour between 9:00 A.M. and 4:00 P.M. daily, it's worth the general admission ($5.00 for those over seventeen). Take a walk through the fort, where artifacts depict living quarters, powder magazine, guardhouse, and artillery used during the Battle of Baltimore in the War of 1812. Try to be at the fort at 4:30 P.M. for the flag ceremony, when the huge flag, similar in size to the one Francis Scott Key wrote about, is lowered.

Return to the hotel via water taxi.

DINNER: Dine in Little Italy, making reservations at **Ciao Bella** (236 South High Street; 410–685–7733). Many restaurants in Little Italy offer complimentary pickup service from Inner Harbor hotels, but if they can't accommodate you, Ciao Bella will deduct the cab fare (less than $5.00) from your tab.

It's as difficult to recommend an entree as it is to select one, but you won't be disappointed no matter what you choose. Both Northern and Southern favorites are featured. The veal dishes are superb. Entrees include Italian favorites like Veal Marsala ($16.95) as well as signature dishes like Veal Chesapeake, a combination of scaloppini and fresh lump crab (market price). Fresh pastas and homemade cannoli top the suggestion list. Moderately priced.

After dinner, try the **Havana Club** (600 Water Street; 410–468–0022) or the **Harbor Club at Pier 5** (711 Eastern Avenue; 410–539–2000) for live entertainment.

LODGING: Hyatt Regency.

DAY 3

Morning

Request a late check out. Board the water taxi at Harbor Place for stop #11, Fell's Point. The fare is $4.50 for adults, $2.00 for children.

BREAKFAST: If you are a fan of the TV favorite *Homicide,* you'll recognize your surroundings as the set for the show. Have breakfast at **Jimmy's** (801 South Broadway; 410–327–3273) just as the cast members on the show did. It's served all day at this local hangout. Moderate.

This neighborhood, Baltimore's original seaport, brims with quaint vitality. Walk around the square, along Thames Street to the "police station" featured on *Homicide.* Venture to the side streets where you'll see colorful scenes painted on the screens of windows and doors. These quaint decorations were developed to provide both privacy and fresh air in the days before air conditioning. The cobbled streets, clapboard and brick row houses with marble stoops, and Irish pubs take visitors back to early days in Fell's Point. It's also a popular antiquing district these days.

Allow ample time for a walk along the river promenade back to the Inner Harbor, about a mile and a half away. You'll pass the Civil War Museum, the Power Plant, the National Aquarium, and the World Trade Center. Pick up the water taxi along the way, if you tire.

LUNCH: Stop for lunch at **McCormick & Schmick's Seafood Restaurant** (Pier 5, 711 Eastern Avenue; 410–234–1300). A large selection of moderately priced lunch specialties and sandwiches. The very tart lemonade and iced tea blend, called the "Arnold Palmer," is the quenching house specialty. Try the spicy Maryland crab soup here. The menu is printed twice daily listing the current forty fresh catches.

Arrange for a shuttle (800–258–3826) for your return to the Baltimore/Washington International Airport and your flight back.

THERE'S MORE

The Star-Spangled Banner Flag House and 1812 Museum, 884 East Pratt Street; (410) 837–1793. After Fort McHenry, stop here to learn how Mary Pickersgill and her daughter hand sewed the giant striped and starred American flag that inspired Francis Scott Key to pen his famous poem. Open Tuesday through Saturday 10:00 A.M. to 4:00 P.M. Guided tours are $5.00 for adults, $4.00 for seniors, and $3.00 for students.

World Trade Center Observation Deck, 401 East Pratt Street; (410) 837–VIEW. Take in the view and exhibits from the twenty-seventh floor of this I. M. Pei five-sided office building. From the harbor, two sides resemble a ship's bough. Open Monday through Saturday 10:00 A.M. to 5:00 P.M., Sunday noon to 5:00 P.M., later during summer. Tickets are $3.00.

B & O Railroad Museum, 901 West Pratt Street; (410) 752–2490. Whether models, china and memorabilia, or the real iron horses of the last century entrance you, you'll find them on display in the beautiful roundhouse of the original St. Clare Station. The museum's open daily 10:00 A.M. to 5:00 P.M. Closed Thanksgiving, Easter, and Christmas. Admission is $7.00 for adults, $6.00 for seniors, and $5.00 for children two to twelve.

Great Blacks in Wax Museum, 1601-03 East North Avenue; (410) 522–9547. Slave ship replica and more than 150 wax figures. Open Tuesday through Saturday 9:00 A.M. to 6:00 P.M., Sunday noon to 6:00 P.M. Closes at 5:00 P.M. from October through January; open daily February, July, and August. Admission is $6.00 for adults, $5.75 for seniors and college students, $4.25 for children twelve to seventeen, and $3.75 for children two to eleven.

National Aquarium in Baltimore, Pier 3, 501 East Pratt Street; (410) 576–3800 for information, (800) 551–SEAT for advance ticket sales. Even if you've visited the 10,000 animals here before, return to experience the newest exhibit *Amazon River Forest,* where giant river turtles, a 300-pound anaconda, and free-roaming exotic birds and reptiles greet you along the journey up a 57-foot river tributary winding through the delicate rain forest. Advance timed tickets are available. General admission is $14.00 for adults, $10.50 for seniors, $7.50 for children three to eleven. Hours vary depending on the season; the aquarium is closed Christmas and Thanksgiving.

National Museum of Dentistry, 31 South Greene Street; (410) 706–0810. This unusual museum is much more fun than going to the dentist and more informative than you might expect. You'll see fifty-two types of vintage extraction tools and learn that bubble gum machines, cotton candy, grape juice, and golf tees were all invented by dentists. One set of George Washington's dentures (they aren't wooden) is on display. Children can dress the part of dentist and patient in the miniature office. Located in the world's first dental school at the University of Maryland. Open Wednesday through Saturday 10:00 A.M. to 4:00 P.M., Sunday, 1:00 to 4:00 P.M. Admission is $4.50 for adults, $2.50 for ages seven to eighteen and seniors.

Port Discovery, 35 Market Place; (410) 864–2654. If traveling with children, especially those between six and twelve, this is a must-see stop. Even without children, the message here is inspirational—it's all about developing the necessary skills to identify and achieve dreams and aspirations by focusing on problem solving, risk-taking and team building. Characters like Ivan Idea, Wanda Whye, and Howie Lovitt were created by the best: Walt Disney Imagineering. Located in the historic 1906 Fishmarket, the adaptive re-use is also of interest. Open daily 10:00 A.M. to 5:30 P.M.; closed New Year's Day, Christmas, and Thanksgiving. Admission is $10.00 for adults, $7.50 for children three to twelve.

Jewish Museum of Maryland, 15 Lloyd Street; (410) 732–6400. The family history center, library, and a modern museum representing some of the collection's 150,000 items are located between two of the oldest synagogues in the United States. The Lloyd Street Synagogue, built in 1845 in Greek Revival style, is open for tours by appointment. The sanctuary features the women's balcony, a stained glass window believed to be the earliest architectural use of the Star of David, and three Torahs rescued from the Holocaust. Visitors can also visit the Orthodox Mikveh (ritual baths) and Matzoth oven in the lower level. B'Nai Israel Synagogue, with gas lights from 1876 and a wooden carved Torah ark, is still in use. Museum hours are Sunday, Tuesday, Wednesday, and Thursday noon to 4:00 P.M. Admission is $4.00 for adults and $2.00 for students and includes docent-led tours at 1:00 and 2:30 P.M. Museum shop.

Inner Harbor Ice Rink, 201 Key Highway; (410) 385–0675. Skating-related activities. Two-hour public skating session costs $3.00 to $5.00.

First Thursdays on Charles Street, Mt. Vernon neighborhood; (410) 837–4636 or (800) 343–3468. Live music, free admission to area attractions, art exhibits, and store specials, beginning at 5:30 P.M.

SPECIAL EVENTS

April. Baltimore Waterfront Festival, Inner Harbor's West Shore and Rash Field. Seafood cooking demonstrations, family activities and entertainment. Free admission. (410) 837–4636 or (800) 343–3468.

May. Preakness Celebration Parade, downtown along Charles and Pratt Streets to Market Place. (410) 837–4636 or (800) 343–3468.

May. Running of the Preakness Stakes, Pimlico Race Course. (410) 452–9400 for ticket information.

July. Artscape, Mt. Royal around Maryland Institute College of Art. Visual and performing arts, national entertainers. Free. (410) 396–4575.

September. Baltimore Book Festival, Mt. Vernon Square. Popular indoor and outdoor literary celebration involving music and arts, authors and publishers, poetry readings, and demonstrations. Free. (410) 837–4636 or (800) 343–3468.

November–December. ZooLights, Baltimore Zoo, Druid Hill Park. Walk-through light show displaying more than 750,000 lights. Admission is $4.50 for adults, $2.50 for children and seniors. (410) 366–5466.

December. Lighted Boat Parade, Inner Harbor to Fell's Point. (800) HAR-BOR–1.

OTHER RECOMMENDED RESTAURANTS AND LODGINGS

Baltimore

Pier 5 Hotel, 711 Eastern Avenue; (410) 539–2000. This upscale, contemporary sixty-five-room boutique hotel is located behind the Baltimore Aquarium. The "Magical Hotel Packages" are a luxurious bargain. Starting at $159, breakfast and passes to area attractions are included. Nouveau-American food is served in the Dish Cafe; (410) 649–5333. Moderate.

Harbor Court Hotel, 550 Light Street; (410) 234–0550 or (800) 824–0076. Probably the priciest hotel in town, with rack rates from $295 to $340, but the rooms are spacious and lovely. The four-star, acclaimed Hampton's Restaurant is expensive, but you won't be disappointed. In addition to the menu, the chef offers prix-fixe four-course menus, from $45 to $90.

The Renaissance Harborplace, 202 East Pratt Street; (410) 547–1200. Connected to the Gallery, a small shopping complex. Weekend rates begin at $134 for the "Two for Breakfast" getaway.

Holiday Inn Inner Harbor, 301 West Lombard Street; (410) 685–3500. Convenient location if you have tickets for a ball game. Newly refurbished with indoor pool. "Great Rates" begin at $119 and include coupons for breakfast in the restaurant. Rates: $89–$159 before travel club discounts.

Scarborough Fair Bed & Breakfast, 1 East Montgomery; (410) 837–0010. Six guest rooms with private baths and other amenities. Near harbor in historic Federal Hill neighborhood. Rates: $129–$159, including breakfast.

Admiral Fell Inn, 888 South Broadway; (800) 292–4667. An eighteenth-century seaman's hostel, now a charming European-style inn on the harbor. Rates range from $139–$399 depending on season, view, and room configuration, including breakfast, parking, and shuttle to various attractions.

Attman's Delicatessen, 1019 East Lombard Street; (410) 563–2666. Serves up the types of sandwiches you'd find in New York City, only at half the price (extra lean corned beef, $5.19). Don't be surprised to find a line out the door of this small establishment. Locals say it's that crowded between noon and 2:00 P.M. daily, but worth the wait. Open every day.

Cafe Hon, 1009 West Thirty-sixth Street (Hampden); (410) 243–1230. Teacup chandeliers, '50s memorabilia, and a menu featuring meat loaf along with nightly specials; sundaes served in coffee mugs have homemade hot fudge. Prices are moderate and the staff is friendly.

Joy America Cafe, American Visionary Art Museum, 800 Key Highway; (410) 244–6500. Visionary southwestern menu to match the museum. Moderate to expensive.

FOR MORE INFORMATION

Baltimore Area Convention and Visitors Association, 100 Light Street, Twelfth Floor, Baltimore, Maryland 21202; (800) 343–3468; www.baltimore.org.

AIRBORNE

Chicago

MORE THAN A WEEKEND'S WORTH

2 NIGHTS

River cruises • Shoppers' paradise • Lake views • Trolley rides
Arts and culture • And the beat goes on

As a lively urban weekend destination, Chicago's popularity among Clevelanders blossoms for several reasons. For starters, it's a quick, inexpensive, nonstop flight. On Southwest Airlines, for example, tourists can choose among frequent comfortable flights, often less than $100 round-trip, to accommodate their time schedules. Logistically, the hour-long flight (considering the one hour time change, even shorter—you get there when you leave) into Midway saves additional time because it's closer to downtown than O'Hare International. And then there's the accessibility of all there is to see, do, and taste, at prices that are more reasonable than in other big cities. Among the most important reasons for getting away: You'll leave your stress behind as you get caught up in the vitality of Chicagoland.

Once you make your air travel arrangements, pick from a long list of sight-seeing and dining opportunities, but don't forget to plan some entertainment and shopping, or at least window shopping. Take advantage of the lakefront recreational possibilities and a unique tour to better acquaint you with the Windy City. Even if you think you know the city well, there's always something new to learn and see since your last trip.

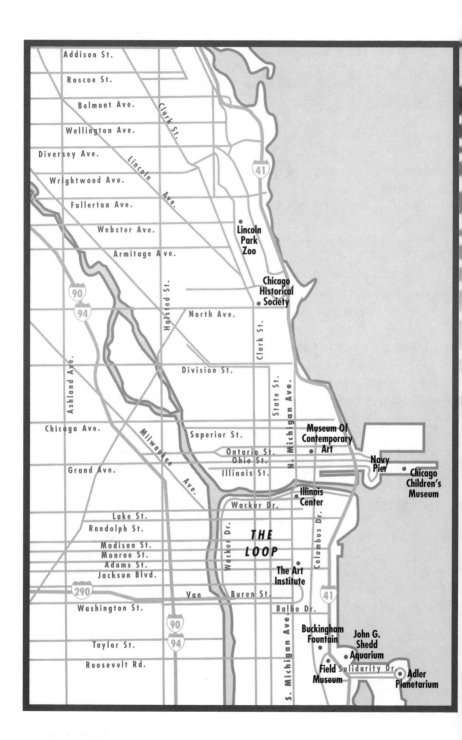

ᶜᔆᶜᴬᴾᴱ ᵀᴴᴿᴱᴱ

AIRBORNE

DAY 1

Morning

Choose a morning flight, departing no later than 11:00 A.M. to include a **Chicago** lunch before the afternoon activities. An interesting and inexpensive ($1.50 per person) ride aboard the Chicago Transit Authority (CTA) rapid transit train gets you to the downtown region known as the loop in a half hour without any traffic delays. You'll have to handle your bags yourself and then take a short taxi ride from the State and Lake stop, but it's about a $3.50 toll in contrast with a $25.00 ride all the way from the airport.

There are, of course, many lodging choices, but a moderately priced one in an easily accessible location is the **Radisson Hotel and Suites** (160 East Huron Street; 312–878–2900 or 800–333–3333). Stop to check in or drop off luggage. Gather up your camera, walking shoes, and a map from the hotel concierge, who will also assist with dinner and evening entertainment reservations.

LUNCH: You might as well get that craving for luscious deep-dish Chicago-style pizza out of the way. There's a **Gino's** right around the corner at 160 East Superior and St. Clair Streets. During warmer months order at the take-out window and eat at one of the outdoor tables. A mini single serving is just $4.00.

Afternoon

You won't get far on a walking tour along North Michigan Avenue if you continually shop and browse, but that's okay. The Magnificent Mile, as it is more widely known, extends from the Chicago River north to Oak Street.

Start at the Michigan Avenue Bridge, one of the city's fifty bascule lift bridges that enable Chicagoans easy access to the opposite side of the Chicago River. If you stop to study its pylons, you'll discover the area's earliest explorers commemorated on the east side. Joliet, Marquette, and LaSalle are among those represented in the carving. Across the street and down the steps, river tours are available from the **Chicago Architecture Foundation River Cruises** (224 South Michigan Avenue; 312–922–3432). This cruise offers dozens of great tours of the city's rich architecture and gives participants an angle not possible from land. For a complete schedule, check www.architecture.org. One of the best tours is the River Cruise, lasting over an hour and departing from the CAF/Mercury Cruise Line ticket booth on the river level of the Michigan Avenue Bridge. Tickets are $21. Tours depart hourly Monday through Friday, 10:00 A.M. to 3:00 P.M., Saturday 10:00

A.M. to 5:00 P.M., and Sunday 9:00 A.M. to 3:00 P.M., June through October. Fewer trips run in the off-season.

Whether you're on a guided boat tour or walking on your own, notice the ornate **Wrigley Building** (400-420 North Michigan Avenue). Many consider it the most beautiful one in the city. The **Chicago Tribune Tower** building is across the street.

As you peruse stores along Michigan Avenue, museums will pique your interest too. In the midst of the Magnificent Mile is the **Terra Museum of American Art** (664 North Michigan Avenue; 312–726–4849). Admission is $5.00 for adults, $2.50 for seniors, free for students and children under twelve, and free on Tuesday and the first Sunday of each month.

Be sure to stop at the Visitor Information Center in the restored pumping station of the Chicago Water Works at Michigan Avenue and Pearson Street for sightseeing information and Hot Tix, a half-price theater ticket outlet. After gathering any sightseeing brochures, stop for coffee or homemade lemonade and an overstuffed "Flat Sammies" sandwich or cinnamon roll at **Chicago Flat Sammies,** also in the Water Works (811 North Michigan Avenue; 312–664–BRED). It's self-serve, but fun and moderately priced.

If you have time, explore some of the museums along South Michigan Avenue, such as the **Chicago Architecture Foundation** (224 South Michigan, on the west side of the street; 312– 922–2431). Stop in for a wonderful selection of Frank Lloyd Wright books. You can sign up here for tomorrow's river cruise or walking tour. Other museums like the **Spertus Museum of Judaica** (618 South Michigan Avenue; 312–322–1747) with its holocaust memorial and archaeological area and the **Museum of Contemporary Photography** (600 South Michigan Avenue; 312–663–5554) are easy additions to the walking tour if you care for a longer outing.

DINNER: A few doors from the hotel, you'll find **Caliterra** in the Wyndham Chicago (633 North Saint Clair Street; 312–274–4444). The innovative gastronomic concept here combines Italian fare with California trends. The chef calls it the "Italiaization" of food and you'll discover what he means by sampling the restaurant's signature appetizer, Santa Barbara shrimp "cigars" served with mustard fruits and aged balsamic syrup ($8.00). Other specialties include brick-oven pizzas, pastas, and such entrees as porcini-crusted cod with vegetable giardinera for $16 or grilled sirloin served with lemon pepper Parmesan fries for $23). The enjoyable dinner is enhanced by an extensive wine collection, piano music, and pleasing contemporary decor. Try to save room for a beautifully presented and deliciously decadent dessert.

Take in some of the city's entertainment, perhaps a theatrical performance (check with the hotel concierge or at the visitors' bureau to find out what's in town) or attend a **Second City** improv show (1616 North Wells Street; 312–337–3992). Tickets are $15 on weekends; no age or drink minimum. If you haven't seen *Shear Madness,* Chicago's longest running play (it's in the *Guinness Book of World Records* for fourteen years of performances), take a short cab ride to the **Mayfair Theatre,** 636 South Michigan Avenue, for an evening of whodunit comedy. Call (312) 786–1920 for ticket information.

DAY 2

Morning

BREAKFAST: Wear comfortable walking shoes for another day of sightseeing, then enjoy a casual breakfast at the **Corner Bakery** (676 North St. Clair; 312–266–2570). There are various locations around town, but this bustling self-serve establishment is more than the usual bakery. Breakfast entrees are available, along with the wide variety of pastries and rolls, and it opens at 7:00 A.M. on weekends for early risers. It's reasonable for budget-conscious travelers and quick, even if you have to wait in line.

Walk back to the Pumping Station of the Water Works to board the **Chicago Trolley** (312–663–0260). The red and green trolleys serve a dual purpose for the day's itinerary. First, the driver will provide an entertaining and informative city tour, pointing out other locations you'll want to visit. Secondly, any time you wish to get off and walk around or visit sights on the trolley stops, do so and then catch a later trolley to continue. Tickets are $15.00 for adults, $8.00 for children three to eleven, and $12.00 for seniors.

The **Art Institute of Chicago** (111 South Michigan Avenue at Adams Street; 312–443–3600) is renowned on many counts, but if you don't have several hours to spend, head directly for the Impressionist and Postimpressionist collections. Open Monday to Friday 10:30 A.M. to 4:30 P.M. (until 8:00 P.M. on Tuesday), Saturday 10:00 A.M. to 5:00 P.M., Sunday and holidays noon to 5:00 P.M. There are three restaurant options. Suggested admission is $8.00 for adults, $5.00 for students and seniors.

The **Adler Planetarium** (1300 South Lake Shore Drive; 312–922–STAR) recently reopened after an extensive $40 million renovation project. Be sure to check out the Gateway to the Universe Gallery and the interactive displays, take a space walk, and watch an awesome performance at Sky Theater. Open Monday through Thursday, 9:00 A.M. to 5:00 P.M., Friday 9:00 A.M. to 9:00 P.M., Saturday and Sunday, 9:00 A.M. to 6:00 P.M. Admission to the museum is $5.00 for adults, $4.00 for children and seniors. There is an additional $5.00 charge for theater shows. Free admission on Tuesdays.

A stop at the **John G. Shedd Aquarium** (1200 South Lake Shore Drive; 312–939–2438) will make you think you're in the Caribbean. The snorkeling is great and you won't get wet. When you're done at the reef, hike the Pacific Northwest all the way up to Alaska. Prices are higher here: $11.00 for adults, $9.00 for children and seniors. Tickets can be purchased through TicketMaster or charge by phone, (312) 559–0200. Open Monday through Friday, 9:00 A.M. to 5:00 P.M., Saturday and Sunday, 9:00 A.M. to 6:00 P.M.

LUNCH: Have lunch at **Foundings Restaurant** at the Aquarium. Prices are moderate, ranging from $7.75 to $11.25, and the view of the city makes for a scenic respite. For a fast food option, try the Bubble Net Food Court.

Afternoon

The **Field Museum** (1400 South Lake Shore Drive; 312–922–9410) is world-famous for taking its guests back centuries to discover historic treasures and to learn about the world's diverse environments and cultures. One of the newest exhibits, the *Underground Adventure,* gives a worm's-eye view of the underground ecosystem. It's larger than life so we humans can fit in, and it's an eye-opening experience. Admission is $7.00 for adults, $4.00 for children, seniors, and students with ID.

Hop back on your Chicago Trolley. Heading north on Lake Shore Drive, you'll pass Buckingham Fountain, where there are light shows at dusk during summer.

Get off the trolley at the **Navy Pier** (600 East Grand Avenue; 312–595–5100 or 800–595–PIER). This landmark has turned into a dynamic mix of restaurants, retail vendors, and an outdoor entertainment park (the 150-foot-high Ferris wheel is visible for miles). There are even theater options, from 3D movies to the Chicago Shakespeare Theater (312–595–5633) where an English-style pub and outdoor garden take you back to the Cotswolds. In winter when outdoor activities close, there's free ice skating.

The pier is also home to the **Chicago Children's Museum** (700 East Grand Avenue; 312–527–1000). It's a must if you're toting kids. They'll want to dig at the Dinosaur Expedition in search of a dinosaur skeleton and wear a raincoat as they create a path for the flowing water at Waterways. Open Tuesday through Sunday, 10:00 A.M. to 5:00 P.M.; open until 8:00 P.M. on Thursday. Admission is $6.50 per person; free on Thursday.

Book a river tour for fabulous skyline views that blend water, architecture, and sky.

Continue on the Chicago Trolley or take the free Navy Pier trolley service along the Grand and Illinois Corridor between the pier and State Street.

DINNER: Visit the Gold Coast area for dinner at a French bistro, **Bistrot Zinc** (1131 North State Street; 312–337–1131). The food and atmosphere are authentic, but prices are moderate. Poulet grand-mère, roasted chicken "grandmother style," is less than $15. Whatever you order, save room for a dessert crepe; the walk back to the hotel covers about 10 blocks of interesting shops to help offset the caloric intake.

After dinner, walk along Rush Street, one of Chicago's hot after-dark areas, stopping at one or more of the clubs, or window shop at the exclusive shops along Oak Street before heading back.

LODGING: The Radisson.

DAY 3

Morning

BREAKFAST: If you have the blues about leaving Chicago, you have to try the Sunday Gospel Brunch at the **House of Blues** (329 North Dearborn; 312–923–2000). It's the most entertaining "feel good" brunch in town. Gospel choirs, some nationally known and others often right off local pulpits, entertain after diners partake in a New Orleans–style spread with all the fixings. Smoked chicken, andouille and sweet potato hash, turnip greens cooked in Dixie beer, and New Orleans bread pudding for dessert are but a few of the items on the all-you-can-eat smorgasbord. The brunch concerts begin at 9:30 A.M. and noon each Sunday. Advance tickets paid for by phone are $32 for adults, $15 for children six to twelve. Children under six are free, but let the reservationist know when you call. Don't leave without taking a good look around. The House of Blues is a wonderful museum of folk art in itself.

After brunch, leave for the airport and your flight back. If you've arranged for a later flight, you can fit in a little more of Chicagoland before returning home.

THERE'S MORE

Bike Chicago, 600 East Grand Avenue, Navy Pier; (800) 915–BIKE. What a fun and energetic way to explore Chicago's lakefront. There's a free 1:30 P.M. guided tour weekdays with any bike rental. Rentals begin at $8.00 hour, but all-day and multiple day rentals are also available.

Museum of Contemporary Art, 220 East Chicago Avenue; (312) 280–2660. Guided tours can be arranged by calling ahead, but audio tours of special exhibits are also available. Try the Mcafe for a relaxing luncheon respite, whether or not you have time to visit the interesting galleries or sculpture garden. Open Tuesday to Sunday 10:00 A.M. to 5:00 P.M., open late on Tuesday and Wednesday. General admission is $6.50 adults, $4.00 for seniors and students; children under twelve are admitted free.

Sears Tower Skydeck, 233 South Wacker Drive; (312) 875–9696. See Chicago and four states from one of the world's tallest buildings. Open October to February, 9:00 A.M. to 10:00 P.M.; March to September, 9:00 A.M. to 11:00 P.M. Admission is $8.00 for adults, $6.00 for seniors, $5.00 for children ages five to twelve, $20.00 for families.

John Hancock Observatory, 875 North Michigan Avenue; (888) 875–8439. See the city from 1,000 feet and take a virtual reality city tour. Open daily, 9:00 A.M. to midnight. Admission is $8.00 for adults, $6.00 for seniors and children ages five to seventeen.

Blue Chicago, 536 and 736 North Clark Street; (312) 661–0100. A night club featuring Chicago-style blues.

National Vietnam Veterans Art Museum, 1801 South Indiana Avenue; (312) 326–0270. Houses expressive artwork created by Vietnam veterans as well as a collection of North Vietnamese and Viet Cong weaponry. Admission is $5.00. Open Tuesday to Friday 11:00 A.M. to 6:00 P.M., Saturday 10:00 A.M. to 5:00 P.M., and Sunday, noon to 5:00 P.M. There is a museum shop and cafe.

SPECIAL EVENTS

Call the Mayor's Office of Special Events for details about these and more free downtown events; (312) 744–3370, TTY (312) 744–2964.

January–March. WinterBreak Chicago Festival. Special events and promotional discounts by merchants, lodgings, restaurants, and sites to promote activities during the winter. Call for a WinterBreak card to use when visiting.

March. St. Patrick's Day Parades, various locations.

May. Mayor Daley's Kids & Kites Festival.

June. Chicago Blues Festival, Grant Park, Jackson and Columbus Streets.

June. Chicago Gospel Festival, Grant Park.

June. Taste of Chicago, Grant Park.

June. Chicago Country Music Festival, Grant Park.

July. Venetian Night, Monroe Harbor, downtown. A parade of decorated boats followed by a fireworks display.

August. Chicago Air and Water Show, North Avenue Beach, North Avenue and lakefront. The oldest and largest show of its type in the country.

August. "Viva! Chicago" Latin Music Festival, Grant Park.

August–September. Chicago Jazz Festival, Grant Park. Some of the best national and international jazz performers gather here to make music.

September. Celtic Fest Chicago, Grant Park. Visual and performing artists from all of the Celtic nations.

November. Magnificent Mile Lights Festival. Ongoing events along Magnificent Mile. Festival procession begins at 6:00 P.M. at Rush and Oak Streets. (312) 409–5560.

November–February. Skate on State Ice-Skating Rink, State Street between Randolph and Washington Streets. Free ice skating. Rentals and refreshments.

OTHER RECOMMENDED RESTAURANTS AND LODGINGS

Brio, 10 West Hubbard; (312) 467–1010. Upscale contemporary Spanish cuisine. Moderate.

Fog City Diner, 33 West Illinois Street; (312) 828–1144. Similar to the original in San Francisco. Moderate.

Giordano's, seven downtown locations, including 730 North Rush; (312) 951–0747. Delicious famous stuffed pizza. Moderate.

ESPN Zone, 43 East Ohio Street; (312) 644–3776. One of the newest interactive eateries in Chicagoland. There's an energetic, gamelike atmosphere and big-screen sportscasts for enthusiasts to enjoy. Even the placemats sport daily news briefs. Menu features some signature dishes and a wide variety of popular American sandwiches, pizza, and entrees. Moderate.

Renaissance Chicago Hotel, 1 West Wacker; (312) 372–7200 or (800) 228–9290. Similar in quality, ambience, and amenities to the Renaissance Cleveland. Theater and shopping packages, several restaurants, and some rooms with bay-window views of Lake Michigan. Weekend specials as low as $139.

The Raphael Hotel, 201 East Delaware Place; (312) 943–5000 or (800) 983–7870. Charming older hotel with nicely furnished oversized rooms; located behind the John Hancock Center. Rates: $169 on weekends; specials range from $89 to $129.

The Tremont Hotel, 1000 East Chestnut Street; (312) 751–1900 or (800) 621–8133. Same management and style as the Raphael Hotel; some standard rooms seem small. Located west of Michigan Avenue. Rates: $169 on weekends.

Hampton Inn and Suites Chicago River North, 33 West Illinois Street; (312) 832–0330 or (800) HAMPTON. One of the best buys in Chicago for suite accommodations. Rooms have Nintendo hookups, refrigerators; a deluxe continental breakfast is included in room rates. Has a neighborhood feel with Frank Lloyd Wright influence in decor and richly appointed rooms. Located near many restaurants; Fog City Diner is in same building and Ruth's Chris Steak House is connected by a skywalk. Rates: $169 with breakfast.

House of Blues Hotel, 133 North Dearborn; (312) 245–0833. A Loews Hotel in the Marina City riverfront complex. Next to the House of Blues Music Hall and Restaurant and similar in style and feeling. Wonderfully artsy, colorful, and upscale. King rooms begin at $159.

FOR MORE INFORMATION

Chicago Office of Tourism, Chicago Cultural Center, 78 East Washington Street, Chicago, Illinois 60602; (312) 744–2400, TTY (312) 744–2947.

Hotel Motel Association of Illinois, 27 East Monroe, Suite 1200, Chicago, Illinois 60603; (312) 346–3135 or (877) 4LODGING.

Illinois Bureau of Tourism, Department of Commerce and Community Affairs, James R. Thompson Center, 100 West Randolph Street, Suite 3-400, Chicago, Illinois 60601; (312) 744–2400 or (800) 2CONNECT.

INDEX

Chicago Trolley, 245
Chicago's Children's Museum, 246
Children's Museum of Indianapolis, 135
Chipotle Mexican Grill, 145
Church Brew Works, The, 36
Ciao Bella, 235
Civil War Museum, 135
Clara's on the River, 210
Clementine's Saloon, 202
Colasanti's Tropical Gardens, 181
Colony Pub and Grille, 16
Columbus Museum of Art, 72
Columbus, Ohio, 68–76
Conkle's Hollow State Nature
  Preserve, 101
Conner Prairie, 130–31
Contemporary Museum, 323
Corner Bakery, 245
Country Music Hall of Fame and
  Museum, 223
Court Street Collection, 107
Coventry Gardens, 180
Cranbrook Art Museum, 193
Cranbrook Institute of Science, 193
Crane's Pie Pantry Restaurant, Bakeries
  and Cider Mill, 204
Cup O' Joe, 70

D

Dagwoodz, 71
Dairy Barn Cultural Arts Center, 107
Daisy Flour Mill, 24
Danville, 161–62
Darfon's, 225
Das Dutchman Essenhaus, 173, 200
Dawes Arboretum, 116
Dee Felice, 159
Detroit Institute of the Arts, 189
Detroit, 187–97
Diamond Lil's at Nemacolin Woodlands
  Resort and Spa, 47
Discovery District, 72
Doc's Smoke Shop, 151

Dover Station, 124
Downtown Partnership, 231
Dr. J. H. Kellogg Discovery Center, 212
Drexel Grandview Theatre, 72
Drover's Inn, 57
Dug Out Restaurant, 212
Duquesne Heights Incline, 39
Dutch Harvest Restaurants, 91–92

E

Eagle Song Studio, 89
Ed Kane's Water Taxi, 234
Eiteljorg Museum of American Indians
  and Western Art, 133
El Campesino Restaurant, 82
Elbert Hubbard Roycroft Museum, 4
Elkhart Bike and Walkway, 173
Elkhart Environmental Center, 173
Elmwood Inn, 161
Erie Canal, 24
Erie Maritime Museum, 12, 14
Erie, Pennsylvania, 12–21
Erie Street, Little Italy of Windsor, 182

F

Fair Lane, 192
Fallingwater, 48
Field Museum, 246
Fifty-five on the Boulevard, 68, 70
Figlio's, 71
Fioriware Art Pottery, 71
First Watch, 130
Fishbone's Rhythm Kitchen Cafe, 189–90
Fisher-Price Toystore, 5
Foot Loose, 115
Fort Ancient State Memorial, 152
Fort McHenry National Monument and
  Historic Shrine, 234–35
Foundings Restaurant, 246
Four Seasons Bakery and Deli, 109
Frank Lloyd Wright's House on Kentuck
  Knob, 48–49

ABOUT THE AUTHOR

MARCIA SCHONBERG has been offering readers getaway ideas for a decade. Her travel articles and award-winning photographs have apeared in regional newspapers and magazines, including the *Columbus Dispatch, Cleveland Magazine, Over the Back Fence Magazine, Country Living Magazine, Michigan Living, Home & Away,* and *Ohio Magazine.* When she isn't researching or writing, she's busy shooting the accompanying photographs for her work as well as making photos for her stock and fine art businesses. Her photos appear in visitors' guides, newspapers, magazines, on posters, postcards and in galleries.

Marcia lives in Ohio with her husband Bill, but covers destinations throughout the United States, Canada, Europe and the Caribbean, searching for the best leisure destinations to share with her readers.

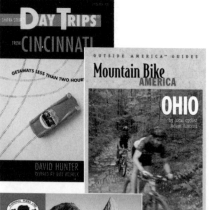
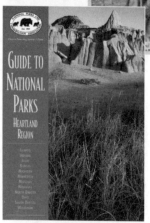